—— T H E ——
WALL
STREET
MBA

THE
WALL STREET MBA

THIRD EDITION

YOUR PERSONAL CRASH COURSE
IN CORPORATE FINANCE

REUBEN ADVANI

New York Chicago San Francisco Athens London Madrid
Mexico City Milan New Delhi Singapore Sydney Toronto

1 2 3 4 5 6 7 8 9   QFR   23 22 21 20 19 18

ISBN   978-1-260-13559-6
MHID   1-260-13559-4

e-ISBN   978-1-260-13560-2
e-MHID   1-260-13560-8

This publication is designed to provide accurate and authoritative information in regard to the subject matter covered. It is sold with the understanding that neither the author nor the publisher is engaged in rendering legal, accounting, securities trading, or other professional service. If legal advice or other expert assistance is required, the services of a competent professional person should be sought.
— *From a Declaration of Principles Jointly Adopted by a Committee of the American Bar Association and a Committee of Publishers and Associations*

Library of Congress Cataloging-in-Publication Data

Names: Advani, Reuben, author.
Title: The Wall Street MBA : your personal crash course in corporate finance / Reuben Advani.
Description: Third edition. | New York : McGraw-Hill, [2019] | Includes index.
Identifiers: LCCN 2018011193| ISBN 9781260135596 (alk. paper) | ISBN 1260135594
Subjects: LCSH: Business enterprises--Finance. | Corporations--Finance. | Accounting. | Wall Street (New York, N.Y.)--Anecdotes.
Classification: LCC HG4026 .A345 2019 | DDC 658.15--dc23 LC record available at https://lccn.loc.gov/2018011193

McGraw-Hill Education products are available at special quantity discounts to use as premiums and sales promotions or for use in corporate training programs. To contact a representative, please visit the Contact Us pages at www.mhprofessional.com.

To Emily, my favorite student and professor

CONTENTS

---------------------------- PART 1 ----------------------------

ACCOUNTING

---------------------------- PART 2 ----------------------------

FINANCE

CONTENTS

ACKNOWLEDGMENTS

A book like this cannot be written without the help of many people. I want to thank my mom, Dolly Advani, who has instilled in me the discipline and drive to take on any task, and my sister, Ramona Advani, who constantly offers her talents to those in need (which quite often is me). My deepest thanks to Ellis Rubinstein, TC Westcott, and Wendy Schneider who have taught me that financial efficiency can increase social impact. I want to thank Noah Schwartzberg at McGraw-Hill for his efforts to bring a third edition of this book to fruition and his immensely helpful suggestions. I owe a great deal of gratitude to Colin Kelley at McGraw-Hill, who originally helped turn my book idea into a reality.

Throughout my career, a number of individuals have offered me guidance, and I truly believe I would not be where I am today without their help. Robert Borghese and Fred Lipman have been tremendous mentors to me and are always willing to offer valuable advice whenever needed. I truly appreciate their help. I want to thank Rakesh Jain and Sajjad Jaffer, my brothers in finance and always great sources of advice. A special thanks is owed to my friends and walking compendiums of all business knowledge, Maziar Akram, Vineet Budhraja, and Vikram Sodhi. Two individuals helped me find my way to Wall Street many years ago, Adam and Richard Pechter, and I owe a very heartfelt thanks to them for helping start my career. I would like to extend an important thanks to Gary Podorowsky and Nick Henny, who helped me learn the corporate side of corporate finance.

I would also like to thank my friends Shom Chowdhury and Nimitt Mankad for their strong support of this book. Thanks is due to my friend Dr. Ravi Goel for showing me just how important finance is to even nonfinancial types. My deepest gratitude is offered to Tomer Rothschild and Matthew Zaklad for their global perspectives.

I also want to thank my friends Brian Buck, Mike Siegel, Oriol Sunyer, and Ignacio Delgado, who help keep me sane during hectic times. A special thanks is owed to Karen Czerniakowski, Chris Czerniakowski, Amanda Reichert, Nora and Estelle who keep me smiling and well fed. Finally, thank you to Emily, Leena, and Leila who provide me with constant support while keeping me on my toes.

INTRODUCTION

Since the publication of this book's first edition, much has happened in the world of global finance. Corporate scandals, overvalued mergers, a global financial crisis, a financial recovery, market volatility . . . and many more developments that can make your head spin! The ups and downs of the global markets create costs that are borne by the investor and consumer public. Misguidance by investment analysts, bankers, accountants, and corporate managers can compound problems and undermine our trust in the institutions that they serve. It has never been more important for each of us to have a basic understanding of corporate finance and corporate accounting. This book was inspired by the tumult created by the financial world.

But here is the bigger problem: finance and accounting are boring! I remember spending long hours in front of dry textbooks while trying to make sense of charts and graphs, let alone the esoteric vernacular. I have a confession to make: after two years at one of the top finance MBA programs, several years on Wall Street, and teaching positions at several respected universities, I still can't tell you what most of those words and symbols mean. And this is coming from someone who has made a good living exploiting those concepts. A lesson that I did learn, however, is that certain MBA themes—if understood within the context of real-world business challenges—can be extremely useful.

Several years ago, I thought to myself, why not put together a book that covers these concepts in a clear, succinct, user-friendly, and entertaining format? With this in mind, I have written this book, which is intended to offer a breakdown of the major concepts covered in a standard MBA finance and accounting program. My objective is to offer a user-friendly, interactive, and fun approach to facilitate understanding and learning. The book draws more on real-life examples and less on theory: it is part textbook, part storybook.

I have yet to find an accounting or finance course that is infused with any degree of passion. Likewise, I have yet to find a student of these studies who has achieved any level of inspiration through them. But who says we can't try? If you can grasp the concepts covered in this book, you will be able to navigate the world of corporate accounting and finance with a heightened sense of confidence. And, I hope, you will never again have to blindly accept the opinions of the so-called experts.

PART 1

ACCOUNTING

1

ACCOUNTING BASICS

Q: What's the definition of an accountant?

*A: Someone who solves a problem you didn't know
you had in a way you don't understand.*

Normally, the mere mention of accounting is enough to send most people into deep REM sleep, and for good reason. Accounting is boring. But as with a lot of other boring things in life, we still do it. Driving to work and getting our teeth cleaned are boring, but we do them because we know that each serves as a means to an end. Similarly, we learn accounting to assist us in tackling a number of business and personal challenges. A clear understanding of accounting, along with the ability to apply the concepts, will lead to better decision making in our business activities. From picking stocks to calculating one's net worth, these concepts are useful. Plus, if we can apply them correctly to real-life vignettes and cases, they will be less boring, more fun, and easier to read and digest.

This chapter will discuss the following:

- Double entry accounting
- Cash versus accrual accounting
- Creative accounting

- Accounting Principles and Standards
- Tax versus book accounting
- Introduction to financial statements

DOUBLE ENTRY ACCOUNTING

In accounting, a system called *double entry accounting* is used. This system is similar in concept to something you might have studied in high school physics class. You may recall that for every action, there is an equal and opposite reaction. A similar principle applies in accounting. The principle is this: money is transferred from a source account to a destination account. In other words, money is neither gained nor lost; it simply is transferred. When a transaction occurs on one side of the financial statements, one or more accompanying transactions occur elsewhere in the financial statements.

Here are a few examples:

Example 1. A company purchases a product for later sale to its customers.
Result: The balance sheet will reflect a decrease in cash and an increase in inventory.

Example 2. A company sells products to its customers and receives payment by credit.
Result: The balance sheet will reflect an increase in accounts receivable and a decrease in inventory.

Example 3. A company borrows money.
Result: The balance sheet will reflect an increase in cash and an increase in debt.

Example 4. Finally, a company purchases a building with a combination of cash and a mortgage note.
Result: The balance sheet will reveal an increase under fixed assets (the purchase price of the building); a decrease of

another asset, cash; and an increase on the liability side of the balance sheet, the mortgage note.

These concepts will become clear when the structure of the balance sheet is reviewed in more detail. For now, simply understand that financial transactions involve a dynamic interplay of accounts that creates this balancing effect.

CASH VERSUS ACCRUAL ACCOUNTING

In financial reporting, there are two basic methodologies for reporting transactions: the cash basis and the accrual basis.

Cash Accounting

With the *cash basis*, as the term implies, transactions are recorded when cash changes hands. Suppose you walk into the local hardware store and purchase a hammer for $10 cash and take immediate possession of it. Under the cash basis, the store owner would record this transaction as a $10 sale because the cash was paid and the item was delivered—the transaction was completed.

Cash basis reporting is not generally accepted in business, but it is allowed for tax purposes in certain businesses that meet some or all of the following conditions (depending on the legal structure of the business):

- The business does not sell products, meaning that it is service-based and therefore has no inventory.
- The business keeps records for cash receipts and payments.
- The business has less than $5 million a year in sales.

For the vast majority of businesses, however, the cash basis is not acceptable. Generally, only small businesses with service-based sales can use cash basis reporting. Most other businesses use accrual basis reporting, including all publicly traded companies.

Accrual Accounting

With the *accrual basis of accounting*, transactions are recorded as they occur. Cash does not necessarily have to change hands, but a transaction must have occurred. Suppose that in a similar transaction you go to the hardware store, purchase your hammer, and take possession of the hammer. However, you pay the $10 with credit. Nonetheless, with accrual accounting, the transaction is recorded as a sale by the store owner.

Accrual basis reporting is used to capture the overall economic activity of the firm. This is done because in finance and accounting, there is a fundamental notion that businesses are assessed not so much on what they have on hand but rather on their expectations or potential. In the universe of financial reporting, what you see is not always what you get. With accrual accounting, the expectation is that the company will receive those payments at some point in the future, although the reality may entail entirely different outcomes. More specifically, companies book sales when goods are shipped, services are rendered, or a long-term contract is signed.

At this point, it is critical to understand the differences between cash accounting and accrual accounting. Suppose ABC Software announces a $500,000 licensing agreement. Under that agreement, ABC will receive payments of $100,000 each year for the next five years. Using the accrual method, what would revenues reflect at the end of this year?

If you answered $500,000, you are absolutely correct, because under the accrual method, ABC would book the full amount—the contract is signed and the services, in theory, are rendered. This assumes that there is no follow-up servicing, and so the software is delivered in its entirety. Using the cash method, how would this result differ?

If you answered that ABC would book $100,000, you are correct once again, because ABC would record only what was collected. In sum, ABC collected $100,000, and that is what was recorded.

CREATIVE ACCOUNTING

As you can well imagine, accrual accounting creates many opportunities for fraud and manipulation. The vague rules governing revenue recognition, along with numerous intangible items, create exciting yet often misleading opportunities for "creative accounting." The best example of this on an industrywide basis has to do with telecommunications companies using network swaps in the late 1990s to inflate their revenues artificially. At that time, loose accounting standards in a nascent industry opened the door to deceptive methods of financial disclosure. The end result of this practice, sadly, was not unlike many of the cases we cover in this book: billions of dollars of hard-earned investor funds evaporated overnight.

For years, large telecom companies were plagued by steadily declining margins in wholesale network bandwidth. At the same time, they faced mounting pressure to reveal strong earnings to Wall Street analysts. To alleviate these problems, those companies began the practice of swapping network bandwidth with other industry players, with both parties booking the sale. This was done by using what were called *indefeasible rights of use contracts* (IRUs), which are long-term contracts for the use of bandwidth. By using these contracts, telecom companies would engage in a practice known as *round-tripping*, in which two companies would engage simultaneously in a purchase and sale of an IRU contract, with each party recognizing the revenue portion. With this technique, one party would book the entire revenue amount resulting from the sale of the IRU contract. The same company would structure a reciprocal deal with its counterpart so that it was simultaneously purchasing a similar bandwidth contract. In the end, no assets were transferred, but both parties booked a sale. The net effect of this transaction was zero because they were effectively exchanging the same bandwidth. However, using accrual basis accounting, they were able to book this revenue.

How did they get away with this? When each side recorded the sale, it booked the full amount of the contract in accordance with the standards of accrual accounting. However, in the buyback, each side spread (amortized) the purchase price of buying access over the course of the deal, which at times meant 25 years or more. Alternatively, the parties might have booked the buyback as a capital expenditure, which would not affect the income statement and in turn would have no effect on earnings. This method of accounting was advocated by Arthur Andersen's Professional Standards Group, which became widely regarded as the arbiter of accounting rules in the industry. As the pressure to meet Wall Street's earnings expectations increased, so did this practice, which was certain to boost earnings. In fact, one famous deal involved two industry leaders, Global Crossing and 360networks. Global Crossing hoped to exchange $150 million of its capacity for $200 million of 360networks' capacity. In the process, both sides would book revenue, although Global Crossing would book less. As a result, 360networks agreed to purchase more at some future date to offset the current shortfall.

Such deals were commonplace and went unchecked for years. As share prices soared, the level of scrutiny of accounting procedures sank. But when such deals failed to compensate for earnings shortfalls, accounting regulators took a closer look at these practices and, more important, at the surrounding disclosures.

ACCOUNTING PRINCIPLES AND STANDARDS

The American Institute of Certified Public Accountants (AICPA) is a professional organization of practicing certified public accountants (CPAs). The recommendations of this organization have been vital to the development of the overall principles that we use in financial reporting and that are known as *generally accepted accounting principles* (GAAP). For the most part, GAAP is considered to be based on the standards and interpretations of the Financial Accounting Standards Board, which is discussed later in this chapter.

If you have been following the news, you know that these methods are far from perfect. There are all types of loopholes that companies may capitalize on, and for that reason, we have seen numerous instances of accounting fraud over the past several years. GAAP is not without its shortcomings, but it is the overriding set of principles used in producing financial statements in the United States.

Who Does What?

A good deal of confusion arises over who is in charge of what when it comes to accounting and financial reporting. Essentially, the prime overseers of corporate accounting regulations and guidelines are the Financial Accounting Standards Board (FASB) and the Securities and Exchange Commission (SEC).

FASB

The Financial Accounting Standards Board serves as an overseeing body whose mission is "to establish and improve standards of financial accounting and reporting for the guidance and education of the public, including issuers, auditors, and users of financial information." FASB is to accounting what the Supreme Court is to the law: the top governing body that issues standards and interpretations that form the basis of all GAAP legislation. Through a series of processes and subcommittees, FASB has been granted the role of determining what is acceptable in financial reporting. FASB is not perfect, but it's the best we've got.

The SEC

After the stock market crash of 1929, a number of changes took place to ensure that such an event would never happen again. To that end, the Securities and Exchange Commission was formed as an independent regulatory agency of the US government. The SEC now regulates all publicly traded companies by making sure that they do the following:

- File annual audited financial statements with the SEC
- Follow accounting standards and practices as recommended by the SEC

- Identify accounting and reporting problems for the FASB to address

International Accounting Standards

Businesses in the United States follow accounting rules prescribed by GAAP. Historically, businesses in other countries tended to use and apply their own countries' standards. These differences in accounting standards affected everything from the treatment of depreciation and amortization to the actual structure of financial statements. Between some countries, such differences were minor. For example, differences between the US and UK versions of GAAP were apparent in the treatment of asset acquisition and the tax treatment of extraordinary income items. Larger differences emerged when accounting standards in the United States were compared with those of some Asian countries. In terms of the structuring of cross-border mergers and strategic alliances, such differences could create untold accounting hassles. For example, a US-based corporation that acquired an Indian-based counterpart would have to account for differences in taxes, intangible expense items, asset valuation techniques, and the like. In large transactions, those differences created millions of dollars' worth of accounting hassles. That was then, this is now.

IFRS

For many years, there was interest in creating a worldwide standard of accounting. As long as each country was confident that it was employing the best standards, however, that interest produced few results. Then came International Financial Reporting Standards (IFRS). As country-based accounting standards in Europe made it difficult to compare results for companies registered in different countries, the International Accounting Standards Board (IASB) was created to provide a single set of standards. As of 2005, publicly traded companies in the European Union (EU) are required to provide financial statements that are based on IFRS. IFRS involves some reclassifications and in some cases alternative valuation methodologies. Countries around the globe have moved to IFRS, and it remains to be seen whether the United States will ever embrace the method completely. Although IFRS is becoming the dominant system worldwide, this book still has a bias toward US GAAP. Sorry, the book after all is called *The Wall Street MBA*, not *The Canary Wharf MBA*. The good news, however, is that the two standards are very similar as a process of convergence began at the onset of IFRS. The best we can do for now is to attempt to understand the basics of accounting and buddy up to distinguished CPAs with years of international experience. If you're having trouble with that, might I suggest *How to Win Friends and Influence People* by Dale Carnegie as some supplementary reading.

TAX VERSUS BOOK ACCOUNTING

Very often, companies will create two sets of financial statements. One is reserved for tax reporting, and the other for investor reporting. This enables a company to present its best performance numbers while minimizing its tax burden. In other words, this is the "have your cake and eat it too" option. Tax accounting is used to make sure that income and deductions reported on tax returns are in compliance with IRS rules and regulations. Book accounting, in contrast, pertains to reporting on a company's financial statements and is usually in line with GAAP standards, though it may not always be in line with tax standards.

Such reporting creates a fair amount of confusion for analysts and investors alike. In fact, companies that tend to maintain tight control over their financial statements and follow very loose reporting standards often capitalize on the differences between tax accounting and book accounting. Companies frequently attempt the balancing act of trying to maximize returns for investors while trying to minimize their tax liabilities for tax purposes. Thus, in essence, it is acceptable for a company to use book accounting for investor purposes and use tax accounting for tax purposes. Companies that follow this approach must reconcile these differences on the basis of an IRS tax schedule so that any changes or differences that exist between the two disclosures are documented.

INTRODUCTION TO FINANCIAL STATEMENTS

Years ago, I was cramming for a high school English final. The exam was to be based on a number of books from the Victorian era, few of which had any relevance in my quest for a Firebird Trans Am. As I fully intended to devote more time to grooming my mullet and as little time as possible to studying Dickens, I devised a revolutionary study technique. To cover several books in a short time, I opted to read every third chapter of each book. By doing this, I could read three books in the time it would take most people to read one. Pretty clever, right? Armed with my new technique and a heck of a lot of confidence, I pored through the classics in record time, and on exam day I pulled a solid A-minus. A few years later I tried this technique in college and failed miserably.

The moral to this story is this: you can read a few chapters of a book and get a feel for the plot, the characters, and the central theme. However, you will never truly understand a story until you have read all the chapters word for word and, more important, have come to understand how they relate to one another.

A similar principle holds true when it comes to financial statements. You should study the balance sheet, income statement, and cash flow statement for a company, but more than anything else, you should understand the links between those statements. Only then will you begin to understand the story behind the company. Unfortunately, because of the obvious time constraints facing high-powered brokers and investors, many on Wall Street use my every third chapter methodology, and this may explain why the world has lost confidence in Wall Street.

The next several chapters are devoted to specific financial statements: how to read, analyze, and project them. We will cover the balance sheet, the income statement, and the cash flow statement, seeking an understanding of what each statement consists of, how each is used, and, most important, how the three statements relate to one another to provide a big-picture analysis. From there, we will learn the best ways to analyze those statements by using trend and ratio analysis. Before we do that, however, take a look at how these statements are disclosed and what generally accompanies them.

Common Public Filings

Financial statements are filed periodically with the SEC by all public companies. Here is a summary guide to the more common filings:

- *10-K.* This covers the company's annual performance and is due after the end of the fiscal year. It contains the following:
  - Income statement
  - Balance sheet
  - Cash flow statement
  - Footnotes to the financial statements
  - Management discussion and analysis
  - Auditor's report
- *Annual report.* Essentially, this is a condensed version of the 10-K with more emphasis placed on marketing the company to investors through colorful charts and pictures.
- *Proxy statement.* This statement is offered around the time of the annual meeting and covers the following:
  - Management compensation
  - Management stock options
  - Related-party transactions
  - Auditor changes
- *10-Q.* The 10-Q is an unaudited statement of the company's quarterly performance that is due after the quarter ends. It includes many performance reports similar to those found in a 10-K.

- *Form 8-K.* This form normally is due after any material event such as a major change in ownership or capital structure.
- *Form 144.* Form 144 is a registration document that discloses when insiders buy or sell stock.

Financial Statement Report

What generally is found in standard financial statement reports such as the 10-K and 10-Q? Aside from the balance sheet, income statement, and cash flow statement, companies offer important accompanying disclosures. This documentation could include management's discussion and analysis, the management's report, the auditor's report, and the explanatory notes and supplementary information. These sections disclose any extraordinary items, any exceptional treatment of certain items, and generally any item that might merit further explanation. The following sections detail each of these reports.

Management's Discussion and Analysis

Commonly referred to as the *MD&A report*, this company-generated analysis offers a strategic overview of the company's performance during the prior year as well as anticipated changes in the coming year. Normally, this occupies a few pages at the beginning of every annual report or 10-K for publicly traded companies. The MD&A report is usually a worthwhile read, as it provides hints about the company's plans, goals, and expectations for the coming year.

Management's Report

Typically a supplement to the MD&A report, the management's report details the responsibilities of individual managers in preparing the financial reports. In the wake of big accounting scandals such as Enron, WorldCom, and Parmalat, it is important to understand who is specifically responsible for the actual preparation of these financial statements.

The Auditor's Report
In the past, this report served as a relatively generic standard seal of approval issued by a company's auditors. However, in the aftermath of the big corporate accounting scandals and the adoption of the Sarbanes-Oxley Act, we have witnessed a new standard in corporate audits. Auditors now explicitly disclose any red flags in their reports.

Explanatory Notes and Supplementary Information
If there's one thing you take away from this section, it should be simply to read the footnotes. There's no possible way I can stress enough the importance of these supplementary notes. To grasp the importance of this, read on.

Read the footnotes! Back in the 1950s, a gentleman by the name of John Rigas was working as a movie house usher in the small town of Coudersport in western Pennsylvania. If you have ever been to Coudersport, you know it is something right out of a Norman Rockwell painting. Behind the colorful five-and-dime store facades and below the cobblestone streets lie the remnants of a cable empire. At the time, Rigas, something of a visionary, read about the new technology of cable television and decided that the good people of Coudersport should have it. With a $300 investment, he commenced building his empire. Within a decade, he had wired most of the town. Over the next four decades, he built a national empire that was managed collectively by him and his sons. By the late 1990s, Adelphia had become a Wall Street darling and the fifth largest cable provider in the United States. All that changed during one quarterly earnings conference call in 2002. This occurred after the Enron scandal surfaced and at a time when Wall Street analysts began asking more pressing questions. On this particular call, one analyst asked a question about a footnote pertaining to company loans to the Rigas family. The footnote stated: "Certain subsidiaries of the company are co-borrowers with certain companies owned by the Rigas family." The question was followed by a vague response and the hasty conclusion of the call.

The stock price collapsed on the news, and over the next several days, a truly remarkable story unfolded that documented instances of the Rigas family borrowing excessively from the Adelphia company bank account. This publicly traded company was treated essentially as the founders' personal bank account. Among other things, they used funds from the company to pay for the construction of a golf course, a private jet, and even shares of Adelphia—not in the company name but in the family name. That, along with clever accounting that included capitalizing millions of dollars in costs that should have been expensed, contributed to the eventual demise of the company. What was ostensibly a conflict of interest later was determined by the courts to be a clear case of fraud.

The moral to this story is simply this: *read the footnotes*. Within that tiny footnote was enough information to turn a multibillion-dollar company into a penny stock. *Read the footnotes*.

2

BALANCE SHEET

A friend of mine used to live by the phrase *leverage your future.* As we were starting our careers in Manhattan, his extravagant lifestyle never ceased to amaze me. From his Park Avenue apartment to his vast collection of Hermès ties, he seemed to possess all the trappings of success. Yet he was always short on cash. In fact, each day he asked to borrow lunch money from me. I was comfortable with that until I realized that these were uncollateralized loans. Thus, when he showed up to work with a new tie each day, I was subsidizing each tie with lunch credits. In fact, his leverage-the-future model was built on his friends' backs. Years later, I realized that numerous companies in corporate America employ this model . . . and my friend now runs such a company.

The balance sheet serves to outline this model by revealing what a company has, what a company owes, and what a company is worth (at least on paper). I like to think of the balance sheet as the doctor's report for a company, because it helps me determine whether a company is in good financial health. It reveals whether the company is strong, and if so, whether it will be around for a while, and if not, what the sources of its weakness are. Specifically, the balance sheet addresses issues of solvency, liquidity, and capital structure. The best way to remember the components of the balance sheet is with this equation:

$$\text{Assets} = \text{liabilities} + \text{shareholders' equity}$$

You might rearrange the equation in this way:

$$\text{Assets} - \text{liabilities} = \text{shareholders' equity}$$

You can slice it and dice it any way you choose, but no matter what, the equation must hold true. If it does not, the balance sheet will not balance and therefore will not be a balance sheet. This chapter will discuss the following:

- Assets
- Liabilities
- Owners' equity
- Sample balance sheet
- Balance sheet games

ASSETS

The balance sheet begins with the assets of the company. The assets describe resources of the firm that are expected to yield some future benefit for the company, such as an increase in cash inflows or a decrease in cash outflows. In other words, they represent what the company possesses. They do not always have to be tangible, but they should represent some value.

Current Assets

The asset section of the balance sheet begins with the assets that are considered to be most liquid, meaning that they can be converted to cash, consumed, or sold within a relatively short period, usually one year. These assets are current assets. Some of the more common current assets include:

- Cash
- Marketable securities
- Accounts receivable
- Inventory

Cash

The first of the current assets is the most liquid of all assets: cash. Most bankers would argue that cash is more liquid than water.

Marketable Securities

After cash, the company may list short-term investments, or what is referred to more commonly as *marketable securities*. These are generally liquid investments that the company realistically could sell within a short period.

Accounts Receivable

Accounts receivable, payments owed to the company, also may appear under current assets. Perhaps the company sold products to a customer on credit. The expected payment is added to the accounts receivable listing on the balance sheet. Even though payment has yet to be collected, for purposes of financial reporting, it is considered an asset. The expectation is that the payment will be received sometime within the next year. In reality, however, this may not be the case. In certain instances, a company may list an allowance for uncollected receivables. This is merely an estimate of what might not be collected, based on historical collection rates. A company may do this to depict the likelihood of collecting receivables more accurately or to create some flexibility in balance sheet adjustments through periodic estimate revisions.

Inventory

In most non-service-based businesses, the next listing probably will be inventory: what the company produced or purchased but has yet to sell.

Noncurrent Assets

Following current assets is noncurrent assets. The assumption with noncurrent assets is that they could be liquidated or consumed in the course of a year. Noncurrent assets generally are grouped into broad categories, which might include the following:

- Tangible fixed assets—usually listed as *property, plant, and equipment (PP&E)*
- Intangible fixed assets—usually goodwill

Tangible Fixed Assets

Usually listed as PP&E, tangible fixed assets might include real estate, manufacturing equipment, furniture, computer hardware, delivery trucks, the corporate jet—anything and everything that constitutes the overall infrastructure of the company. Suppose you buy a dusty old dirt farm with your uncle and cousins. You would record the amount paid for that land on your balance sheet. Next, you purchase a shiny red Dodge Charger, weld the doors shut, and paint a flag on the roof. In this case, you also would list the price you paid for the car on your balance sheet. Thus, your PP&E reflects the land and the car. Over time, your uncle starts to produce moonshine on the land, and your car has earned a reputation as the fastest in the county. Clearly, both have appreciated in value. However, for purposes of balance sheet reporting, both are still listed at historical cost. In a moment, you will see how most assets are assumed to lose value over time, even when the market might reveal something entirely different.

Intangible Fixed Assets

Occasionally, an item will be listed as goodwill under noncurrent assets. Goodwill is a by-product from an acquisition and results from the difference between the price paid for an asset and what is considered its fair value. For example, when one company buys another, the purchase price is distributed among the separate units of the acquired business and is based on the appraised value of the underlying assets. If the purchase price is higher than the value of the underlying assets, the excess is recorded as goodwill (which is usually the case). The idea behind this premium is that the acquirer believes the acquired firm will generate profits over time and the value of those future profits is recorded today as an asset.

Depreciation

A very important concept in finance and accounting concludes the asset section of the balance sheet: depreciation. This affects not only the balance sheet but the income statement and cash flow statement as well. In theory, depreciation reflects the loss of value of a fixed asset over its expected life. As you can imagine, there is no scientific way to assess this. However, financial analysts and accountants try their best to estimate this by using a variety of schedules and tables. On the balance sheet, the depreciation listed is accumulated over the lifetime of the asset. To understand depreciation, consider the following example.

If you have ever purchased a car, you know that the minute you drive that car off the lot, its value decreases. This happens because a certain amount of depreciation is associated with it. Suppose you buy that shiny Dodge Charger that was mentioned earlier. You spend $10,000 on it. The expected life of this car is 10 years. If the car depreciates on a straight-line basis, meaning that it loses an equal portion of its value each year, it would lose $1,000 in value after one year.

On your balance sheet, you would record the following under fixed assets after one year:

YEAR 1 FIXED ASSETS	
Property, Plant, and Equipment:	$10,000
Accumulated Depreciation:	$ 1,000
Property, Plant, and Equipment, net:	$ 9,000

Thus, the loss of $1,000 in value is listed next to accumulated depreciation and subtracted from property, plant, and equipment. How would your second year look?

At this point, you would add another year's worth of depreciation to accumulated depreciation, which would appear on your balance sheet in the following way:

YEAR 2 FIXED ASSETS	
Property, Plant, and Equipment:	$10,000
Accumulated Depreciation:	$ 2,000
Property, Plant, and Equipment, net:	$ 8,000

Accumulated depreciation is the total of each of the prior years' depreciation. This continues until the asset is fully depreciated.

Depreciation is often a breeding ground for manipulation. For the most part, there are at least five commonly accepted methods of calculating depreciation, although companies often use their own interpretation of those methods or choose the one that best fits their objectives. For example, a company seeking to minimize its tax liability might use an accelerated depreciation schedule, meaning that a certain asset depreciates more in the early years and less in the later years. In some instances, a company might have more than one depreciation schedule pertaining to a particular asset.

Depreciation becomes particularly complicated in new asset categories. In such cases, companies will use their own discretion to determine how to depreciate a particular asset. The result can have a dramatic impact on the balance sheet, and as you will see later in this book, it can have an even stronger impact on the income statement because depreciation for that particular year will affect the company's earnings and in turn the amount of taxes paid. Depreciation is an area that companies very often seek to maximize for tax purposes but minimize for investor reporting purposes.

LIABILITIES

On the other side of the balance sheet, you will find liabilities. Liabilities, simply put, represent the debts of the company, or what the company owes. Like assets, liabilities begin with current liabilities: those that in theory come due within the course of a year.

Current Liabilities

Current liabilities might include any form of short-term debt, such as the following:

- Lines of credit (amount outstanding)
- Accounts payable
- Current debt
- Current portion of long-term debt

Lines of Credit

This lists the amount drawn from any credit facilities. As with credit cards in personal finance, lines of credit enable companies to obtain short-term funding with few transaction costs. For this item, only the amount outstanding would appear on the balance sheet. For example, a company might have a $5 million credit line from which only $1 million has been borrowed. Only the $1 million would be reflected on the balance sheet despite the fact that the line of credit is substantially larger. When it comes to lines of credit, size doesn't matter.

Accounts Payable

This refers to amounts owed by the company to vendors or suppliers. Perhaps the company purchased raw materials for manufacturing but has yet to pay for them. Again, the assumption is that the company will have to pay within one year.

Current Debt

This might include any type of short-term bond or note issued by the company.

Current Portion of Long-Term Debt

Often, when a company issues long-term debt, the amount due in the current year will be listed here.

Noncurrent Liabilities

Below current liabilities are noncurrent liabilities. Noncurrent liabilities usually take the form of long-term debt: any debt that comes due after the course of one year. Certain debt instruments will pay down principal each year as seen under the current portion of long-term debt. Therefore, only the portion of debt that comes due after one year is listed under noncurrent liabilities.

OWNERS' EQUITY

Finally, there is owners' equity, or what is commonly referred to as *shareholders' equity*. Owners' equity represents the book value of the company, or its value on paper. This is not to be confused with the market value, which will be discussed later in this book. It is the difference between assets and liabilities, in other words, what is left after the company pays everything it owes with everything it owns. Owners' equity consists of two components: direct owners' equity and indirect owners' equity.

Direct Owners' Equity

Direct owners' equity represents funds that are invested directly into the company by the firm's shareholders. This might include a sole proprietor of a small business investing seed capital to start the business, or it might be the funds raised from the investment of thousands of investors in a public offering. Either way, the funds invested directly into the company represent direct owners' equity. In the case of the hardware store mentioned in Chapter 1 (we'll call it Cunningham Hardware), assume that it was started by one owner with an investment of $10,000. That $10,000 investment would be listed on the company balance sheet under direct owners' equity, or what is commonly referred to as *paid-in capital*. Suppose that after 10 years the business has grown substantially. The hardware store has expanded into a national chain with stores in all 50 states. At this point, a need for significant capital has arisen, and so the owner decides to take the company public. In this initial public offering, $100 million is raised. These funds are also listed under direct owners' equity or paid-in capital as they represent funds invested directly into the company.

Indirect Owners' Equity

The other component of owners' equity is indirect owners' equity, commonly referred to as *retained earnings*. Retained earnings represent the buildup of equity through the generation of income. This tends to be a bit more complex than most balance sheet items, so brace yourself. Retained earnings very often are overlooked or, worse, taken for granted. In fact, many smaller companies simply plug in this number by using mathematical deduction, which ignores any deceptive accounting or fraud.

Going back to Cunningham Hardware, suppose the company reports $20,000 in net income on its income statement this year, and suppose it issues a dividend to shareholders that in total amounts to $5,000. When the dividend payment is subtracted from net income, the remainder is $15,000. That $15,000 is recorded on the balance sheet as part of retained earnings. It then is added to the retained earnings account. Thus, retained earnings represents the amount left after net income is calculated and dividends are paid out. The balance sheet shows the cumulative of this account, which changes each period. The amount calculated on the income statement, which will be discussed in Chapter 3, is based on the performance for that particular year.

SAMPLE BALANCE SHEET

Figure 2-1 presents a balance sheet for Cunningham Hardware. The company lists its assets on one side and its liabilities and owners' equity on the other side, a common format for a balance sheet. Sometimes, however, assets will be listed above liabilities and owners' equity.

The first items are the current assets of the company, beginning with $8,000 cash, which represents the total cash reserves of the company. Next is $10,000 in accounts receivable, representing the total of payments owed to the company. The company has sold $10,000 worth of merchandise but has yet to collect payment for it. The reality might be that the company will collect only a portion of this; this is very often the case. Nonetheless, the full

FIGURE 2-1 Sample Balance Sheet

Cunningham Hardware Co.

ASSETS		LIABILITIES	
Current Assets		**Current Liabilities**	
Cash	$ 8,000	Accounts Payable	$ 3,000
Accounts Receivable	$ 10,000	Accrued Expenses Payable	$ 5,000
Inventory	$ 14,000	Income Tax Payable	$ 1,000
Prepaid Expenses	$ 2,000	Total Current Liabilities	$ 9,000
Total Current Assets	$ 34,000		
Noncurrent Assets		**Noncurrent Liabilities**	
Fixed Assets	$ 45,000	Notes Payable	$19,000
Accumulated Depreciation	$(23,000)		
Total Noncurrent Assets	$ 22,000	Total Noncurrent Liabilities	$19,000
Total Assets	$ 56,000	**Shareholders' Equity**	
		Paid-In Capital	$ 8,000
		Retained Earnings	$20,000
		Total Shareholders' Equity	$28,000
		Total Liabilities & Shareholders' Equity	$56,000

amount outstanding is listed here as a current asset, though it is not entirely liquid. Again, in financial statements, what you see is not always what you get.

Next is inventory, which represents the value of what the company produced but has yet to sell. The company reveals $14,000 worth of inventory. Whether the company sells this is inconsequential. For the purposes of balance sheet reporting, it is listed as a current asset. Again, what you see is not always what you get.

The final current asset is prepaid expenses. This represents expenses that were prepaid and designated for this account in the amount of $2,000. Perhaps the company signed a contract with a vendor that spans more than one year. In that case, the total amount to be paid is recorded to this prepaid expense account and expensed periodically. In total, Cunningham Hardware has current assets of $34,000.

Next are the noncurrent assets, beginning with fixed assets. Again, fixed assets often are referred to as *property, plant, and equipment*: the hard assets or the infrastructure of the company.

The assumption here is that these assets would require a course of time greater than one year to liquidate. The total value of the fixed assets is $45,000, which is based on historical cost. When these assets were acquired, they were worth $45,000. Finally, the accumulated depreciation of $23,000 is subtracted from the fixed assets, and net noncurrent assets of $22,000 remains. The total value of current and noncurrent assets is $56,000.

On the other side of the balance sheet are the current liabilities. The company has accounts payable of $3,000. These are accounts that it owes to any company that has allowed it to purchase items or pay for services on credit. Perhaps Cunningham purchased several cases of hammers to sell in the store. The amount that Cunningham purchased these items for totals $3,000, which is what it owes to its suppliers. It also has accrued expenses payable representing expenses that have been incurred but are not due yet. Accrued expenses are the opposite of prepaid expenses and are expected to be paid in the period in which they have been incurred. Common accrued expenses include wages and interest. In total, Cunningham has accrued expenses in the amount of $5,000. Finally, it has income tax payable in the amount of $1,000, which represents the portion due to the government but not yet paid. Companies make tax payments on the basis of estimated income. This account helps reconcile the differences between estimates and what is owed. In total, the company has current liabilities of $9,000.

Next on the liabilities side of the balance sheet are noncurrent liabilities. Again, the assumption here is that these noncurrent liabilities come due in a course of time greater than one year. The first and only item is notes payable. In this case, there is a note payable in the amount of $19,000. Therefore, the total of noncurrent liabilities is $19,000.

Last but not least is shareholders' equity or owners' equity. Remember, owners' equity usually consists of direct and indirect owners' equity. In most cases, direct owners' equity is listed as paid-in capital, which here totals $8,000. This represents the amount that the owner or shareholders of the company have invested in the company. Indirect owners' equity is listed as retained earnings, which in this case is $20,000. These retained earnings are generated through the accumulation of income minus dividends over time. Each year, after net income is recorded and any dividends are subtracted out, what remains is retained earnings.

Thus, total shareholders' equity is $28,000. Add this to current and noncurrent liabilities to come up with total liabilities and shareholders' equity of $56,000, which is a number that, not coincidentally, is equal to the total assets. The balance sheet balances and therefore is a proper balance sheet.

BALANCE SHEET GAMES

One of my fondest childhood memories was exploring my dad's great big Craftsman toolbox. In it, he reserved the cavernous bottom compartment for the tools that he owned, and on the top tray lay the tools that were borrowed from friends. Thus, in a way, his toolbox functioned much like a balance sheet. If there were any tools he did not want me to find, well, those were usually hidden somewhere else in the garage—much like a balance sheet.

The balance sheet in many instances creates a great hiding spot for corporate managers. Nowadays, the use of this statement for such purposes is becoming increasingly complex. It is easy to understate a few billion dollars in liabilities or overstate a few billion dollars in assets on the balance sheet. Before we get to the how, we should consider the why. As was discussed earlier, the balance sheet serves as the doctor's report for a company. In other words, it reveals the company's state of financial health. This is important to investors, analysts, creditors, and credit rating agencies. For this reason, corporate managers will go to great lengths to reveal a clean bill of health, which will often involve a clever scheme. Manipulation of this statement can occur in the following ways:

- Improperly recording the value of assets or liabilities
- Mark-to-market accounting
- Removing liabilities from the balance sheet entirely

Improper Valuation

As was just shown, most asset values on the balance sheet are recorded at historical cost. However, new standards have evolved by which certain items may be adjusted to current market price. Items such as marketable securities are relatively volatile while being fairly liquid; therefore, accounting standards necessitate that they be reflected at their fair market value. Other, less volatile assets may be adjusted downward but not upward. As a result, financial managers often are given the freedom to interpret these values.

As pressure to meet certain requirements for funding becomes greater, financial managers must ensure that their financial ratios fall in line with what is expected. For example, most commercial lenders require that a company achieve a certain debt-to-equity ratio as well as current ratio: the ratio that compares current assets with current liabilities (see "Ratio Analysis" in Chapter 6 for more information). Thus, when a company's current ratio falls below a certain required level, a financial manager may choose to overvalue specific current assets such as marketable securities. How and when those securities are valued will affect the end result and in turn the current ratio. The standards are loose and the enforcement of these standards even looser.

Mark-to-Market Accounting

An obscure accounting topic made front-page headlines during the financial crisis of 2008. Why? To put it mildly, the fate of the global banking system became highly susceptible to the assumptions used in a method of accounting known as mark-to-market accounting. Mark-to-market accounting is used to assign value to an asset on the basis of its current market price. The idea came about in the nineteenth century, when futures traders used it in an effort to mark their positions to the current market price. Although futures may simply serve as contracts to buy or sell something at some point in the future, they maintain some value during their life. With mark-to-market accounting in place, the changes in value of these instruments are recorded on a regular basis on the financial statements of the company holding them.

In other words, they are marked to market rather than listed at cost (what was paid for them).

Imagine that 10 years ago you purchased a home for $100,000. Three years ago, your home's value was assessed to be $200,000. If you were to use mark-to-market accounting, you would list this increase in value on your personal financial statements and show an increase in your noncash income. Did you benefit from this increase? Not directly. It doesn't affect your household income or available cash because you have not sold the home. However, it does increase your net worth on paper, which means that in theory, you might be able to borrow more. In fact, you probably could obtain a larger home equity loan or line of credit on the basis of this increase in net worth. Having access to this capital appears to place you in a stronger financial position.

Let's consider another scenario: the home you purchased 10 years ago for $100,000 is worth $70,000 today because of a drop in home prices. Using mark-to-market accounting, your noncash income would be reduced on the basis of the drop in market value and, more important, your net worth would have dropped as a result. Although your household income is not affected and this represents no significant change to your lifestyle, your ability to borrow could be diminished. This may present some problems should you be in need of a home equity loan or some other source of capital.

Fortunately, we have little need for mark-to-market accounting in personal finance, but what happens when some of the largest corporations in the world use this technique? That is what happened in 2007 when financial institutions were required by the Financial Accounting Standards Board (FASB) to use this method to disclose the values of various financial instruments. Some of those instruments, such as mortgage-backed securities, were highly complex in that they were based on massive bundles of other instruments, such as home mortgages. Quantifying their values became increasingly difficult when those instruments were not actively traded. In other words, when such instruments are actively traded, assigning a mark-to-market value is relatively simple. It becomes the price that buyers and sellers agree on. But what happens when these instruments are no longer traded? Then you have the makings of a major financial crisis.

As the appetite for these instruments waned in late 2007, financial institutions found it difficult to sell them. Without a liquid market, those institutions were forced to use broad-based estimates to determine their values. In essence, they moved from mark-to-market accounting to mark-to-model accounting. The results were ugly. As the housing market collapsed, the values determined by those financial models were shockingly lower than they had been in past quarters. As a result, major banks around the world were writing down those assets at a rapid pace while lowering their profits and eroding investor confidence. As investors lost confidence because of those massive write-downs, stock prices fell to reflect this.

The world is divided on mark-to-market accounting. There are those in favor of it because it increases transparency in financial disclosure. As the argument goes, if something loses value, the financial statements should reflect the loss of value. The opposing argument is based on the idea that trying to estimate market values can do more harm than good and ultimately prove misleading, especially in illiquid markets.

Off-Balance-Sheet Items

If a company is seeking to maintain a solid debt-to-equity ratio, it may simply remove certain liabilities from its balance sheet. How is this possible? you ask. With a wonderful invention called the *off-balance-sheet transaction*. By meeting certain ownership stipulations, some balance sheet items can be transferred from the parent company's balance sheet to that of an affiliate company. It's that simple.

Most off-balance-sheet structures involve the use of special-purpose entities (SPEs). These are some of the many culprits behind several large accounting scandals in corporate America, including Enron and Cendant. An SPE is formed as a separate entity loosely affiliated with a parent company and is based on specific rules of ownership. The SPE is created by designating a specific entity to carry out an activity or series of transactions related to a defined purpose. It is formed through one of the following structures:

- Limited partnership
- Limited liability company
- Corporation
- Trust

A minimum investment is contributed by a third-party investor, representing a legal equity ownership interest in the SPE. In exchange for this investment, the third-party investor controls the SPE's activities while assuming the risks and rewards of its ownership in the SPE assets. For the SPE to be an arm's-length entity (not consolidated into the sponsor's financial statement), the third-party investor must bear the risks of the investment as well. Through such a structure, any number of items can be moved off the company's balance sheet, something that was done quite liberally by Enron (see Chapter 5 for more information on Enron).

SPEs are not considered inherently problematic or deceptive. However, thanks in part to Enron and a number of other companies, they have come under a great deal of scrutiny because of their ability to disguise liabilities. An SPE, when structured and disclosed in a legitimate manner, can be quite effective. A company can use it as a funding source to lower its cost of financing. When assets such as receivables are isolated in an SPE, the SPE can use them as collateral on debt. An SPE also can create research-and-development joint ventures with other companies, avoiding significant liability on the holding company's balance sheet. Additionally, it can finance real estate through tax-beneficial transactions. In fact, the majority of large corporations use some form of off-balance-sheet structure. An SPE also can provide a needed asset without the accompanying liability. For example, suppose Cunningham Hardware continues to receive shipments of inventory from overseas. This is problematic because these shipments will arrive throughout the year regardless of demand for the products. The store is simply too small to display all items, and the cost of renting a facility is too high. Instead, management decides to build a small warehouse. By doing this, Cunningham Hardware can hold the inventory and pull from it when demand increases.

To finance the construction, the store will need to borrow funds. This will involve a significant capital outlay, which undoubtedly will affect the balance sheet. At this crucial stage in its growth cycle, the store would rather not reflect excessive amounts of debt on the balance sheet even if it is for a good reason. Furthermore, Cunningham is considering a private placement or public equity offering, both ways of accessing capital, and wants investors to see the strongest balance sheet possible. The best option would be to create an SPE to build the new warehouse. In doing this, the warehouse (the asset), along with the debt to finance it (the liability), would be excluded from the store's balance sheet. Cunningham can rent the space from the SPE for a nominal fee and have complete use of it without any substantial impact on its financials. Most investors will recognize this if it is disclosed properly and probably will take little issue with it. However, problems arise when this disclosure is omitted or obscured.

Wouldn't it be great if everything had an off-balance-sheet counterpart? A poor grade in a course could be transferred to an "off-report card," or a poor round of golf could be ignored as an "off-scorecard" round. Not a bad way to go through life. Soon those clever enough to use this tool would be able to reportedly excel at virtually everything life has to offer. This is the mindset that fueled some of the biggest corporate scandals in the early twenty-first century and subsequently raised questions about the use of off-balance-sheet structures.

3

INCOME STATEMENT

During my Wall Street days, I worked with a guy who made self-aggrandizement a sport. While the rest of us were pulling all-nighters to update spreadsheet models, he devoted his time to creating a certain image for himself. He made sure each of his superiors had at least a once-a-day telling of his latest dirty joke, a recap of last night's game, and, of course, a brief update on the projects he was working on. What was most remarkable about his approach was not so much his ability to charm his bosses but, more important, his ability to disclose information selectively. Most of his project summaries revolved around assignments that were in progress, were on their way, or had been allotted time on his busy schedule. His self-initiated performance report was a paradigm of good public relations. He would overemphasize positive developments and underemphasize negative ones. Ultimately, he was judged more on the potential of those projects to come to fruition than on their actual completion. Needless to say, they often remained unfinished. Each year, however, he received the highest employee rating among any of my colleagues.

This approach to performance caught my attention on many levels. Most significantly, I saw that not only did my colleague use this approach effectively, most of corporate America did as well. In fact, most companies had an official format for this in which they could highlight their most recent performance on the basis of things that had yet to happen, plus they could highlight other items that seemed more relevant to their strategic objectives. This format has a name. It is called the *income statement*.

I like to think of the income statement as the report card for a company, because it is intended to help gauge the overall performance of that company. How did this company perform on an operating basis? What were its margins? Are sales increasing? Essentially, the income statement helps analysts and investors determine whether a company is optimizing its potential on a day-to-day basis—at least in theory. However, in the world of finance, it's the student and not the teacher issuing the grade. The underlying problem with this is that the disclosure requirements are vague and leave far too much to the discretion of the company's management. A company can highlight certain items with the hope that Wall Street and the investor public will look more favorably on it based on that emphasis. Simply stated, the problems include the following:

- Revenues do not accurately reflect what the company has collected.
- Expenses do not accurately reflect the cash that was paid.

The income statement is not entirely useless, however. It does have a purpose in that it reports the overall performance of the company, though often this performance may not be actualized. For example, as you will see shortly, the sales of a company do not reflect the cash the company has received. This is the basis of accrual accounting, which was discussed earlier in this book. The idea here is that a company's performance is based more on its expected payments than on its collected payments. At the same time, a company may expense or deduct what has yet to be paid. Ultimately, the timing of payments is not overly important in determining a company's performance. This chapter will discuss the following:

- Income statement components
- EBITDA, EBIT, and EBT

- Revenue recognition
- Inventory and cost of goods sold
- Depreciation
- Earnings release

INCOME STATEMENT COMPONENTS

A good income statement reveals a company with earnings that are stable, predictable, and sustainable. Of course, these are relative measures, and so they must be compared with overall industry measures. Some of these comparisons will be discussed in Chapter 6. It is important to remember that the income statement reflects the financial standing of a company over a period of time. This differs from the balance sheet, which is a snapshot of a company at one particular time. If you recall, when the balance sheet was reviewed, assets, liabilities, and shareholders' equity were listed. The value of each of these items was based on the end of the period. The income statement, in contrast, tracks changes occurring during the period. To analyze the income statement, one must examine its three basic subcomponents.

Revenues

Revenues are a reflection of market demand and represent payments recorded in exchange for goods and services. The term *revenues* is loosely synonymous with *sales*, and so if it is listed as sales, one must understand that they are essentially the same thing. Sometimes revenues are listed as *net sales* rather than sales, which represents sales adjusted for discounts and returns. Because most companies use accrual accounting, revenues are rarely a reflection of cash payments.

Expenses and Costs

There is a distinction between *expenses* and *costs*, although the terms often are used interchangeably. Costs reflect what is paid to produce or acquire goods and services. More specifically, they are the costs associated with each unit sold. Thus, in a company that manufactures widgets, the cost of the raw materials involved in the manufacturing will be listed under cost of goods sold, or cost of sales. Expenses pertain to what is paid to run the company on a day-to-day basis. Items such as salaries, rent, utilities, legal, marketing, accounting, and telecommunications will be included in expenses.

Income, Earnings, and Profit

Income, often referred to as *earnings* or *profit*, is what is left over after expenses and costs are subtracted from revenues. If expenses and costs exceed what is listed as revenue, the income statement will show negative net income, or a net loss. Otherwise, income will be listed as *net income*.

Common Items on the Income Statement

There are various items that frequently appear on income statements.

Sales or Revenues

This item represents proceeds, either cash or credit, received in exchange for products or services.

Cost of Goods Sold

Also listed as *cost of sales*, these are costs that are tied directly to production. However, this is listed only upon the sale of an item. Therefore, when an item is sold, the cost to produce or acquire it is reported here.

Selling, General, and Administrative (SG&A)

This covers most day-to-day operating expenses, such as those mentioned in the previous section. Sometimes these items are listed line by line, but more often than not they are grouped into this broad category. This is done for the sake of simplicity or to obscure specific items. For example, when salaries appear unusually high, they can elicit an excessive amount of scrutiny from analysts and investors. Rather than face questions about their executive compensation, corporate managers tend to prefer to obscure this number in SG&A.

Depreciation

Depreciation is a noncash expense that is based on the reduction in the fixed value of assets. You saw accumulated depreciation, the depreciation collected over time, on the balance sheet. On the income statement, you see just the depreciation for that particular year, which is treated as a noncash expense.

Interest

This pertains to payments made to service debt.

Taxes

This will vary depending on how the company treats taxes and, more specifically, whether the company defers taxes.

Net Income

This is the company's profit, or its bottom line: what is left over after all these expenses and costs are subtracted from revenue.

EXAMPLE Figure 3-1 shows the income statement for our favorite hardware store. Cunningham Hardware is a company not unlike many others, public or private. Its income statement follows a standard format, beginning with revenues and descending through the different levels of profitability.

FIGURE 3-1 Sample Income Statement

Cunningham Hardware Co.

INCOME STATEMENT	
Sales	$100,000
Cost of Goods Sold	$ 60,000
Gross Profit	$ 40,000
Selling General & Admin.	$ 24,000
EBITDA*	$ 16,000
Depreciation	$ 4,800
EBIT†	$ 11,200
Interest Expense	$ 1,600
EBT‡	$ 9,600
Tax	$ 3,200
Net Income	$ 6,400

* Earnings before interest, taxes, depreciation, and amortization
†Earnings before interest and taxes
‡Earnings before taxes

As you can see in Figure 3-1, at the very top, sales are listed. In the most recent year, the company recorded $100,000 in sales. Next is cost of goods sold. This represents all the costs associated with that $100,000 in sales, which total $60,000. That $60,000 is subtracted from the $100,000 in sales; a gross profit of $40,000 is left.

Cunningham's selling, general, and administrative costs appear next. This item incorporates all the operating expenses of the company. In this case, as with most companies, they are combined into one category, totaling $24,000. Corporate managers strongly support this item, as it enables them to obscure the specific breakdowns of their expenses—especially executive salaries!

Next, SG&A is subtracted from gross profit to calculate *EBITDA* (earnings before interest, taxes, depreciation, and amortization), which is $16,000. From there $4,800 in depreciation is subtracted to arrive at *EBIT*—earnings before interest and taxes. Once the interest expense of $1,600 is subtracted, *EBT*, earnings before taxes, remains. Finally, taxes are subtracted to arrive at a net income of $6,400.

EBITDA, EBIT, AND EBT

Banker-speak is riddled with the fabled terms *EBITDA* and *EBIT*. These numbers are useful for three reasons. First, they measure profitability at different levels. Second, they enable companies to highlight their strongest level of profitability. Third, they make bankers seem more sophisticated than they really are. As for the first reason, it is useful insofar as it enables one to draw consistent comparisons between one company and the next or between one company and a peer group. In doing so, one can account for the differences that exist between companies. For example, Cunningham Hardware makes interest payments of $1,600. Its nearest competitor, by contrast, perhaps does not have any interest charges because it does not have any debt to repay. Perhaps this competitor is financed entirely through equity. Aside from this difference, assume that the two businesses are virtually identical. They have a similar customer base, similar products, and comparable revenues and expenses. If you were to compare the two companies on a net income basis, all other things being equal, you would see that the competitor might perform somewhat better because of the missing interest. However, this is misleading, as it does little to explain how the companies perform on the basis of their ability to generate profits. Rather, it underscores a difference in their capital structures, which is another issue entirely. To draw a fair comparison, we look at these two companies and evaluate their profitability before interest is subtracted. To do this, we compare them on the basis of earnings before interest and taxes—EBIT.

What happens if Cunningham Hardware has depreciation of $4,800 and its competitor has no depreciation because it has no fixed assets? If there are no fixed assets, there is no depreciation. Perhaps the competitor simply leases its property, plant, and equipment. If you were to compare the profitability of these two companies, all other things being equal, you would see that the competitor might perform somewhat better than Cunningham because of these depreciation expenses. These differences might be skewed further as a result of the leasing charges that the competitor assumes for its assets. Regardless, a fair comparison is difficult to make because of depreciation, and thus, it may be more useful to compare the profitability of the two companies on earnings before interest, taxes, depreciation, and amortization basis—EBITDA. Amortization, like depreciation, involves the expense or payment of an obligation over an extended period. Rather than the item being expensed at one time, it is distributed over a period of time in installments. This might be helpful when a company has assumed significant research-and-development costs for a product that has yet to be launched. When these costs are expensed over time, the profits do not fall drastically in any one year.

To summarize, EBITDA, EBIT, and EBT are used to account for the differences in interest, taxes, depreciation, and amortization—all variables that can affect net income. In an effort to analyze company profitability exclusive of these variables, several levels of profitability can be considered. As you will see later in this chapter, such profitability measures are also useful in valuation.

REVENUE RECOGNITION

The income statement is becoming increasingly important in detecting accounting fraud as a result of issues pertaining to revenue recognition. Earlier, we discussed the differences between cash accounting and accrual accounting. You saw that most companies report their financial performance on an accrual basis, which means that revenues may not reflect payments that actually were received. Thus, many company managers have gone to great lengths to book anything and everything that remotely resembles revenues even when the probability of actually collecting is slim. For that reason, revenue recognition has become a major concern for the Financial Accounting Standards Board (FASB), the Securities and Exchange Commission (SEC), and the investor public.

In 1999, the SEC issued *Staff Accounting Bulletin 101* (SAB 101) to address the issue of when revenue is realized or realizable. The bulletin describes a basic framework for analyzing revenue recognition by focusing on four bedrock principles established in GAAP. Those principles state that revenue generally is realized or realizable and earned when all the following criteria are met:

1. Persuasive evidence of an arrangement exists.
2. Delivery has occurred or services have been rendered.
3. The seller's price to the buyer is fixed or determinable.
4. Collectability is reasonably assured.

The general framework and foundation for SAB 101 could not be simpler—it is based on the commonsense notion that revenue on a sale should not be recognized until the seller has fulfilled its obligations to the buyer under the sale arrangement. For the most part, the terms outlined by the SEC seem relatively straightforward. However, the point regarding collectability has raised a number of issues, especially in the aftermath of some particularly noteworthy scandals.

Informix

One of the best examples of creative revenue recognition comes from a company called Informix. In the mid-1990s, Informix, a database software company, made an aggressive play to compete with its larger competitors, Oracle and IBM. Informix cooked up a number of dubious schemes to boost revenue that had little chance of ever being collected. Once it was discovered that Informix was involved in such practices, the company's shares fell from about $24 to around $5 in a matter of months. The former CEO was convicted on several counts of securities fraud, and Informix eventually settled a multitude of shareholder lawsuits that forced the company to take a $94 million charge on its income statement. Eventually, the company was restructured, with the majority of it sold to IBM.

What happened? Essentially, Informix management was exaggerating the numbers by booking revenues before end-user sales were completed and by structuring loose barter arrangements with customers. From time to time, Informix would enter into licensing contracts with certain customers, such as computer hardware manufacturers. The parties called such contracts *pools of funds*. Under this arrangement, the manufacturer would resell Informix's software to end users. Then the Informix customer would agree to make payments to Informix over time in exchange for those resale rights. Informix entered into two pool-of-funds agreements in 1996. In both cases, the companies maintained the right to resell Informix's software for a period of time as well as the right to make payments under the contracts to Informix. One of the agreements required that the company pay Informix approximately $6.4 million, $3.2 million, and $3.2 million by three separate deadlines. The other obligated the company to pay Informix approximately $4.7 million, payable as the software was resold, but with the total balance due by late 1997.

Informix also would recognize revenue from a pool-of-funds contract at the time it entered into such a contract provided that payment was due within 12 months from the contract's signing. As a result, this benefited Informix's revenue numbers by allowing the company to include these anticipated payments even if they were not actually made by the customer until a subsequent reporting period.

In the mid-1990s, GAAP rules allowed for the recognition of anticipated payments only if certain strict requirements were met. These requirements were unique to the software industry and included the following:

- Informix had delivered the software to the customer.
- Informix had no continuing obligations under the contract.
- The customer's payment, as stipulated in the contract, was fixed, and collectability of that payment was probable.

However, it was alleged that Informix management would enter into side agreements with customers, allowing them to cancel and seek a refund for payments made to Informix pursuant to those contracts. The side agreements rendered Informix's recognition of revenue from these contracts on financial statements improper and not in accordance with applicable accounting principles.

Suppose a company tells you that you can use its product for a few years and you do not have to pay until later. Furthermore, you can return it for a full refund at any time. What if it is a product that becomes outdated after a few years? What Informix did was give some of its preferred customers the option to use its software for a specified period of time, at the end of which they were expected to make the payment for its use. However, if the customer team was disappointed with the product, it could simply return the product to Informix for a refund of the balance paid. Not a bad deal. Informix realized that it could book revenues very easily by using this method. In turn, it could inflate its net income, which would, it hoped, boost the stock price.

INVENTORY AND COST OF GOODS SOLD

The assessment of inventory values is a concept that significantly affects the income statement. Generally speaking, there are two common methods of accounting for inventory: FIFO and LIFO. FIFO stands for "first in, first out," and LIFO stands for "last in, first out." Under FIFO, product costs are charged out to cost of goods sold, in chronological order. Thus, when items are sold, the value that is disclosed under cost of goods sold is done in order of the items' original purchase. A LIFO system, in contrast, charges out product cost in reverse chronological order: the last item purchased is the first listed under cost of goods sold.

Confused? Well, you should be. This is a tricky concept. Perhaps the best way to understand it is to use an example. Suppose you acquire four units of a product, one at a time. The first time you purchase the merchandise, you pay $10. A couple of weeks later, you buy another unit, but the price has gone up, so you now pay $12. A few more weeks later, you acquire a third for $14. Finally, the following week, you pay $16 for the fourth. In total, you spend $52 to acquire these four units.

Next month, you decide to sell those units in your store. At the end of the quarter, you have sold only three of the four units. Under FIFO, you sell the first three that you purchased: the $10 unit, the $12 unit, and the $14 unit. That gives you a total of $36 to list under cost of goods sold on your income statement. On your balance sheet, the $16 unit, the last one you purchased, remains in inventory. Essentially, the first units you purchased are the first ones out the door. The advantages of FIFO include the following:

- Inventory costs are closer to replacement costs.
- Expense and sales numbers are better matched chronologically, which is helpful in gross margin analysis.

The other method, LIFO, "last in, first out," selects the last item purchased and then works backward until the total costs for the units sold during the period are removed. Going back to the original example, you acquire four units of a product, one at a time. You pay $10, $12, $14, and $16, for a total of $52. At the end of the quarter, you have sold three of those four units. You have sold the $16 unit, the $14 unit, and the $12 unit, for a total of $42. The first unit, which you purchased for $10, ends up in inventory. On your income statement, $42 is listed under cost of goods sold. The advantages of LIFO include the following:

- Taxable income will be lower during times of rising costs.
- Assigning the most recent costs of purchased products to cost of goods sold more accurately depicts the current replacement cost on the income statement.

To understand how these two methods can affect a company's financial report, take a look at the two methods in practice. Figure 3-2 shows two inventory purchases. On January 1, Cunningham Hardware purchased 100 screwdrivers for $10 each. On January 15, it purchased another 100 screwdrivers for $12 each. Whether Cunningham uses FIFO or LIFO, the result is identical for the purchases. Cunningham records $1,000 for the first

FIGURE 3-2 FIFO Versus LIFO

Cunningham Hardware Co.

Inventory Transactions	FIFO	LIFO
Jan. 1, Buy inventory (100 screwdrivers @ $10)	$1,000	$1,000
Jan. 15, Buy inventory (100 screwdrivers @ $12)	$1,200	$1,200
Income Statement		
Sales (100 units @ $20)	$2,000	$2,000
Cost of goods sold	$1,000	$1,200
Pretax income	$1,000	$ 800
Taxes (40%)	$ 400	$ 320
Net income	$ 600	$ 480
Balance Sheet		
Inventory	$1,200	$1,000

purchase and $1,200 for the second. The differences arise when one looks at the income statement.

Suppose the store sells 100 units at $20 a unit. Using FIFO, the store books $2,000 in sales: $20 multiplied by 100 units. Using LIFO, it books the same amount, as the techniques do not differ in terms of sales reporting. You begin to see differences when you examine cost of goods sold. Under FIFO, $1,000 in cost of goods sold is noted because Cunningham is recording the first purchase of inventory: the first item purchased is the first one sold—first in, first out. Under LIFO, $1,200 is recorded under cost of goods sold because the $1,200 pertains to the second purchase, or the last purchase—last in, first out.

In looking at pretax income, subtract out cost of goods sold from sales, and a pretax income of $1,000 remains using FIFO. Compare this with pretax income under LIFO, which shows $800. Now notice what is paid in taxes. Under FIFO, the store pays $400, assuming a tax rate of 40 percent on that pretax income of $1,000. Under LIFO, the store pays $320, which is 40 percent of the $800 booked in pretax income.

Finally, the net income under FIFO is $600, whereas under LIFO it is only $480. Using FIFO, the store pays more in taxes but at the same time records higher net income. Under LIFO, less is paid in taxes, but there is also lower net income.

As you can see, there is a trade-off that a financial manager faces in determining which method to use: a trade-off between lowering the tax burden and maximizing income. Imagine for a moment that this is a multimillion-dollar company by adding six zeros to each of those numbers. The impact is staggering. We see tax differences of $80 million and income differences of $120 million. Thus, this simple accounting technique can account for millions of dollars in tax savings or millions of dollars in net income.

DEPRECIATION

Depreciation is treated like any other expense except that it involves no cash outlay. It is imputed, meaning that it is based on a specific portion assigned to a specific time period. As you saw on the balance sheet, it is listed in its accumulated form, whereas on the income statement it is listed as an expense specific to that period. Depreciation is usually based on the useful life of an asset and therefore can be subjective. Often, companies deal with new classifications of assets, especially in areas such as technology, biotech, and pharmaceuticals. In the case of new asset classes, it is not entirely clear what the useful life should be. For that reason, determining depreciation schedules sometimes is left to the discretion of the company.

As with most intangible items, a number of problems are associated with depreciation. When businesses use an accelerated schedule, they will deduct more depreciation in early years, meaning they probably will see much larger tax savings in the near term. However, they also are going to see lower net income, which can be perceived as a negative from an investor's perspective. Furthermore, different depreciation schedules frequently pertain to different asset classes. Any new asset class will have few parameters. For that reason, financial managers may take great liberties in the way they determine depreciation for it.

EARNINGS RELEASE

Each quarter, Wall Street analysts and investors behave like eager little children on Christmas morning. This behavior results from anticipation of the quarterly earnings statement that is issued by most public companies and can bring forth all kinds of surprises. This is essentially a condensed form of a company's income statement and offers a report card of sorts for the company. The most important grade on this report card is the earnings per share number. It simply records the company's net income applicable to each share of common stock outstanding. This number is compared with what Wall Street analysts predicted, and a number that exceeds this prediction usually will trigger an increase in the company's stock price, whereas a number that falls short can mean a drop. Of course, like almost everything else in financial reporting, this number can be manipulated (see Chapter 5).

Earnings per share is a very important number in this process of examining overall company performance. It is important because it enables investors to gauge how much they earned on an investment—how much net income per share they earned. Earnings per share numbers are calculated by taking net income and dividing it by total shares of common stock outstanding.

For example, a company reports $2 million in net income. If the company has 500,000 shares of stock outstanding, what is its earnings per share number? It would be $4 ($2 million in earnings divided by 500,000 shares of stock). This is a number disclosed by all public companies, and it affects their market value. It tends to be one of the ways investors assess the performance and, in turn, the value of a company.

In 1997, the Financial Accounting Standards Board instituted a rule requiring companies to report earnings per share in two ways, basic and diluted. Basic refers to net income minus preferred dividends divided by total shares outstanding. Diluted reports options, warrants, preferred stock, and convertible debt, reflecting their impact if they were exercised, or converted to shares of common stock. The growth of stock options as a form of compensation reached unprecedented levels in the 1990s, and concerns arose that if and when those instruments were exercised, they would dilute the holdings of existing shareholders. For that reason, FASB instituted this rule stating that earnings must be reported on both a basic and a diluted basis because any increase in the number of shares outstanding will indeed affect the earnings attributed to each share.

4

CASH FLOW STATEMENT

One of the proudest days of my life was the day I landed my first job. It was an unforgettable thrill that was compounded by the fact that at a relatively young age, I soon would assume a great deal of responsibility. I was in charge of a business unit at a high-growth company. In that capacity, I managed logistics, procurement, and customer relations, and at the end of the day I often reviewed the accounts. That process taught me a great deal about generating income and, more specifically, cash. More than anything, I soon recognized the importance of generating cash flow. Payments often were made by credit or check, but ultimately the strength of the business was built around its ability to generate cash. And my keen ability to reconcile cash and credit receipts soon earned me a promotion to the drive-through along with unlimited french fry privileges.

The cash flow statement is what I like to think of as a company's checkbook. It shows how much cash the company generated during the prior period, which leads to how much cash the company has currently. The cash flow statement determines whether a company builds cash on the basis of its operating activities, investing activities, and financing activities. Essentially, it takes the accrual-based numbers from the balance sheet and income statement and works backward to reconcile the changes in cash (see Figure 4-1). What is left over, usually listed at the end of the cash flow statement, is the change in cash for the period. That change is added to the cash position on the balance sheet from the end of the last period, which in turn is added to the cash position at the end of the current period. This represents the link between the cash flow statement and the balance sheet.

FIGURE 4-1 Financial Statements: Primary Links

Balance Sheet

ASSETS			LIABILITIES		
Current Assets			**Current Liabilities**		
Cash	$ 8,000		Accounts Payable		$ 3,000
Accounts Receivable	$ 10,000		Accrued Expenses Payable		$ 5,000
Inventory	$ 14,000		Income Tax Payable		$ 1,000
Prepaid Expenses	$ 2,000		Total Current Liabilities		$ 9,000
Total Current Assets	$ 34,000				
			Noncurrent Liabilities		
Noncurrent Assets			Notes Payable		$19,000
Fixed Assets	$ 45,000				
Accumulated Depreciation	$(23,000)		Total Noncurrent Liabilities		$19,000
Total Noncurrent Assets	$ 22,000				
			Shareholders' Equity		
Total Assets	$ 56,000		Paid-In Capital		$ 8,000
			Retained Earnings		$20,000
			Total Shareholders' Equity		$28,000
			Total Liabilities & Shareholders' Equity		$56,000

Ending cash balance links to cash account on the balance sheet

Net income less dividends plus previous year's retained earnings balance links to retained earnings account on the balance sheet

Net income forms starting point of the cash flow statement

Income Statement

Sales	$100,000
Cost of Goods Sold	$ 60,000
Gross Profit	$ 40,000
Selling General & Admin.	$ 24,000
EBITDA*	$ 16,000
Depreciation	$ 4,800
EBIT†	$ 11,200
Interest Expense	$ 1,600
EBT‡	$ 9,600
Tax	$ 3,200
Net Income	$ 6,400

* Earnings before interest, taxes, depreciation, and amortization
† Earnings before interest and taxes
‡ Earnings before taxes

Cash Flow Statement

Cash Flow from Operating Activities		
Net Income		$ 6,400
Accounts Receivable Increase	$(3,200)	
Inventory Increase	$(3,900)	
Prepaid Expense Increase	$ (600)	
Depreciation	$ 4,800	
Accounts Payable Increase	$ 300	
Accrued Expense Increase	$ 500	
Income Tax Payable Increase	$ 100	
Cash Flow from Operating Activities		$ 4,400
Cash Flows from Investing Activities		
Purchases of Property, Plant, & Equipment		$(5,000)
Cash Flows from Financing Activities		
Short-Term Debt Increase	$ 800	
Long-Term Debt Increase	$ 1,200	
Stock Issue	$ 300	
Dividends Paid	$(1,600)	
Cash Flows from Financing Activities		$ 700
Change in Cash		$ 100
Beginning Cash		$ 7,900
Ending Cash		$ 8,000

This chapter will discuss the following:

- Cash flow
- Sample cash flow statement
- Why cash flows?
- Managing cash flows

CASH FLOW

The cash flow statement is divided among operating activities, investing activities, and financing activities, each of which is detailed next.

Cash Flows from Operating Activities

Cash flow from operating activities is based on the transactions that normally affect the generation of operating income. This portion of the cash flow statement is used to compute just the cash component of these items. In doing so, it examines the various changes in certain accounts to determine the amount of cash generated or lost.

Cash Inflows
- Sale of products or services
- Other extraordinary revenue

Cash Outflows
- Purchases of inventory
- Operating expenses
- Interest expenses

To build a cash flow statement, the preferred method is to begin with net income and then work backward to reconcile the changes in cash position.

Cash Flows from Investing Activities

Cash flows from investing activities involve transactions related to the purchase and sale of securities, land, buildings, equipment, and other assets not generally held for resale. Investing activities are not classified as operating activities because they have an indirect relationship to the central, ongoing operation of a business (usually the sale of goods or services).

Cash Inflows
- Sale of plant assets
- Sale of a business unit
- Sale of investment securities

Cash Outflows
- Purchase of plant assets
- Purchase of investment securities

Cash Flows from Financing Activities

Cash flows from financing activities deal with the flow of cash to or from the shareholders (equity financing and dividends) and creditors (debt financing). For example, in issuing new shares of stock, the company raises cash, which is in effect a cash inflow. Similarly, when a company issues debt, the cash brought in is treated as a cash inflow. When a company pays down debt or buys back shares of stock, those actions are treated as cash outflows. Finally, the payment of a dividend is treated as a cash outflow.

Cash Inflows
- Issuance of company stock
- Borrowing (bonds, notes, mortgages, etc.)

Cash Outflows
- Dividends to stockholders
- Repayment of principal amounts borrowed
- Repurchase of shares of stock

SAMPLE CASH FLOW STATEMENT

Imagine that Cunningham Hardware is reporting strong profits each year but failing to achieve its expansion goals. Suppose the owner, Mr. C., is hoping to open new stores and perhaps even expand into new areas such as auto repair garages. In fact, his son's best friend has built quite a practice in that area repairing motorcycles. The possibility of expanding into this industry offers numerous advantages. First, adding a service business to a product-based business usually helps boost margins. Second, the strong relationships with hardware suppliers could lead to better purchasing power for automotive parts and tools. Third, the close ties to someone with experience in this business could offer trustworthy guidance in entering this new market.

So what is the problem? Although the company is generating decent profits, cash flows are weak. Ultimately, the decision to expand is a function of having sufficient liquidity or, more specifically, cash flow. Acquiring the building, inventory, employees, and so on undoubtedly will involve a fair amount of cash. Profits alone will not cover this, as profits do not necessarily imply cash. Within that profit number are payments not yet received; therefore, a company can continue to generate strong profits while consistently falling short of cash. This cash shortage has slowed efforts to expand and is likely to create liquidity problems.

In an effort to understand his lack of cash flow, Mr. C. consults with a business-savvy friend who owns the burger and malt shop in town. After reviewing the financial statements, they draw the conclusion that the store is not generating enough cash to meet the goals of expansion. They quickly decide that some combination of the following would increase cash flow:

- Increase collections
- Sell fixed assets
- Raise funds through a debt or equity offering

Figure 4-2 presents the complete statement of cash flows for Cunningham Hardware (this is the same cash flow statement that appears in Figure 4-1). Each cash flow statement begins with net income, which is pulled directly from the income statement, as you can see in Figure 4-1. In this case, the store has net income of $6,400. From there, we work backward to reconcile the cash and noncash charges, which in turn will lead to a net change in cash for the year.

FIGURE 4-2 Cash Flow Statement

Cunningham Hardware Co.

CASH FLOW STATEMENT

Cash Flow from Operating Activities

Net Income		$ 6,400
Accounts Receivable Increase	$(3,200)	
Inventory Increase	$(3,900)	
Prepaid Expense Increase	$ (600)	
Depreciation	$ 4,800	
Accounts Payable Increase	$ 300	
Accrued Expense Increase	$ 500	
Income Tax Payable Increase	$ 100	
Cash Flow from Operating Activities		$ 4,400

Cash Flows from Investing Activities

Purchases of Property, Plant, & Equipment		$(5,000)

Cash Flows from Financing Activities

Short-Term Debt Increase	$ 800	
Long-Term Debt Increase	$ 1,200	
Stock Issue	$ 300	
Dividends Paid	$(1,600)	
Cash Flows from Financing Activities		$ 700
Change in Cash		$ 100
Beginning Cash		$ 7,900
Ending Cash		$ 8,000

Cash Flows from Operating Activities

Receivables

The first thing the cash flow statement in Figure 4-2 shows is an increase in accounts receivable in the amount of $3,200. Therefore, this increase must be subtracted on the cash flow statement. This is done because an increase in receivables between last year and this year indicates that the increase was booked as part of sales on the income statement, though the payments have not actually been collected. The sales line on the income statement reflects that increase, but the underlying cash is not there. In this case, the change is positive because the receivables went up. Because the receivables went up, that difference is subtracted since the cash is not in the company's hands. It is important to note that this is the change in receivables between last year and this year, not the actual amount that appears on this year's balance sheet. The number on the balance sheet at the end of this year is the total accounts receivable.

Inventory

The next figure shows an increase in inventory. Inventory is not something that appears on the income statement. It is nonetheless a cash outflow because the company had to pay to acquire it. Inventory becomes an income statement item only when it is sold, and at that point it is listed under cost of goods sold. Until then, it remains listed as inventory on the balance sheet. Here inventory went up by $3,900, which was a cash outflow, and so it must be subtracted. Again, the purpose of the cash flow statement is to reflect changes in cash. Thus, the increase in inventory is subtracted out.

Prepaid Expenses

The company also reports an increase in prepaid expenses. These expenses do not show up on the income statement but are still cash outflows that must be subtracted. On the cash flow statement, only the portion due in that particular period is expensed.

Depreciation

The cash flow statement shows a depreciation charge of $4,800, which also was listed on the income statement. On the income statement, it was subtracted much like any other expense. However, on the cash flow statement, it is added back because it is a noncash expense. Although this was listed as a deduction on the income statement, that amount was not actually paid in cash. Again, the purpose of the cash flow statement is to see how much cash was generated or lost during the period, and so depreciation is added back to the net income.

Accounts Payable

Next, the increase in accounts payable is reported. Accounts payable increased, and so the amount owed to vendors has gone up as well. Hence, that number must be added back. This is done because although this amount is expensed on the income statement in some form, it has not actually been paid yet. Thus, the cash position is effectively higher.

Other

Accrued expenses went up, and those expenses also are added back much like accounts payable. Finally, there is an income tax payable increase, meaning the company has a payable due to the IRS. Again, this may have been expensed but has not actually been paid, and for that reason it must be added back. After summing these items, the total cash flow from operating activities equals $4,400. Note that net income is $6,400, but cash flows from operating activities are substantially less.

CASH FLOW FROM OPERATING ACTIVITIES	
Net Income:	$ 6,400
Accounts Receivable Increase:	$(3,200)
Inventory Increase:	$(3,900)
Prepaid Expense Increase:	$ (600)
Depreciation:	$ 4,800
Accounts Payable Increase:	$ 300
Accrued Expense Increase:	$ 500
Income Tax Payable Increase:	$ 100
Cash Flow from Operating Activities:	$ 4,400

Cash Flows from Investing Activities

The next segment on the cash flow statement is cash flows from investing activities. In this case, purchases of property, plant, and equipment amount to $5,000. Again, cash flows from investing activities pertain to one-time purchases or sales that do not show up on the income statement. The assumption is that these one-time transactions are not necessarily part of the day-to-day operating activities of the company, and for that reason, they remain off the income statement. Nonetheless, they are listed on the cash flow statement because they represent cash inflows or outflows.

CASH FLOW FROM INVESTING ACTIVITIES	
Purchases of Property, Plant, & Equipment:	$(5,000)

Cash Flows from Financing Activities

Finally, cash flows from financing activities are listed. Any increases or decreases in financing (debt, equity, dividends) appear in this section.

Debt

This cash flow statement shows an increase in short-term debt. The company borrowed from a short-term debt vehicle, perhaps a line of credit, and in that process raised $800, representing a cash inflow. Next, it reports an increase in long-term debt of $1,200, meaning that the company issued some form of long-term debt and in the process raised $1,200.

Equity

The company also issued equity, meaning that it sold shares of stock to raise $300.

Dividends

Last, dividends paid to shareholders are reflected on the statement. That amount paid is listed here as a cash outflow because it did not show up on the income statement. Since it is still a cash outflow, it is subtracted. The total of these cash flows from financing activities reveals a cash increase of $700.

CASH FLOW FROM FINANCING ACTIVITIES	
Short-Term Debt Increase:	$ 800
Long-Term Debt Increase:	$ 1,200
Stock Issue:	$ 300
Dividends Paid:	$(1,600)
Cash Flows from Financing Activities:	$ 700

Ending Cash

The last step on the cash flow statement is to sum the three categories: cash flows from operating activities, cash flows from investing activities, and cash flows from financing activities. In doing so, a net increase in cash of $100 is calculated. During the period, cash has gone up only $100 despite the fact that income was listed as $6,400.

Often, such dramatic differences between cash flows and income exist. This is related to the differences between accrual accounting and cash accounting. The cash flow statement is designed to reconcile these differences. In this case, the increase in cash of $100 is applied to the cash position that the company started the year with, which is listed on the balance sheet as last year's cash balance. The beginning cash balance, listed in the statement as $7,900, is the same cash that the company had at the end of last year (the end of last year is the same as the beginning of this year—see Figure 4-1). The cash flow statement shows a cash gain of $100, which leads to an ending cash position of $8,000. That $8,000 is now transferred to the balance sheet and in turn reflects the cash position for the end of this year—again, see Figure 4-1. This is the common link between the cash flow statement and the balance sheet. The cash flow statement shows how much cash was produced or lost during the period and is applied to the cash position from last year to get the current cash position.

A Quick Recap of Financial Statements

Now that each of the financial statements—the balance sheet, the income statement, and the cash flow statement—has been described, take time to note the essential elements of each. Figure 4-3 presents a summary.

FIGURE 4-3 Financial Statements Summary

Balance Sheet

- Assets = liabilities + owners' equity
- Balance sheet numbers reflect positions at one point in time
- Fixed assets are listed at original cost
- Liabilities and owners' equity provide sources of financing
- Current assets can be liquidated within one year
- Current liabilities must be paid within one year
- Retained earnings represent income left after dividends paid

Income Statement

- Income = revenues – expenses
- Income statements track changes over a period of time
- Income does not necessarily equate with cash
- Expenses may include noncash items
- Revenues may include payments not yet received
- Net income less dividends equals retained earnings

Cash Flow Statement

- Cash flows are based on operating, investing, financing activities
- Cash flows track changes over a period of time
- Cash flows reconcile differences between accrual and cash accounting
- Cash flows lead to the amount of cash generated or lost during a period

WHY CASH FLOWS?

At this point, you are probably convinced that the cash flow statement is an entirely confusing waste of time. Right? Not so fast. Cash flow statements have been required for all US-based publicly traded companies since 1987, when FASB issued Statement No. 95. Before 1987, a less formal statement of general funds was used to summarize changes in balance sheet items, but unfortunately, it lacked clear guidelines. As a result, companies offered creative interpretations of such changes, rendering the statement all but useless. The new cash flow statement offered a standard format and a clear way to link the flows of cash to the ending cash balance. Over the past two decades, the need to understand a company's ability to generate cash has been on the rise. If a company continues to report strong profits while burning cash, that company will not be around for very long. This is something Wall Street loses sight of from time to time. Therefore, the cash flow statement is an important piece in the financial performance puzzle of a company.

The cash flow statement has been gaining in popularity in light of the proliferation of accounting fraud disguised through various income statement items. However, most Wall Street analysts and many investors tend to focus on the income statement at the end of the quarter, giving supreme weighting to profits. They often stress the fact that cash flows, by contrast, are generally erratic and fail to capture the true performance of a company. For example, a company can report positive cash flows one period and negative cash flows the next. Although the company might continue to grow by increasing sales and decreasing expenses, its cash flows could still be negative. In fact, the company might prove to be exceptionally profitable even though cash flows are increasingly negative. Cash flows, more than anything else, are dependent on the timing of payments and the reconciliation of noncash items.

Perhaps the best example of this is seen periodically in the automotive industry. Consider those great offers of zero percent down, zero percent financing. When automakers offer such compelling deals, sales may spike. Even though they are booking sales and in turn increasing income, the cash is not there. It could take years before they start to collect. Because of accrual accounting, the income statement is rich with profits, whereas cash might be weak, with few payments coming in. However, this may be offset if the company has an independent financing arm that assumes the receivable while making the payment to the manufacturer.

MANAGING CASH FLOWS

Considerations

What should a company focus on when trying to manage its cash flows? (Pay attention, because this is applicable in personal finance as well.) These are the main questions a financial manager must ask to manage cash flows effectively:

Sales. What are the company's sales for the period compared with the same period last year? Are there any dramatic changes?

Bank balance. How much cash is in the bank?

Receivables. How much outstanding is owed to the company by its customers?

Payables. How much does the company owe to its vendors and suppliers? How does this compare with receivables?

Capital expenditures. How much is the company spending on purchases of property, plant, and equipment? Are these purchases necessary?

Financing. Is the company paying down debt or buying back stock? If so, is there surplus cash to do this? Is the company paying a dividend? Is this something that has been done in the past? Does the company's performance support this?

Steps to Stronger Cash Flows

Companies face significant pressure to manage their cash flows optimally. In fact, I have yet to see a company that falls short in this area stay in business. No matter what the other financial statements say about a company, it needs cash to survive. Most respected companies tend to emphasize the following procedures in an effort to maximize cash flows:

Preparing detailed forecasts. Keeping track of detailed budgetary needs and expected revenues will help a company better manage its cash flows.

Setting up sufficient cash reserves. This goes without saying—keeping something in the bank will prevent a liquidity crunch during slower times.

Creating effective inventory management. Inventory is costly on many levels, and so keeping just enough to meet demand while avoiding surplus will contribute to stronger cash flows.

Leasing instead of purchase. Although this will increase operating expenses on the income statement, it no doubt will lower capital expenditures, which should benefit cash flow.

Accelerating receivables. The sooner those outstanding payments are collected, the stronger cash flows will be.

Decelerating payables. Hanging on to those payments due a bit longer also can help cash flows. But hanging on to them for an extended period can lead to questions about a company's creditworthiness.

How Much Cash?

A question that invariably arises is, How much cash should a company have? The simple answer to this question is that it depends on the type of business. On the one hand, every business requires sufficient cash reserves to cover the day-to-day changes in the business. However, excess cash can mean lost opportunities. On the other hand, deficient cash can mean delinquent payments and lower credit ratings. Business managers often face this balancing act of maintaining just the right amount of cash.

In the late 1990s, Microsoft came under fire for building up billions of dollars in cash reserves. Critics argued that the company was not using that cash to engender growth, namely, through acquisitions and new businesses. However, Microsoft took a more conservative approach to cash management, and a few years later, when technology companies were hit particularly hard by a weak economy, it was able to continue operating as before, with few dramatic cost-cutting initiatives.

Free Cash Flow

Free cash flow is a term that often is used in the world of investment banking. Investment bankers drop this phrase whenever possible but rarely take the time to explain it. In fact, as I discovered many years ago, there is no single definition for it. It can have a number of meanings, a few of which are listed here:

- Net income plus depreciation plus any other intangible expense during the period
- Cash flow from operations
- Cash flow from operations minus some or all of the capital expenditures during the year

The bottom line here is simply to ask, How is free cash flow being defined? Frequently, financial analysts and investment bankers choose the definition that best suits their objectives.

5

FRAUD AND MANIPULATION

In the late 1980s, a musical duo captivated the hearts of millions. With catchy beats, clever lyrics, and dazzling good looks, they kept young adults singing and dancing around the world. In addition to selling millions of albums, they won a Grammy. Yet every now and then, something just did not seem right. Suspicions arose that perhaps they were not actually singing during their concerts. But as they continued to sell albums, many fans cast aside their doubts. Eventually, the truth surfaced that not only were these performers lip-synching in their concerts, they were lip-synching on their albums as well!

Nearly a decade later, corporate America was enjoying the fruits of the greatest bull market ever. Soaring earnings and skyrocketing stock prices became the norm for companies across industries. Although suspicions mounted that the numbers were not entirely accurate, few voiced any serious concerns. As long as the accountants, lawyers, and bankers were paid well, there was little cause for concern. Soon, however, irregularities surfaced, and certain creative accounting techniques that were employed across industries proved to be blatantly deceptive. Before long, investors and analysts came to realize that the numbers did not add up. We all know what happened next. Baby, don't forget the numbers.

History has taught us one thing: as long as companies are managed by human beings, fraud and manipulation will occur. However, as corporations become larger, so does the financial and social impact of such avarice. The boom years of the 1990s raised the need to exceed analysts' expectations and boost shareholder value to unprecedented levels. As a result, corporate managers went to great lengths to deceive Wall Street, investors, and the government. Through elaborate schemes involving sales skimming, misappropriation of funds, improper revenue recognition, overstatement of assets, and understatement of liabilities, corporation managers created paper wealth of untold proportions. And as the web of deception unraveled, a costly price was paid by the stock market and the overall economy. If any good came of this, it was the painful reminder that each and every one of us should understand the basics of financial analysis and, more important, know the ways to detect corporate fraud. This chapter will discuss the following:

- Types of fraud
- Enron
- Profit smoothing
- Detecting fraud
- Pro forma financials

TYPES OF FRAUD

Most types of fraud can be assigned to one of the six areas detailed below.

Money Laundering

Money laundering is essentially taking money from illegal sources and passing it through another business to make the money appear legitimate. For example, an organized crime syndicate involved in the drug trade might create a chain of dry cleaners to pass through money from drug sales in an effort to "wash" those funds.

Sales Skimming

Sales skimming involves the deliberate omission of revenue to lower taxable income. This could very well be the case with small businesses that only accept cash, as it would be difficult to track their sales receipts. It becomes a much larger issue when we are talking about Fortune 500 companies that use creative methods to defer revenue or simply hide revenue, as was the case in many of the recent corporate fraud scandals.

Overstating Expenses

This type of fraud often takes the form of running personal expenses through a business to lower taxable income. This is something that might occur in small private companies, and generally it goes unnoticed when done on a small scale. It becomes a larger concern in publicly traded companies, in which a CEO might decide to expense his private art collection to the company.

Bribes and Payoffs

Often committed by large businesses seeking to fix prices or land contracts, this is the type of thing that occurs when a large company is seeking to capture a portion of an international market to secure a large account. Usually some type of bribe or payoff is offered to local government officials or business leaders to gain their approval. In my naive younger days, while I was working as a financial advisor in Latin America, I found it a strange coincidence that when a lucrative privatization contract was awarded to a foreign bank, it seemed to coincide with the minister of commerce's purchase of a brand-new Hummer.

Shifting Sales and Expenses Between Businesses and Operating Subsidiaries

Often large corporations will shift expenses from a less profitable unit to a more profitable unit. This allows for a smoother distribution of profits, and in some cases it can reduce the overall tax burden. For example, the more profitable unit may be facing an excessive tax bill. When expenses are added to its income statement, that burden may ease.

Phony Off-Balance-Sheet Financing Schemes

Overall, off-balance-sheet entities are not considered to be inherently deceptive. However, a combination of creative accounting and lax observance of ownership rules has created an opportunity to hide liabilities in them. As you saw in Chapter 2, a special-purpose entity is created to take on the debt of a parent company, and in the process, the liability essentially is hidden. The perception is that the holding company has a much stronger balance sheet, something that analysts and investors prefer.

ENRON

The granddaddy of all corporate fraud tales has to be that of Enron. A number of other scandals rival it in size and scope, but the Enron story involved such elaborate schemes, crafted by some of the most respected leaders in corporate America, that we probably will be talking about it for decades to come. More significantly, we have only begun to scratch the surface in terms of what was occurring behind the scenes.

The Enron story began in the early 1990s when the company incurred large amounts of debt to help it evolve from a simple energy pipeline operator to a sophisticated energy trading house. Within a few years, the vast majority of its revenues were derived from the trading business. Soon afterward, the company was trading everything from telecom bandwidth to pollution emission credits. In fact, Enron officials boasted that they could trade anything, including weather! Enron continued to receive accolades and acknowledgment for its innovative ideas, aggressive culture, and astronomical growth. In 2001, it was named the most innovative company in America by *Fortune* magazine—a well-deserved honor had it pertained to accounting practices.

The Enron story started to unravel when the company took large write-downs in its telecom and water businesses. In October 2001, Enron announced a restatement of earnings for the past five years, and between October 2001 and February 2002 the company lost approximately $80 billion in market value. In fact, even while executives were selling some $1 billion worth of stock as the scandal unfolded, Enron officials were encouraging their employees to buy more stock.

What happened? Unfortunately, we may never know exactly. Thousands of pages of documents were lost or shredded, and the parties allegedly involved have offered conflicting accounts of what occurred. What we do know is detailed in the following sections.

Special-Purpose Entities

Some 3,000 special-purpose entities (SPEs) were created to hide billions of dollars of debt through skillfully devised off-balance-sheet limited partnerships. They included names such as Chewco Investments and Joint Energy Development Investment (JEDI). Any idea where those names came from? Enron's management and employees were so captivated by the *Star Wars* movies that they went so far as to disguise their capital base by using characters' names from them. (Enron headquarters was affectionately termed *The Death Star*.) Enron funded the SPEs with its own stock, and the SPEs issued dividends on Enron's stock to create an artificial source of revenue. This system worked as long as stock prices increased.

Shifting Expenses

Enron hid expenses by shifting them from one SPE to another. This allowed the company to inflate profits artificially.

Revenue Manipulation

Enron would purchase oil and gas rights and record the value of reserves as revenues by using mark-to-market accounting. This type of accounting involves adjusting items to their fair market value. However, in the case of Enron, the company used this as justification to value the reserves off the expected returns discounted to present value. Essentially, those revenues were grounded entirely in speculation.

Enron also would sell ownership of power projects to its SPEs, which in turn would sell contracts for that power back to Enron.

Additionally, Enron would sell fiber-optic cable contracts to the SPEs and record earnings from the sales.

Price Fixing

Enron was involved in a major energy price-fixing scheme that led to energy shortages in California.

Why Did This Occur?

Two questions invariably follow a discussion on Enron: How did this occur, and why didn't someone say something sooner? The why tends to be simpler. When lawyers, bankers, and accountants are paid a lot of money, who stops to ask questions? Indeed, many company insiders and affiliates sensed that something was rotten in the state of Texas, but as long as times were good and people were paid well, few questions were asked.

So how did everyone fail to see this? This is a bit more complex. Take a look at this footnote from page 38 of Enron's 2000 annual report:

> *Securitizations. From time to time, Enron sells interests in certain of its financial assets. Some of these sales are completed in securitizations, in which Enron concurrently enters into swaps associated with the underlying assets, which limit the risks assumed by the purchaser. Such swaps are adjusted to fair value using quoted market prices, if available, or estimated fair value based on management's best estimate of the present value of future cash flow. These swaps are included in Price Risk Management activities above as equity investments.*

Aside from revealing management's mastery of the written word, this passage reveals little more. In fact, rather than clarify an issue, it further complicates it. First, it fails to specify which assets were sold or when this occurred. Second, it offers little detail on the securitizations and even less on the swaps associated with them. Third, it gives virtually no indication of how the swaps are valued, being so bold as to state that this might be based on "management's best estimate." Such disclosures are prevalent throughout Enron's financial statements.

To understand how most of Wall Street failed to uncover such egregious fraud, take a look at Enron's income statement from 2000, which is reproduced in Figure 5-1. Here you can see a company that reports over $100 billion in revenues using no more than four lines to outline what contributed to it. In fact, the financials for Cunningham Hardware are more comprehensive than this. This combination of limited financial disclosure, vague footnotes, and a soaring stock price will serve to limit the number of questions about how a company does business—for some time, at least.

PROFIT SMOOTHING

Nowadays we hear a lot about *profit smoothing*. This is a broad term that is used to describe the practice of intentionally deflating or inflating profits, depending on the objective. In fact, many publicly traded companies engage in some form of profit smoothing for reasons ranging from beating analysts' expectations, to displaying steady growth, to reducing tax liabilities. Managers may do this by deferring revenues and expenses to subsequent periods. By waiting to book revenues or prepaying expected expenses, a company can limit its tax burden in the near term. Such tax savings can be of particular use to a cash-strapped company. A company seeking to boost earnings in an effort to appease Wall Street analysts and shareholders might record a pending sale in the current period. This practice is highly suspect and in most cases is considered outright fraud, yet companies have been doing it for years. In reviewing financial statements, it is important to read the footnotes and understand exactly how revenues are treated and, more important, when they are recorded.

FIGURE 5-1 Enron's Income Statement

ENRON CORP. AND SUBSIDIARIES
CONSOLIDATED INCOME STATEMENT

(In millions, except per share amounts)	Year ended December 31,		
	2000	1999	1998
Revenues			
Natural gas and other products	$50,500	$19,536	$13,276
Electricity	33,823	15,238	13,939
Metals	9,234	-	-
Other	7,232	5,338	4,045
Total revenues	100,789	40,112	31,260
Costs and Expenses			
Cost of gas, electricity, metals and other products	94,517	34,761	26,381
Operating expenses	3,184	3,045	2,473
Depreciation, depletion and amortization	855	870	827
Taxes, other than income taxes	280	193	201
Impairment of long-lived assets	-	441	-
Total costs and expenses	98,836	39,310	29,882
Operating Income	1,953	802	1,378
Other Income and Deductions			
Equity in earnings of unconsolidated equity affiliates	87	309	97
Gains on sales of non-merchant assets	146	541	56
Gain on the issuance of stock by TNPC, Inc.	121	-	-
Interest income	212	162	88
Other income, net	(37)	181	(37)
Income Before Interest, Minority Interests and Income Taxes	2,482	1,995	1,582
Interest and related charges, net	838	656	550
Dividends on company-obligated preferred securities of subsidiaries	77	76	77
Minority interests	154	135	77
Income tax expense	434	104	175
Net income before cumulative effect of accounting changes	979	1,024	703
Cumulative effect of accounting changes, net of tax	-	(131)	-
Net Income	979	893	703
Preferred stock dividends	83	66	17
Earnings on Common Stock	$ 896	$ 827	$ 686
Earnings per Share of Common Stock			
Basic			
Before cumulative effect of accounting changes	$ 1.22	$ 1.36	$ 1.07
Cumulative effect of accounting changes	-	(0.19)	-
Basic earnings per share	$ 1.22	$ 1.17	$ 1.07
Diluted			
Before cumulative effect of accounting changes	$ 1.12	$ 1.27	$ 1.01
Cumulative effect of accounting changes	-	(0.17)	-
Diluted earnings per share	$ 1.12	$ 1.10	$ 1.01
Average Number of Common Shares Used in Computation			
Basic	736	705	642
Diluted	814	769	695

DETECTING FRAUD

So how do we spot these red flags? Among other things, it is absolutely imperative that we read the financial statements as well as the footnotes. In particular, we should be aware of certain items that can be a cause for concern. These include the following:

Stock option awards. Stock options, when exercised, can have a strong dilutive effect on existing shares. It is important to understand what that impact might be, and so the best recourse is to discuss this with company management or investor relations if it is not specifically outlined in the footnotes.

Pending lawsuits and investigations. Any type of adverse news can undermine company valuation. Again, it is important to understand the potential outcome of these lawsuits and investigations.

Segment information. It is very important to understand the specific segments in which the company operates and how the company has performed within those segments. Segment laggards tend to bring overall company performance down, and unfortunately, not all companies disclose the way they perform on a segment-by-segment basis.

Off-balance-sheet entities. Anytime you see discussion related to more off-balance-sheet entities or other special-purpose entities, it is important to ask how those entities were structured and for what purpose. Off-balance-sheet entities can mean hidden liabilities.

PRO FORMA FINANCIALS

The use of pro forma financials has raised a number of concerns recently. Pro forma financials are essentially adjusted financial statements. For our purposes, pro forma financials tend to fall into one of two broad categories:

- Adjusted earnings
- Projections

Over the past few years, companies have encountered a fair amount of scrutiny when it comes to pro formas. The simple reason has to do with the loose standards governing their preparation. Several years ago, the SEC released the following statement about this:

> ... we believe it is appropriate to sound a warning to public companies and other registrants who present to the public their earnings and results of operations on the basis of methodologies other than Generally Accepted Accounting Principles ("GAAP"). This presentation in an earnings release is often referred to as "pro forma" financial information.

Pro forma financials are derived from selective editing of information, which can easily mislead investors. Through their use, a company can effortlessly present a deceptive view of operating performance. In fact, statements about a company's financial results that are true may still be misleading if they omit material information. From time to time, companies will use a pro forma disclosure to reflect a loss as if it were a profit. Consider the case of Amazon. In 2001, the company announced its first pro forma profit by excluding charges for stock compensation, restructuring charges, and amortization of goodwill. Simple exclusions provided a huge public relations coup for the company, and the stock market loves good PR.

Adjusted Earnings

This is used to determine variations on earnings by omitting or including certain extraordinary items on the income statement. One-time charges and write-offs can be overlooked easily, thus turning a loss into a profit. Because there are no consistent standards or regulations for this, companies are able to use their own discretion in crafting informal disclosure and press releases to boost investor appeal. Reasons for this practice include the following:

- Providing a meaningful comparison to results for the same period in prior years
- Emphasizing the results of core operations
- Exceeding Wall Street analysts' expectations
- Impressing shareholders

The more common exclusions include the following:

- Restructuring charges
- Write-downs of assets
- Stock option expenses
- Write-offs of research and development costs
- Litigation costs
- Merger-related expenses

In the sample income statement shown in Figure 5-2, notice how any of the several extraordinary items can be excluded to create stronger earnings numbers.

FIGURE 5-2 Sample Pro Forma Income Statement

Actual Numbers			Pro Forma		
Net Sales		$3,589,234	Net Sales		$3,589,234
Cost of Goods Sold		$1,567,321	Cost of Goods Sold		$1,567,321
Gross Profit		$2,021,913	Gross Profit		$2,021,913
SG&A		$ 890,487	SG&A		$ 890,487
Other Charges			EBITDA		$1,131,426
Amortization of Goodwill	$ 23,965				
Impairment of Assets	$ 14,864		Depreciation		$ 134,965
Associated Merger Charges	$ 106				
Total Other Charges	$ 38,935		EBIT		$ 996,461
Depreciation		$ 134,965	Interest		$ 34,688
Interest		$ 34,688			
			EBT		$ 961,773
Income Taxes		$ 276,851			
Net Income		$ 645,987	Other Charges		
			Amortization of Goodwill		$ 23,965
			Impairment of Assets		$ 14,864
			Associated Merger Charges		$ 106
			Total Other Charges		$ 38,935
			Income Taxes		$ 276,851
			Net Income		$ 645,987

Projections

Companies often use pro formas to show the impact of a planned transaction or to spell out expected results. Such statements are useful provided that they are detailed and are understood to be based solely on estimates. For example, a company might use pro forma financials to illustrate the expected capital structure and performance of a company after a merger. The company then would issue a pro forma balance sheet, income statement, and cash flow statement. Such disclosure would be useful for planning purposes. A company also might detail the impact of a capital-raising transaction such as a stock or debt offering. In that process, a pro forma balance sheet is revealed. Finally, for purposes of valuation, pro formas are a must. Future cash flows and multiples usually are based on some expected results, which necessitate the creation of pro formas.

How are projections formed? Unfortunately, there are no clear rules for developing financial projections, yet many financial decisions are based on analysis stemming from projections. Whether it is valuation or capital budgeting, a projection forms the most time-intensive component of the process.

Financial models are useful for the following:

- Building forecasts and budgets
- Assessing funding requirements
- Creating marketing or operational strategies
- Doing business planning
- Raising capital
- Conducting financial analysis
- Determining valuation

There are several ways to form projections, but the best ones tend to have a line-by-line justification for each assumption. Among the more common techniques are the following:

- Line-by-line forecasts for all components of the balance sheet, income statement, and cash flow statement

- Simple growth rate based on historical averages applied to the individual components of financials
- Economic growth rate applied to company performance

Among these methods, the first is by far the most widely accepted and, when done correctly, the most credible. What does it mean to build a credible forecasting model? For starters, the company has to reflect a current set of financials from which to build on. It can project out any number of years provided that it has sufficient information, but five years tends to be the standard in most industries. With the most recent balance sheet, income statement, and cash flow statement, a company can start to construct its projections. Usually, more emphasis is placed on income statement projections, yet more time is devoted to the sales aspect of them. If you have ever taken an introductory economics course, you may recall that sales are a function of the following:

$$\text{Price } (P) \times \text{quantity } (Q) = \text{total sales}$$

Therefore, assumptions will have to be made for both P and Q in each projected period. The company would have to consider the price of each product and the expected quantities to be sold year after year. As you can imagine, in a large corporation, this can prove to be a daunting task.

So come take a stroll with me down memory lane as I seek to reconstruct the steps in creating a forecasting model. Feel free to read out loud to your friends and family so that they too can share in the joys of building a financial model!

Step 1. Choose the right mood music—it's always a good idea to set the mood when one is preparing a good financial model. Since you probably will be spending the next several dozen or so hours staring at a computer monitor, this will soothe the pain. My favorite selections in the past included "Pressure" by Billy Joel and "Please Shoot Me," a little something I put together and enjoyed serenading my coworkers with during my Wall Street days. Unfortunately, the lyrics are not provided in this book, so you will have to make up your own, which should be no trouble.

Step 2. Review the current financials along with those of the prior three years. Pay close attention to any trends, extraordinary items, and changes in accounting policies.

Step 3. Begin to forecast your income statement. Take a look at current sales and determine the best method for doing this. In the most detailed models, you would form volume forecasts for each product. You would multiply those volume numbers by pricing estimates for each product.

Step 4. Measure all variable costs, namely, your cost of goods sold. You can model them individually on the basis of estimated price forecasts or on the basis of a percentage of sales.

Step 5. Estimate operating expenses for each of the next five years. This can be fairly simple if you expect operating expenses to remain relatively flat. In particular, you must give thought to number of employees, salaries, marketing, legal, utilities, and so on. If you are projecting substantial sales growth, of course these things should rise as well. How much they rise depends on the level of efficiency the company expects to achieve over time. Most publicly traded corporations will boast projected sales growth while claiming to trim operating expenses. In some instances, this might happen, but it is far from the norm.

Step 6. Taxes should not be overlooked in the forecasting process. Clearly, they form a large part of any company's budget and should be treated accordingly. The estimated percentage that will be paid in taxes should be multiplied by pretax income. This amount is subtracted from pretax income to arrive at net income.

Step 7. With a complete income statement, you can begin to construct a cash flow statement. Normally, detailed cash flow projections would have to be crafted in tandem with balance sheet projections, which can be time-intensive, not to mention highly speculative. Specifically, estimating changes in accounts receivable, accounts payable, inventory, and so forth can be painstakingly tedious. For this reason, many analysts prefer to look at simplified variations on cash flows such as EBITDA. By forecasting EBITDA, they are simply working from the income statement and, for the most part, producing numbers closer to cash. In some cases they subtract any extraordinary items such as capital expenditures, but in the end it begs the question, Who really cares? These are all guesses anyway.

Summary. At this point, you can build out the cash flow and balance sheet changes. Usually, such models are dynamic and are built into spreadsheets so that certain accounts will adjust automatically to reflect changes in other accounts.

To review, the items to build into your projections include the following:

- Accumulated depreciation
- Bad debt provisions
- Capital expenditures
- Changes in debt
- Depreciation rates
- Dividends
- Fixed-asset values
- General overhead
- Intangible assets
- Interest rates
- Inventory
- Material costs
- Research and development
- Sales volumes
- Selling and distribution costs
- Selling prices
- Share issues
- Tax rates

You can always come up with more, but these form a good starting point. Enjoy!

6

FINANCIAL ANALYSIS

In my early days in finance, I was given the opportunity to invest in one of two businesses. The first business was selling a branded product for which the demand was very high. The second was selling a product that the business both produced and sold to the consumer. That product, however, lacked brand appeal, something that inevitably leads to slower sales growth. Failing to do any further analysis, I chose to invest in the first company. I soon realized this was a big mistake, as that business eventually failed while the second business went on to achieve remarkable success. But I learned a valuable lesson from this, something that Wall Street has been teaching for years and that has stuck with me ever since. Basically, numbers are good, but analysis is better. Just because the sales numbers and profit numbers are strong, that does not mean that the company is. Or in this case, a business that posts meager results may in fact reveal untold future potential after further analysis. A few of the following measures of financial analysis could have saved me from making a poor investment:

- Profit margins
- Sales growth projections
- Return on equity
- Inventory turnover

In fact, if I had done this kind of analysis, I would have uncovered information that showed that the company I chose to invest in had the following:

- Lower profit margins as a result of the high cost of acquiring the product
- Slower sales growth because of increased competition in a crowded space
- Lower return on equity because of multiple investors
- Lower inventory turnover because management had overzealously ordered too much product to meet aggressive sales forecasts

To this day, I regret not investing in the second company, which performed exceptionally well. In fact, the founder earned the distinction of being called the Lemonade King in our neighborhood, whereas the company I invested in petered out like most of the other Kool-Aid stands on the block.

This chapter will discuss the following:

- Financial statement analysis
- Trend analysis
- Ratio analysis
- Economic value added (EVA)

FINANCIAL STATEMENT ANALYSIS

At this point, we transition to financial statement analysis. We already have taken a close look at the balance sheet, the income statement, and the cash flow statement. We saw that the balance sheet is essentially the doctor's report, because it tells us whether a company is in good financial health. We took a look at the income statement, which serves as the report card by helping to gauge a company's performance. Then we took a look at the cash flow statement, which helps determine how much cash a company is generating; it serves as the checkbook for the company.

Examining these statements is useful for making comparisons with prior years and, more important, with other companies. For that reason, there is an entire school of finance that is based on financial statement analysis. Wall Street research analysts, investment bankers, commercial bankers, financial managers, and traders commonly use this type of analysis.

Nowadays, financial analysis has particular relevance as corporate managers are rewarded on the basis of their ability to meet certain benchmarks. For example, a CEO's compensation will have some component that is dependent on certain levels of quantifiable achievement, which might include return on equity or profit margins. Furthermore, financial statement analysis can be useful in drawing performance comparisons between individual divisions of a company or between companies in an entire industry. Next, we will take a look at these techniques to understand what they are used for and who uses them.

TREND ANALYSIS

One of the primary methods used to assess a company's performance is known as *trend analysis*. This takes many different forms. The two most common methods are detailed here.

Year-to-Year Change Analysis

The most common way to assess a company's performance from one year to the next is called *year-to-year change analysis*. For example, look at a company's sales growth. If the company over time has increased its sales approximately 10 percent per year, that figure can be compared with the industry average. If the industry average reveals a trend in which sales throughout the industry have grown 20 percent, the conclusion can be drawn that the company has underperformed the industry. If, in contrast, the industry trend is sales growth of 5 percent, the company seems to be doing reasonably well by outperforming the industry average. Year-to-year change analysis allows for the examination of virtually any item on the financial statements to determine a company's growth. From there, comparisons can be made with other items on the company's financials or with other companies in the industry.

Index-Number Trend-Series Analysis

Another method used to measure trends is called *index-number trend-series analysis*. This method is used for longer-term trend comparisons. It involves choosing a base year for all financial statement items and expressing each item, such as sales, as 100 percent. Every year after the base year, the sales number is adjusted above or below the base number to reflect the change. This process is helpful in assessing how those items have changed over an extended period. An example is shown in the following table.

	YEAR 1	YEAR 2	YEAR 3	YEAR 4	YEAR 5
Sales	100	150	175	200	250
Index-number trend	100%	150%	175%	200%	250%

RATIO ANALYSIS

The most common method of analyzing companies is called *ratio analysis*. If you watch stock investment shows, read Wall Street equity research reports, or work with bankers and accountants, you probably have encountered some type of ratio analysis. These ratios are helpful in determining the relative strength, performance, and value of a company. In fact, there are several different categories of ratios, each pertaining to a specific set of users. For example, operations managers focus on performance activity. Short-term bank and trade creditors focus on the immediate liquidity of a firm. Longer-term creditors such as bondholders are interested in the long-term solvency of a firm. Managers examine the profitability of a firm, whereas investors monitor returns. Finally, market traders and equity analysts are most interested in overall market performance. For each group of financial professionals, there tends to be a corresponding set of ratios.

It is important to understand that ratio analysis helps provide an overall profile of a firm, its economic characteristics, and its competitive strategies. A primary advantage of ratio analysis is that it allows comparison among firms of different sizes. However, the construction of such ratios invariably involves a process of standardization, and in any such process, specific differences between the companies pertaining to capital structures, extraordinary items, and accounting methods tend to be ignored. For example, two very similar companies may use entirely different methods to calculate depreciation. If one uses a decelerated schedule and the other uses an accelerated one, the financial statements will reflect this; more specifically, so will several profitability and asset-based ratios. The ratios themselves will not disclose this difference in accounting treatment, though the comparative analysis certainly will be affected.

What can be done? It is unwise to disavow one of the fundamental tools of financial analysis completely, as tempting as that might be. Rather, it is important to understand that one should not rely exclusively on ratio analysis to make a definitive conclusion about a company. Ratio analysis should be used as one part of the entire analysis process.

There are six broad categories of ratio analysis. Below is a brief description of each one, along with the group that tends to use it:

1. *Activity analysis.* This first category enables the evaluation of revenues and output generated by the firm's assets. Activity analysis is useful for operations managers as well as management consultants. In fact, a number of large consulting firms have built their practice around this type of ratio analysis.
2. *Liquidity analysis.* This measures the adequacy of a firm's cash resources and its ability to meet near-term cash obligations. Liquidity analysis is particularly useful for commercial bankers and, to a lesser degree, investment bankers, because it enables the lenders or issuers to understand whether a firm has sufficient cash resources to meet the obligations of a particular offering.

3. *Long-term debt and solvency analysis.* This examines a company's capital structure, its mix of financing sources, and, more important, the ability of the firm to satisfy its longer-term debt and investment obligations. Investment bankers and fund managers often use this type of analysis.

4. *Profitability analysis.* This measures the income of a company relative to its revenues and invested capital. Profitability analysis is particularly useful for investment analysts, private equity investors, and, of course, company managers.

5. *Return analysis.* This examines the returns on assets, total capital, and equity in an effort to measure investment performance. Investors of every type use return analysis.

6. *Market analysis.* This measures value, income, and dividends relative to one another. This is useful for investors and market traders.

Let's examine each category in greater depth.

Activity Analysis

Activity analysis describes the relationship between a firm's level of operations and the assets needed to sustain those operating activities. It is helpful in assessing the overall efficiency of a business.

Inventory Turnover Days

Inventory turnover days is a very common measure of a company's efficiency. This measure shows how frequently a company is converting its inventory to sales. This is important because inventory, to put it mildly, is costly for a number of reasons. For one thing, there is the cost of storage. If the company produces or purchases inventory, it must store it. Whether the company owns its property or leases it, there will be a cost associated with storage. The longer it takes to sell the inventory, the longer the company must store it and the more costly it becomes. At the same time, there are risks associated with inventory. Every time a piece of inventory is produced but not sold, the company faces the risk that eventually that inventory will become obsolete. The longer the inventory is held, the more likely it is to end up liquidated at a discount or not sold at all. Also, the cost of financing inventory can create concerns for a company. The longer the inventory is held, the more the company assumes in financing costs. Thus, there are numerous reasons why inventory is costly, and because of this, company managers look at inventory turnover days.

$$\text{Inventory turnover days} = 365/(\text{cost of goods sold}/\text{average inventory})$$

As this formula shows, inventory turnover days is calculated by taking 365 days in the year and dividing that number by the ratio of cost of goods sold to average inventory. Suppose a company has a cost of goods sold of $1 million and average inventory of $100,000. We take the $1 million and divide it by $100,000, which gives an inventory turnover of 10 times. In other words, inventory turns over (sells) 10 times per year. Then we divide that turnover of 10 into 365 days in the year to calculate inventory turnover days of 36.5. By using this, we can conclude that every 36 to 37 days, inventory converts to sales. Is this a good number? That depends. To decide, we measure it against an industry average. If the industry average is 72 days, 36.5 days is a very good number, because competitors are taking roughly double the amount of days to convert their inventory to sales. If the industry average is 18, then 36.5 is not so strong. Here competitors are converting their inventory in half the time.

Inventory turnover days is a useful measure because, as we just saw, inventory is costly. The sooner inventory turns, the better. In fact, inventory turnover becomes increasingly important in certain industries. One company in particular—see if you can guess which one—serves as a shining example of how far inventory turnover can propel a business. This company maintained a relatively level stock price during the early part of the new millennium while its competitors were experiencing precipitous drops in share prices. Wall Street was quick to recognize that this company's low inventory turnover days number was freeing up cash and lowering the risk of excess inventory, both of which are serious concerns in an industry marked by new product innovations and liquidity problems. Give up? Dell Computer has a world-class system of supply chain management that creates numerous advantages in the process of inventory management. By building computers to order, Dell maintains lower inventory for a shorter period than most of its competitors. This lowers financing costs, storage costs, and obsolescence risk, all of which has helped Dell build billions of dollars in shareholder wealth.

Accounts Receivable Turnover Days

Like inventory, accounts receivable poses some concerns. The longer receivables remain outstanding, the more costly they become. The longer a company holds on to its receivables, the less likely it is to collect them. Furthermore, if there are receivables outstanding, the company is losing interest on those payments. To measure average collection rate, use accounts receivable turnover days.

$$\text{Accounts receivable turnover days} =$$
$$365/(\text{credit sales/average accounts receivable})$$

With accounts receivable turnover days, we take 365 days in a year and divide that number by the ratio of credit sales to average receivables. If the company has $1 million in credit sales and $100,000 in average receivables, the accounts receivable turnover days are 36.5—every 36 to 37 days, receivables convert to payment. Is this a good number? Again, it must be compared with the industry average. This is an important measure in service industries because those industries typically are characterized by installment billing. Often, a service is performed with the expectation that payment will be received at some point in the future. Attorneys, accountants, physicians, and consultants spend a fair amount of time focusing on collecting these payments. In corporate America, financial managers spend their time computing their accounts receivable turnover days.

Accounts Payable Turnover Days

The flip side of accounts receivable turnover days is accounts payable turnover days. This shows on average how long it takes a company to pay off its outstanding payables.

Accounts payable turnover days =
365/(purchases/average accounts payable)

To calculate this, take 365 days in the year and divide it by the ratio of purchases to average accounts payable. Purchases are defined as the cost of goods sold plus changes in inventory. Thus, if a company has $1 million in purchases and $100,000 in average accounts payable, its accounts payable turnover days equals 36.5. Again, is this a good number? You know the answer. The idea here is to obtain as large a number as possible, because the longer the company has to turn over its payables, the better off it is—the longer it keeps that cash on hand. Of course, a lot of things can be done with that cash. The company can reinvest it or deploy it in some manner to create added benefit for itself. In theory, then, the longer it can hold on to the cash, the better off it is. However, the company does have to be careful not to overdo it. Too much of a good thing can cause problems. If analysts sense that this number is excessive, they may assume that the company is facing liquidity problems.

Cash Conversion Cycle

A formula that combines the different turnover numbers is called the *cash conversion cycle* (*CCC*):

CCC = A/R days + inventory days − A/P days

As you can see, it is calculated by taking accounts receivable (A/R) days, plus inventory days, minus accounts payable (A/P) days, and it is a good measure of a company's immediate liquidity.

Averages

The term *average* is prevalent throughout much of ratio analysis: *average inventory, average receivables,* and *average payables* are some of the more common applications. Each represents a balance sheet item, which, if you recall, reflects a snapshot at a particular point in time. For example, inventory would reflect the inventory at the end of the last reporting cycle. That may not reflect what occurred during the reporting cycle accurately, and therefore an average inventory number is needed. More often than not, that average number is calculated by taking the inventory number from the end of the most recent year plus the inventory number from the prior year and dividing the sum by 2. It is not perfect, but it works. A similar method of averaging can be used for any of the other balance sheet items when needed.

Liquidity Analysis

Liquidity analysis shows whether a company has sufficient liquid resources to cover its near-term obligations. This is of particular interest to most commercial banks, which often base their determination of a company's creditworthiness on these ratios.

Current Ratio

The first and most common measure of a company's liquidity is the current ratio.

$$\text{Current ratio} = \text{current assets}/\text{current liabilities}$$

The current ratio is calculated by dividing current assets by current liabilities. You might recall that current assets—which include cash, marketable securities, accounts receivable, and inventory—are assets that can be converted to cash within a year and current liabilities are assets that come due within a year. With the current ratio, the hope is that current assets will exceed current liabilities, resulting in a ratio greater than 1. This proves that the company has sufficient liquidity to cover its near-term obligations, which is a good position to be in. If current assets fall below current liabilities, the company would have a current ratio less than 1—and, more important, a big problem on its hands. In other words, it does not have sufficient resources to cover its near-term obligations. In this case, the company could either sell off fixed assets or issue long-term debt. Either strategy would improve the current ratio. However, issuing more short-term debt would leave the company in a potentially weak position. Although it would generate cash, it would commensurately boost current liabilities.

Quick Ratio

A variation on the current ratio is the quick ratio.

$$\text{Quick ratio} = (\text{cash} + \text{marketable securities} + \text{accounts receivable})/\text{current liabilities}$$

The quick ratio adds cash, marketable securities, and accounts receivable and then divides the sum by current liabilities. The primary difference between the quick ratio and the current ratio is the exclusion of inventory in the quick ratio. For reasons discussed earlier in this chapter, inventory often is seen as not truly liquid. It is difficult to sell and eventually can become obsolete. For that reason, many analysts believe the quick ratio is a better measure of a firm's immediate liquidity, because it uses a purer form of liquid assets.

Cash Ratio

The cash ratio adds cash to marketable securities and divides the sum by current liabilities.

$$\text{Cash ratio} = (\text{cash} + \text{marketable securities})/\text{current liabilities}$$

With the cash ratio, both inventory and accounts receivable are excluded because the view is that both are inherently problematic as a result of the difficulty of converting them to cash.

Long-Term Debt and Solvency Analysis

Long-term debt and solvency analysis is useful in determining whether a company is optimally capitalized.

Debt-to-Capital Ratio

The first and most common of these ratios is what is called the *debt–to–capital ratio* (*debt-to-cap ratio* in banker-speak).

Investment bankers commonly use this to measure relative levels of debt. It is calculated by taking total debt (current debt plus long-term debt) and dividing it by the sum of total debt and total equity:

$$\text{Debt-to-capital ratio} = \text{total debt/}$$
$$(\text{total debt} + \text{total equity})$$

In other words, the debt-to-capital ratio measures debt outstanding relative to the company's entire capital structure. For example, a company's 50 percent debt-to-capital ratio could be compared with an industry average. If the industry average is 20 percent, this company is clearly overleveraged. This proves useful in financing decisions, such as deciding on the appropriate mix of debt and equity financing. Investment bankers love the debt-to-capital ratio because they can tell their clients either "You're overleveraged; we should issue some equity to pay down that debt" or "You're underleveraged; we should issue more debt." Either option results in hefty underwriting fees!

Debt-to-Equity Ratio

The debt-to-equity ratio is a simple variation on the debt-to-capital ratio. In this case, take total debt and divide it by total equity:

$$\text{Debt to equity} = \text{total debt/total equity}$$

Times Interest Earned Ratio

Finally, analysts use the times interest earned ratio, or what is commonly referred to as the *interest coverage ratio*. This is a popular measure not just in corporate finance but in personal finance as well. If you have ever sought a loan of any type (e.g., home equity loan, school loan, auto loan), someone at a commercial bank took a look at your times interest earned ratio. The person who did this wanted to gauge your capacity to cover the interest expense. This was done by taking your earnings before interest and taxes and dividing it by your interest expense:

$$\text{Times interest earned} = \text{EBIT/interest}$$

The interest coverage ratio helps determine whether a company has sufficient EBIT to cover the necessary interest payments on debt outstanding.

Profitability Analysis

Profitability analysis is an effective way of measuring the various levels of profits relative to sales. You might recall from Chapter 3, which discussed the income statement, that companies exhibit different levels of profitability. Starting at the very top of the income statement, gross profit, EBIT, EBITDA, EBT, and net income are revealed. These levels of profitability are effective in measuring profitability among companies with varying operating and capital structures. This principle is observed in profitability ratios as well.

Gross Margin

Gross margin is the greatest ratio ever. It is hard to manipulate and offers an exceptional measure of a company's profitability at the highest level. It is calculated by taking gross profit and dividing it by sales:

$$\text{Gross margin} = \text{gross profit/sales}$$

Corporate managers are concerned with gross margin because the number is a measure of a company's distribution efficiency. Specifically, a company with higher gross margins derives more from a sale than does one with lower margins even though their profits may be comparable. Investors prefer a company with a higher gross margin because this indicates greater efficiency.

The best illustration of the importance of gross margins can be observed in the supermarket industry, which generally is characterized by low gross margins. In this industry, cost of goods sold tends to be very high relative to sales. An apple might cost the supermarket $0.32, and the supermarket might sell it for $0.35. For that reason, supermarkets are driven by volume.

Additionally, a number of trends have emerged over the past decade that improve gross margins:

1. As supermarket chains consolidate, they are able to increase their buying power and achieve better pricing from wholesalers. Additionally, because competition has been eliminated, prices may increase, further improving gross margins.
2. By diversifying into new products and services such as organic produce and banking services, supermarkets are able to capitalize on higher-margin offerings.

Additionally, consolidation among supermarket chains can lead to savings in operating expenses by eliminating overlapping functions. This will boost other margins.

Operating Margin

The software industry typically is characterized by very high gross margins. Software traditionally exhibits these high gross margins because its cost of goods sold tends to be very low. The cost of goods sold for software is really the cost of disseminating the software, either on disc or through Web-based applications. That tends to be a very small percentage of overall sales. In software, however, there are much higher operating expenses, which usually involve a significant amount of research and development. These expenses are distributed incrementally, or amortized, over some period. Research and development tends to be a large part of a software company's expense structure, and so the company's operating margin is much lower. Operating margin pertains to operating income divided by sales:

Operating margin = operating income/sales

Profit Margin

Finally, the most common measure of profitability is the profit margin, net income divided by sales:

Profit margin = net income/sales

Return Analysis

Return analysis frequently is referred to as *return on investment* (*ROI*), a very common term among investment managers. "What is the ROI on this investment?" is a question often heard within the walls of venture capital firms. ROI can be calculated a number of different ways.

Return on Assets

Return on assets is calculated by taking net income and dividing it by total assets:

Return on assets = net income/total assets

Return on Total Capital

Another way to calculate return on investment is by calculating return on total capital. Here net income is divided by the sum of total debt plus total equity:

Return on total capital = net income/
(total debt + total equity)

Return on Equity

Finally, ROI can be calculated as return on equity. This is done by taking net income and dividing it by total equity (shareholders' equity):

Return on equity = net income/total equity

Market Analysis

Last, there is a category known as *market analysis*. If you have ever seen an investment show or if you follow the market, you probably are familiar with one or more of the terms described in this section. They are useful for gauging stock price performance, dividend payout, and valuation. These ratios are used commonly by Wall Street traders as well as mom-and-pop investors. This information used to be part of an esoteric language spoken by the so-called industry analysts and experts. Nowadays, though, with the advent of the Internet, this information is much more readily available.

Price-to-Earnings Ratio

The first of the market ratios is the price-to-earnings ratio, or P/E ratio. The P/E ratio is useful because it enables an analyst to gauge the relative value of a company. It is measured by dividing the company's stock price by its earnings per share:

Price-to-earnings ratio = stock price/earnings per share

The share price of a company's stock reflects that company's ability to generate profits. The P/E ratio reveals the price an investor must pay to capture a dollar of earnings. A company's P/E ratio is measured relative to an industry average or peer group. If the P/E ratio of a company exceeds the P/E ratio of the industry, it is usually thought that the company is overvalued. If the P/E ratio of the company is less than the industry average, it is observed that the company might be undervalued. If the P/E ratio of the company is equal to the industry average, the company is probably fairly valued.

As was mentioned earlier, ratios should seldom be the sole evaluation criterion. Rather, they should be used in conjunction with much more detailed analysis. They're merely a starting point. However, in many, many instances the P/E ratio is useful for valuation purposes.

There are instances when the P/E has fallen below the market average for good reason and the company is not considered undervalued. For example, a company that is awaiting a ruling in a lawsuit that could be unfavorable probably would exhibit a lower P/E ratio than the market average.

Suppose a company has a market price per share of $20. If this company has earnings per share of $2, its price-to-earnings ratio is 10. If the industry average is 15, the company is probably undervalued. Again, there could be reasons for this, but at first glance, it appears that the company is undervalued. If the industry average is 7, the company might be seen as overvalued.

Earnings Yield

Earnings yield takes earnings per share and divides it by the market price per share. It's the inverse of the P/E ratio or, in other words, the earnings you buy with a dollar's worth of stock.

$$\text{Earnings yield} = \text{earnings per share}/\text{market price per share}$$

If the company has earnings per share of $2 and a market price per share of $20, its earnings yield is 10 percent.

Dividend Yield

Dividend yield takes dividends per share and divides it by market price per share. This helps assess how much the company is paying in dividends relative to its market price per share, or what percentage of the market price that dividend is. Also, that can be compared with an industry average to see if the company is paying more or less than the industry average.

$$\text{Dividend yield} = \text{dividends per share}/\text{market price per share}$$

If the company pays out $1 in dividends with a market price per share of $20, the dividend yield is 5 percent. If the industry average is 10 percent, the company is paying less than the industry. Is that a good yield? Since dividends tend to be one of the more controversial topics in finance, this is difficult to determine. There are those who believe that dividends should be paid out regularly and those who believe that they tend to compromise company growth. When a dividend is paid out, it represents the loss of funds that could have been used to grow the company through research, development, new product launches, and acquisitions. Certain companies consistently pay out very strong dividends and are praised for that, and other companies pay out few or no dividends and have performed reasonably well using this model.

Dividend Payout Ratio

The dividend payout ratio takes dividends per share and divides them by earnings per share:

$$\text{Dividend payout ratio} = \text{dividends per share} / \text{earnings per share}$$

If a company pays out $1 in dividends and has $2 in earnings, its dividend payout ratio is 50 percent. Again, whether this is a good or a bad number depends on industry averages. The remaining $1 is transferred back to the balance sheet in the form of retained earnings.

Price-to-Book Ratio

Finally, the price-to-book ratio takes market price per share and divides it by book price per share:

$$\text{Price-to-book ratio} = \text{market price per share} / \text{book price per share}$$

Market price per share is the price observed in the open market. For a publicly traded company, this is the stock price. The book price per share is the price or the value observed on the balance sheet that is listed as owners' equity, and it usually is not considered a good indicator of company value. Market value is based on the demand for the company or its shares, and it is commonly accepted as a starting point in the sale process. Rarely are these two numbers the same. Usually market price will exceed book price, though there are instances when the two numbers converge, which is often seen as a buying opportunity. In fact, many private equity investors will look for these rare instances because they seek to acquire companies for very little, restructure them, and resell them at a higher value. Through these acquisitions and restructurings, significant value is unlocked, creating a strong return on investment and in turn a higher price-to-book ratio.

ECONOMIC VALUE ADDED

Economic value added, or EVA, is a relatively recent performance measure developed to help companies calculate their true economic profit. One of the major advantages of EVA is that it can be used to measure performance on a divisional level, unlike other methods of analysis and valuation. EVA essentially does this by taking net operating profits after taxes minus a charge for the opportunity cost of invested capital. In other words, it measures a company's performance after deducting its cost of capital from its tax-adjusted operating profit. Some uses for EVA include

- Strategic goal setting
- Bonus determination
- Capital budgeting
- Valuation
- Equity analysis

The derivation of the formula for EVA is as follows:

Net sales − operating expenses = operating profit

Operating profit − taxes = net operating profit after taxes

Net operating profit after taxes − capital charges
(capital × cost of capital) = EVA

Or simply put:

EVA = net operating profit after taxes −
(capital × cost of capital)

EVA is used to measure profitability after a company accounts for its cost of invested capital. This capital charge is what really drives the EVA analysis. Although the company is seemingly profitable, it must exceed the cost of capital to benefit the shareholders. Suppose you manage a large multidivisional, multinational corporation. EVA provides a useful and user-friendly performance measure. You can measure EVA on the basis of operating divisions or even on a regional basis. It is a simple standard that most shareholders can understand, and aside from the cost of capital, it is rarely subject to manipulation. Although EVA is gaining ground in application, it still has a way to go before being universally accepted.

7

MANAGERIAL ACCOUNTING

When I was a kid, I made more than a few visits to the local amusement park. As much as I delighted in the thrills that the park had to offer, I was put off by the lengthy lines for the best rides. Unfortunately, this meant that I took multiple turns on the merry-go-round when all I really wanted was one turn on the corkscrew. If only someone had used managerial accounting to develop financial and process efficiencies. This would have allowed loyal customers like me to enjoy more rides in less time and allowed the park to service more customers. Had that been the case, I could have spent more time soaring upside down instead of nodding off on a plastic horse.

Imagine a world in which accounting allows you to turbocharge the process of strategic business decision making leading to enhanced efficiency and, in turn, profitability. Sure, balance sheets, income statements, and cash flow statements prove useful when evaluating a company's current and past financial performance. But what if those numbers could be used to help company decision makers with things like cost management, margin enhancements, or even production efficiencies? Wouldn't that be something? Well, that world does exist, and it's largely driven by managerial accounting.

Managerial accounting is designed almost exclusively for internal decision making. Managers use managerial accounting tools, some standard and others customized, to form better decisions that will hopefully lead to enhanced company performance. In other words, managerial accounting tends to have an internal bias, while financial accounting has an external one. Additionally, managerial accounting tends to be forward looking, while financial accounting tends to be backward looking. The table summarizes the major differences between financial accounting and managerial accounting.

	FINANCIAL ACCOUNTING	vs.	MANAGERIAL ACCOUNTING
Targets	Outside company		Inside company
Time	Past		Future
Rules	GAAP/IFRS		None
Metrics	Financial		Financial and nonfinancial

To put this all into perspective, let's suppose that Beanbag Beds, Inc. is hosting its annual shareholders' meeting next month. In preparation for this meeting, the finance team will prepare the balance sheet, income statement, and cash flow statement for the past four quarters with particular focus on how key items have improved or worsened. Let's suppose that in the next month, senior management has an important strategy meeting scheduled. In preparation for this meeting, senior management will develop a plan to grow the business while making it more efficient. In essence, management will look at where key metrics stand today and work to improve these numbers going forward.

The beauty of managerial accounting is that there are few rules defining what can be measured and, more important, how things can be measured. A clever manager can invent a metric with a convincing story to support it. Granted, being too clever can alienate other managers and stakeholders, so measuring some aspects of business performance is often a balancing act of sorts. This chapter will discuss the following:

- Costing analysis
- Activity-based costing (ABC)
- Operations management

COSTING ANALYSIS

Costing analysis can help a manager arrive at the most cost-efficient decisions surrounding the sourcing of a product. An essential part of this is what is called *contribution margin*. Contribution margin is a close cousin of gross margin, which we reviewed in Chapter 6. If you recall, gross margin is the ratio of gross profit (sales – cost of goods sold) divided by total sales. It reveals how much you earn on a product sold relative to sales. A high gross margin reveals that your costs of procuring or producing the product is low relative to its sale price. Contribution margin goes a step further by incorporating other variable costs into the equation. It's based in the equation:

Sales – cost of goods sold – other variable costs

With contribution margin, you will better understand your real cost of procuring or producing the product. Suppose you're in the business of selling plastic sandals. Each pair sells for $20. Materials cost $8, labor $2, machine operation $1. Your contribution margin would be $20 less the material cost, labor cost, and machine operation cost, or $9. If your fixed costs total $9,000, you must sell 1,000 plastic molded sandals before you generate a profit. After selling these 1,000 sandals, each additional pair sold will boost your profit by $9.

As you can see, contribution margin reframes the profit picture by allowing you to determine how many units you need to sell before you are able to cover your fixed costs. It's a remarkably effective tool, but as you might imagine, determining all the appropriate variable costs can sometimes prove challenging.

Transfer Pricing

Transfer pricing is the price at which one division sells goods and services to another division. This is important because it affects divisional performance and may have tax consequences as well. For example, if pricing is too low, the division may sell externally. If the division is in a higher tax bracket comparatively, it may make sense to price high to maximize the tax benefit to the company.

The Incredible Ink Company produces ink in a variety of colors for pens and markers. Fine Tip Industries is a leading manufacturer of ballpoint pens and markers. Fine Tip recently acquired Incredible Ink with the hopes of reducing Fine Tip's cost of ink. By offering low transfer pricing to Fine Tip, Incredible Ink's contribution margin increases. Now, suppose that a worldwide shortage of red ink has occurred due to a global recession causing financial losses. Incredible Ink, once the leading supplier of red ink, can no longer fulfill the growing demand for red ink as it must fulfill the orders at cost for its parent, Fine Tip, before it can sell to external customers. In other words, the low transfer pricing has created a formidable dilemma for Fine Tip. Does Fine Tip suspend orders so that Incredible Ink can fulfill orders externally at a higher price point? This could help boost Incredible Ink's profit, but it would hurt margins on Fine Tip's pens as they would be forced to source ink elsewhere. Or worse yet, they may have to suspend sales, which would prove even more problematic. What is a manager to do?

One of the more popular examples of this has to do with the nearly omnipresent question facing managers: Do I build it or do I buy it? Suppose Car-E-Oki requires a key part for its next generation Car-E-Oki machine. The part currently costs $20 per unit. If the company were to manufacture the part, the unit cost would drop to $10. However, manufacturing the part in-house would require fixed costs of $200,000 to purchase equipment needed to produce the part. So does the company build or buy? This all depends on how many machines it would expect to sell. A simple, one-term analysis can help answer this question. Consider the following:

1. Unit savings from manufacturing the part = $10/unit
2. Fixed cost needed to acquire the machine to manufacture the part = $200,000 (assume costs for running the machine are variable and included in the $10/unit cost)

To answer the question, we use the following equation:

Fixed cost to purchase equipment/cost savings
per unit = total units to achieve breakeven

$200,000/$10 = 20,000 units must be sold to
achieve the same profit as buying the part

In other words, if the company expects to sell more than 20,000 machines, it makes sense to buy the machine and manufacture the parts in-house. Of course, there are more involved considerations that include how long until it sells 20,000 machines, the expected life of the machine, and the annual depreciation on the machine. Managerial accounting calculations can easily expand, and all those numbers and calculations can sure look snazzy in a PowerPoint presentation to a board of directors.

ACTIVITY-BASED COSTING (ABC)

Don't let the name fool you. ABC is not always as easy as 123. While complex, ABC can be immensely useful in business decision making. First used in the manufacturing sector, ABC focuses on assigning costs to the production process. This method accounts for costs assigned to a task or product based on how the resources are assigned to the process by assigning percentages to overhead.

Suppose you own a business that produces muffins and cupcakes. It sells 200 muffins and 200 cupcakes each month. At the end of the month, you receive your bill from the utility company, which is $400. A hefty sum, but nearly all of it is used to power the ovens that bake the goods. In this case, how would you divide your utility bill between the muffins and cupcakes? Of course, you could divide the $400 utility bill by 400 total muffins and cupcakes. The result is $1 per baked good. What if it takes more power to bake a muffin than a cupcake? Perhaps it takes $1.50 worth of power to produce a muffin and $0.50 to produce a cupcake (our customers like their muffins well done). These types of costs are often difficult to allocate, but if we can determine the cost per item, it can help us make better pricing decisions. By knowing that muffins use three times as much power as cupcakes, we can run our business more efficiently.

Production Overhead

Using ABC in the following example, we calculate $0.50 per cupcake in setup costs and $0.50 per cupcake in production costs for a total production overhead per cupcake of $1.00.

ABC	
Setup:	$100
Batch units:	200
Overhead per unit:	**$0.50**
Overhead per production hour:	$50
Cupcakes per hour:	100
Overhead per cupcake per hour:	**$0.50**
Total production overhead per cupcake:	$1.00

Using basic cost analysis, our production overhead is a mere $0.50 per cupcake. While this looks better, it fails to account for the impact that setup costs will have on our units of production.

BASIC (NO ABC)	
Setup:	$0
Batch units:	NA
Overhead per unit:	NA
Overhead per production hour:	**$50**
Cupcakes per hour:	100
Overhead per cupcake per hour:	**$0.50**
Total production overhead per cupcake:	$0.50

Let's consider a more complex example based on a manufacturing company that produces one product. The production process can be segmented into two parts: the setup for production and the production itself. Overall, the company spends $200,000 in production overhead with $40,000 of that amount associated with the setup process. Since there are 100 total setups each year, the cost per setup works out to $400 ($40,000 setup overhead/100 annual setups). Since we have 2,000 units in each batch, the setup overhead per unit works out to $0.20 ($400 overhead per batch setup/2,000 units per batch). If the number of units in the batch increases, the setup overhead per unit will decrease.

The $160,000 in overhead relates to the overall production hours. In this case, we have 40,000 hours per year, which means we spend $4 per hour on production overhead ($160,000 production overhead/40,000 production hours). And if we produce 50 units per hour, our unit overhead works out to $0.08 ($4 production overhead per hour/50 units per hour). When we compare the analysis with and without ABC, we see that the overhead per unit is much higher when using ABC than when not using ABC. We can conclude that we need to increase the number of units in the batch in order to bring down our production overhead per unit. A production manager can run various sensitivities to determine what happens when these numbers are adjusted and how it affects unit costs. Meanwhile, a pricing manager can adjust retail pricing such that the product produces sufficient margins in line with forecasts. Who said accounting wasn't exciting?

	ABC	NO ABC
Production overhead for setup	$ 40,000	$ —
Total setups	100	NA
Production overhead per setup	$ 400	$ —
Total production overhead	$ 200,000	$ 200,000
Less cost assigned to machine setups	$ 40,000	$ —
Production overheads costs allocated to machine hours	$ 160,000	$ 200,000
Machine hours	40,000	40,000
Production overhead per machine hour	$ 4.00	$ 5.00
Production overhead	$400 setup per batch + $4.00 per hour	$5.00 per hour

	ABC	NO ABC
Production overhead for setup	$ 400	$ —
Units in batch	$ 2,000	NA
Production overhead per unit	$ 0.20	NA
Production overhead per machine hour	$ 4.00	$ 5.00
Units per hour	$ 50	$ 50
Production overhead per unit	$ 0.08	$ 0.10
Total overhead allocted per unit	$ 0.28	$ 0.10

OPERATIONS MANAGEMENT

One of the more intriguing areas of managerial accounting focuses on inventory production. While inventory production analysis falls under the broader umbrella of operations management, certain production measures are part of managerial accounting. As discussed earlier, inventory can prove costly. And the sooner the inventory is sold, the sooner the company benefits from it.

In order to understand the managerial accounting measures used in analyzing inventory processes, it's important to first understand key terminology. *Throughput* is the number of units flowing through a business over a given period of time. For example, a business would have throughput of 10 cupcakes per hour if that is the average number of cupcakes produced each hour. *Flow time*, a concept related to throughput, is the total amount of time that a unit spends in a particular business process. And finally, *inventory*, in the context of operations management and managerial accounting, is the number of units in any given time in a process.

MBA programs around the world like to run simulations to illustrate how production time is a function of effectively managing the production process. Suppose it takes three people to make one cupcake. The first person removes the cupcake from the oven, allows it to cool, and walks it over to the second person. The second person removes the cupcake from its tray and adds frosting. The third person places the frosted cupcake in its wrapper. The time for each step is listed below:

- Person 1: Time = 15 seconds (throughput is 4 cupcakes per minute)
- Person 2: Time = 60 seconds (throughput is 1 cupcake per minute)
- Person 3: Time = 30 seconds (throughput is 2 cupcakes per minute)

The process time for one cupcake is 105 seconds or 1.75 minutes. The process reveals that person 2 takes the longest amount of time leaving both person 1 and person 3 with idle time. In fact, person 2's production time is the throughput of the entire process. What happens if there are three cupcakes ahead of one person's order of one cupcake? Little's Law can explain this based on what is referred to as *work in process* (*WIP*):

Inventory = throughput × flow time

With three cupcakes ahead of the one just ordered, total inventory is four cupcakes. Throughput is one cupcake per minute based on person 2's production time. The flow time, therefore can be solved using the equation below:

4 cupcakes = 1 cupcake/minute × flow time

Flow time = 4 minutes

It takes four minutes for a person to get his or her cupcake. Now the fun part. In managerial accounting, one might analyze ways to increase throughput to improve efficiency and production. Perhaps the simple solution is to replace person 2 with someone more skilled in the fine art of cupcake frosting techniques.

PART 2
FINANCE

8

COST OF CAPITAL

At this point, you have made it reasonably far into this book and are feeling pretty good about yourself. That's all fine and dandy, but no good book on financial concepts would be complete without a section that causes you to rethink your intellect and, more important, your value as a contributing member of society. For that reason, I give you cost of capital.

Almost everyone has a friend who dates only people who are volatile and high risk. When things are good, they're really good, and when things are bad, they're really bad. The relationship is a veritable roller coaster with constant highs and lows. And of course, almost everyone has a friend who dates only people who are stable, secure, and low risk. Monotony and routine supersede excitement and thrills. For the former, payoffs can be huge or can be disastrous. For the latter, payoffs are usually adequate. In the world of finance, we use the term *cost of capital* to measure payoffs and risk.

You will hear the term *cost of capital* quite a bit in financial circles, yet it is rarely explained. What is the cost of capital? That depends on the context. For example, a simple definition pertains to the rate required or charged for the use of funds. If you go to the bank and take out a loan, your cost of that loan is what you pay in interest. Therefore, interest rates are a good example of the cost of capital. Now you can look at a related concept, the *opportunity cost of capital*, which is the rate of return offered by equivalent investment alternatives in the capital markets, essentially the cost of capital based on the opportunity that is forgone. The opportunity cost of capital is also referred to as the *discount rate* or the *hurdle rate*.

Consider the following:

- You invest $100,000 today into Project A.
- Project B, an ongoing project, is as risky as Project A.
- Project B's expected rate of return one year from today is 20 percent.
- If you invested $90,000 in Project B today, based on historical performance, you would expect to have $108,000 one year from now (you earned 20 percent on that $90,000 investment).
- What is the opportunity cost of capital if you invested in Project A?

Your opportunity cost of capital would be 20 percent, which is the expected return from the investment opportunity forgone from Project B. Therefore, the expected payoff from Project A would be $100,000 times 120 percent, giving you a total of $120,000 (by applying that 20 percent opportunity cost of capital to Project A).

In practice, investors normally do not know what the exact return on a project is, but they will use a benchmark on an equally risky investment to help calculate another project's expected return. The cost of capital measures the amount charged for the use of funds, and it usually is expressed in annual percentage terms. The opportunity cost of capital measures the opportunity forgone by investing in a project of similar risk.

The question now arises: How do you decide on that appropriate opportunity cost of capital? Opportunity cost of capital depends on the risk involved in the project. In fact, investors typically expect a higher rate of return if they deem a project to be riskier than any other opportunity in the market. The simple reason for this is that they want to be compensated for the higher risk involved. This has been observed throughout history. In the

1980s, corporations issued high-yield "junk" bonds to fund risky projects. For assuming an excessively high level of risk, the bondholders were paid a commensurately high rate of interest because they were to be compensated accordingly for the extra risk. That is, they were compensated for the possibility that the project might not come to fruition or might dissolve altogether, in which case they would lose their entire investment.

Before we take a look at calculating the cost of capital, ponder a final question: Why the heck do we even care about the cost of capital? Cost of capital is useful in the world of finance for two primary reasons:

1. It serves as an effective performance benchmark.
2. It enables the calculation of present values of future payments—something extremely useful in valuation analysis.

As a performance benchmark, cost of capital is useful in determining how much a company must earn on its assets to meet the expectations of investors and creditors. For example, if a company's cost of capital is 18 percent, any return above 18 percent will enhance the company's perception and, the company hopes, value. In other words, a company that returns in excess of its cost of capital should see an increase in its stock price. Logically, this makes sense, because any excess over what was expected should serve to attract new investors. The price should continue to rise until it reflects the company's cost of capital, which in this case is 18 percent. Conversely, a company that underperforms its cost of capital should see a share price adjustment downward to reflect that.

As a valuation variable, cost of capital will affect the overall value of a company when based on future returns (cash flows, EBITDA, etc.). This will be covered in much more detail in Chapter 9, where the cost of capital will be related to what is commonly termed the *discount rate*. This chapter will discuss the following:

- Cost of equity
- Weighted average cost of capital

COST OF EQUITY

The cost of equity is essentially the return expected by the share-holders of a company. Unlike debt, where the debt holders are promised a certain rate, equity offers no clearly defined return. As a result, there are several ways to calculate this. The two methods examined here are among those more commonly used by Wall Street analysts and bankers. The first is called the *dividend growth model*, and the second is called the *capital asset pricing model* commonly referred to as the *CAPM*.

Dividend Growth Model

The dividend growth model is considered the easiest way to estimate the cost of equity capital. It is predicated on the notion that the firm's dividend will grow at a constant rate. The dividend growth model is written as follows:

$$r_E = (D_1/P_0) + g$$

where

r_E = return on equity (cost of equity)
$D_1 = D_0 \times (1 + g)$
D_0 = most recent dividend payment
P_0 = current stock price
g = estimated dividend growth (use historical rates or
    analysts' forecasts)

As you can see, in this model, the return on equity (r_E), or the cost of equity, is equal to the dividend after the first period (D_1) divided by the current stock price (P_0), which then is added to the growth rate (g).

To understand the model, we must review the components in more detail. The first component, the dividend after the first period, is calculated by taking the last or most recent dividend payment (D_0) and multiplying it by 1 plus the growth rate. The stock price is the current market price per share, and the growth rate is the estimated dividend growth.

There are a couple of ways to estimate dividend growth. One method is simply to look at historical rates and take an average of the past several years. Another method involves analysts' forecasts for the company or might even involve the forecast for the entire industry.

To understand this, look at this sample problem:

A utility company paid a dividend of $2 per share last year, which is expected to grow at 6 percent per year indefinitely. If the company has a current share price of $60, what would its return on equity be, based on the dividend growth model?

Apply the dividend growth formula to the sample problem here. This company paid a dividend of $2 per share last year, and the company is expected to increase the dividend at a rate of 6 percent per year for the foreseeable future. With the shares of the company at $60, calculate its return on equity or cost of equity based on the dividend growth model.

To begin, calculate D_1 by taking the most recent dividend payment, $D_0 = \$2$, and increasing it by the growth rate of 6 percent, which equals $2.12 ($2 \times 1.06 = $2.12). Then take that $2.12 and divide it by the company's share price of $60 to get 3.5 percent. Next, add that to the growth rate of 6 percent to arrive at 9.5 percent. Thus, as determined by the dividend growth model, the cost of equity is 9.5 percent. The advantage of this model lies primarily in its simplicity. However, a number of problems arise with this approach. For one thing, it is applicable only to companies that pay dividends. Furthermore, the dividends must grow at a constant rate, and the result is highly sensitive to that growth rate. Finally, risk, which is a key measure of return on equity, is not considered explicitly. To account for these shortcomings, an alternative method—the capital asset pricing model—often is used to calculate the cost of equity.

Capital Asset Pricing Model

The capital asset pricing model (CAPM) is useful in measuring the cost of equity because it measures risk explicitly. It is also applicable to companies that may not have steady dividend growth. In its simplest form, the CAPM states that the expected return on a stock is the sum of the rate of return on a risk-free security and some expected risk premium rate. This usually is measured in correlation with the market risk premium.

It is important to understand that the CAPM is defined in terms of expectations, and as a result, investors are compensated in the expected sense. Actual returns typically deviate from these expectations, but the expectations form a useful estimation. The CAPM prices securities relative to their market risk premium, meaning that market risk is a key input in this process. The expected risk premium on a security is proportional to the risk premium expected for the overall market.

At this point, you should be entirely confused. The CAPM is fairly difficult to grasp initially, but with some work, it should become manageable soon. Here is the formula for the CAPM:

$$r_E = r_f + \beta(r_m - r_f)$$

The expected rate of return, or the return on equity (r_E), is equal to the risk-free rate (r_f) plus beta (β) multiplied by the return on the market (r_m) minus the risk-free rate. Perhaps it is better explained as the sum of the risk-free rate plus some risk premium associated with that particular security. The individual components are discussed below.

Risk-Free Rate

How is a risk-free security defined? A risk-free security is a security whose rate of return is guaranteed. Specifically, there is no risk of default on these payments because the payments have no associated risks aside from inflation. Typical risk-free securities are government securities such as Treasury bills, Treasury notes, and Treasury bonds. Usually, Treasury bills are considered the safest because they have very little to no risk of interest rate fluctuation, unlike their T-note and T-bond counterparts. These securities are considered risk-free because the US government has never defaulted on its debt...at least not yet. Therefore, a good risk-free rate would be the rate on Treasury bills.

Market Rate

To understand the market rate, it is necessary to understand the concept of a market portfolio. A market portfolio is designed to cover all the securities in the market or to be a representation of the securities in the market. This provides a clear benchmark for overall market performance. A typical market portfolio would be the S&P 500 index. Although only 500 companies are included in this index out of several thousand publicly traded companies, those 500 account for a substantial portion of the value of all stocks traded. For that reason, the S&P 500 index often is used to represent the market portfolio. Thus, the market rate would be based on this.

Beta

Ah, beta. Many use it but few understand it, and that is quite all right. In fact, I have yet to meet an investment banker who can derive beta. Beta measures the correlation of the returns on individual stocks relative to the returns on the overall market. It is assumed that the beta of the overall market is 1. This is the case because the market is the portfolio of all stocks, and so the average stock should have a beta of 1. Stocks with betas greater than 1 would tend to amplify market movements. Stocks with betas between zero and 1 would tend to move in the same direction as the market, but not by as much. For example, assume that the market returns 10 percent. A stock whose beta is 1.5 would return 15 percent, because it would go up one and a half times as much as the market. Suppose this stock has a beta of 0.5. If the market goes up 10 percent, this stock would go up 5 percent because it would move by half as much as the market.

Beta is derived through some complex calculations. Statisticians and some portfolio managers actually calculate beta by taking the covariance between the return on the stock and the overall market and dividing it by the variance on the overall market return:

$$\beta = s_s s_m / s_m^{\,2}$$

where

$s_s s_m$ = covariance between the return on stock S
and the overall market return

$s_m^{\,2}$ = variance of the market return

These are challenging concepts that you should not worry yourself over. In fact, beta usually can be found easily on virtually any financial website or in any number of publications. If you are interested in calculating beta, take this quiz to determine if you are qualified:

Have you ever been to a *Star Trek* convention?	Y	N
Are you fluent in Wookie or Ewok?	Y	N
Did your college alma mater name include "Tech"?	Y	N
Do you value your friends on the basis of the number of computer languages in which they can program?	Y	N
Do you read comic books?	Y	N
Do you wear a pocket protector?	Y	N
Have you ever received a wedgie?	Y	N
Do you prefer calculus problems to crossword puzzles?	Y	N
Did you actually buy this book?	Y	N

If you answered yes to any of these, you are probably qualified to calculate beta. Take a moment to review your understanding of beta with a couple of questions:

Q: If a company has a beta of 1.5, is it riskier or less risky than the market?

A: Technically it would be riskier because it tends to amplify the overall market movements.

*Q: Suppose another company has a beta of 0.8.
Is it riskier or less risky than the market?*

A: It would be slightly less risky.

Finally, take a moment to set up the capital asset pricing model and calculate the expected rate of return on stock S (r_s), using the following information:

Risk-free rate of return (r_f) = 4%

β of stock S = 1.2

Rate of return on market (r_m) = 7%

Plug those numbers into the CAPM formula:

$$r_s = r_f + \beta(r_m - r_f)$$

$$r_s = 4\% + 1.2(7\% - 4\%)$$

$$r_s = 7.6\%$$

As you can see, to calculate the rate of return on stock S, take the risk-free rate of 4 percent and add it to the result of a beta of 1.2 multiplied by the difference between the return on the market of 7 percent and the risk-free rate of 4 percent. What you get is 7.6 percent, the return on equity for stock S.

In the following example, you can calculate the beta of stock X by using the capital asset pricing model. Here you might use the resulting beta as a proxy for that of a similar company. For this example, the risk-free rate of return is 5 percent, the return on the market is 13 percent, and the rate of return on stock X is 6.9 percent. For quick reference, set up the "givens" this way:

Risk-free rate of return (r_f) = 5%

Rate of return on market portfolio (r_m) = 13%

Rate of return on stock X (r_x) = 6.9%

Once again, plug the numbers into the CAPM formula:

$$r_x = r_f + \beta(r_m - r_f)$$

$$6.9\% = 5\% + \beta(13\% - 5\%)$$

$$\beta = 0.24$$

What you did here was to set the return on stock X, 6.9 percent, equal to the rest of the equation, which included the risk-free rate of 5 percent plus beta, which you were solving for, multiplied by the return on the market of 13 percent minus the risk-free rate of 5 percent. If you work backward through that and solve for beta, you arrive at something that is roughly 0.24. Thus, if the market goes up 10 percent, this particular stock's return will be about 2.4 percent. More important, this can be applied to a company that behaves in a similar manner.

At this point, it should be clear that risk is proportional to the expected return on a security. The capital asset pricing model is predicated on this relationship between risk and the expected rate of return. The basic benchmark for the CAPM formula is the risk-free rate, which usually is tied to Treasury bills. The CAPM assumes that if a company has debt in its capital structure, any risk associated with the security on that debt is already priced into its beta. What does that translate to? It essentially means that we are making some loose assumptions here about debt, and therefore the CAPM is really useful only insofar as we are looking at equity. It more or less accounts for the risk associated with equity.

WEIGHTED AVERAGE COST OF CAPITAL

To reach an assessment of what the overall cost of capital is for a firm, you must use what is called the *weighted average cost of capital* (WACC). This is the most commonly used method to measure the overall cost of capital. The major advantage of the weighted average cost of capital is that it takes into account financing decisions—the mix of debt and equity and, more specifically, their weighted averages. Furthermore, the WACC also takes into account the fact that interest payments are tax-deductible, and therefore it is important to look at the cost of capital on an after-tax basis.

How does this work? Suppose a company issues debt and pays a 10 percent coupon on that debt. If this company is in a 30 percent tax bracket, what would its after-tax cost of debt be? Given the fact that the interest payments are tax-deductible, the after-tax cost of debt in this case would actually be 7 percent:

$$\text{After-tax cost of debt} = r(1 - T)$$

where

r = coupon rate
T = tax rate

The weighted average cost of capital takes this into consideration, with tax affecting the debt interest. The weighted average cost of capital looks like this:

$$r_{WACC} = (1 - T)r_D D/V + r_E E/V$$

where

T = tax rate
r_D = rate of return on debt
   (usually the yield, not the coupon rate)
D = total debt outstanding
V = total capital of the company ($D + E$)
r_E = rate of return on equity
E = market value of equity

As the last equation shows, the weighted average cost of capital is equal to 1 minus the tax rate, multiplied by the rate of return on the debt multiplied by the ratio of the total debt outstanding to the total capital of the company. This is added to the return on equity multiplied by the ratio of equity to the total capital of the company.

Capital structure here is denoted by V, and that represents debt outstanding plus the market value of equity. The return on equity can be calculated by using what has already been covered:

either the dividend discount model or the capital asset pricing model. Some analysts use both and take an average; others, when possible, simply use the capital asset pricing model because it tends to be a bit more detailed and is perceived as being more credible.

Generally speaking, the weighted average cost of capital is the preferred method for all cost of capital measures. It takes into account the firm's overall capital structure as well as the tax benefits or the tax deductibility of interest.

In the next example you also solve for the weighted average cost of capital. In this example, the return on debt of 9 percent, the tax rate of 35 percent, and the ratio of debt to overall capital structure of 30 percent are all given. Return on equity has already been calculated at 15 percent by using the dividend growth model. Succinctly written, we have:

$$r_D = 9\%$$

$$T = 35\%$$

$$D/V = 30\%$$

$$r_E = 15\% \text{ (assume this was already calculated using the dividend growth model)}$$

We are now ready to set up the formula for the weighted average cost of capital and then substitute:

$$r_{WACC} = (1 - T)r_D(D/V) + r_E(E/V)$$

$$= (1 - 0.35)0.09(0.3) + 0.15(0.7)$$

$$= 0.1226, \text{ or } 12.26\%$$

(Note that $E/V = 1 - D/V = 1 - 0.3 = 0.7$
[or 70%], because $V = D + E$.)

In solving this problem, first take 1 minus the tax rate of 35 percent, which is then multiplied by the weighted average cost of capital return on debt of 9 percent, multiplied by the ratio of debt to the overall capital structure of the company of 30 percent. This is added to the return on equity of 15 percent, which is multiplied by the ratio of equity to the overall capital structure of the company of 70 percent. This is an additional calculation that had to be made, because the value for E, the value of equity, was not given. The total value (V) of the company is composed of total debt (D) and total equity (E). Therefore, if 30 percent of the company is debt, the other 70 percent is presumed to be equity. After all these variables are inserted, the end result is a weighted average cost of capital of 12.26 percent.

As was shown earlier, return on equity can be calculated either with the dividend growth model or with the capital asset pricing model. In the next example, calculate the weighted average cost of capital by using the following information: a return on debt of 8 percent, a tax rate of 35 percent, an equity to capital structure of 40 percent, a beta of 1.2, a risk-free rate of 6 percent, and a return on the market of 14 percent.

$$r_D = 8\%$$

$$T = 35\%$$

$$E/V = 40\%$$

$$\beta = 1.2$$

$$r_f = 6\%$$

$$r_m = 14\%$$

Given this information, it is clear that the capital asset pricing model needs to be employed to solve for the equity component. The first step is to use the capital asset pricing model to find the return on equity. Once you have the return on equity, you can plug that number into the weighted average cost of capital model.

First, calculate r_E by using the CAPM formula:

$$r_E = r_f + \beta(r_m - r_f)$$

$$= 0.06 + 1.2(0.14 - 0.06)$$

$$= 0.156, \text{ or } 15.6\%$$

You were given the risk-free rate of 6 percent, which you added to a beta of 1.2, which was multiplied by the difference between the return on the market and the risk-free rate, 14 percent minus 6 percent. The end result is a return on equity of 15.6 percent.

Next, plug in r_E and calculate after-tax WACC:

$$r_{WACC} = (1 - T)r_D(D/V) + r_{E(}E/V)$$

$$= (1 - 0.35)0.08(0.6) + 0.156(0.4)$$

$$= 0.0936, \text{ or } 9.36\%$$

(Note that $D/V = 1 - E/V = 1 - 0.4 = 0.6$
[or 60%], because $V = D + E$.)

The first thing done with the weighted average cost of capital model was to take 1 minus the tax rate of 35 percent, multiplied by the return on debt of 8 percent, multiplied by the ratio of debt to the overall capital structure of 60 percent. Then that was added to the return on equity derived above of 15.6 percent, multiplied by the ratio of equity to overall capital structure. In solving those numbers you come up with a weighted average cost of capital of 9.36 percent, which is the discount rate or the number you use to discount future cash flows to find their present value. (We will see how discount rates are used in Chapter 9.)

Finally, here is another weighted average cost of capital problem in which the following information is given. This company has debt outstanding of $75 million. This company has return on debt of 9 percent. Its equity outstanding is 2 million shares at $42 per share. Calculate the return on equity given the following assumptions—assumptions that feed into the dividend growth model. The historic dividend is $5. The price per share is $37.14, and the growth rate is 4 percent. Last but not least, the tax rate is 35 percent.

First, set up the assumptions so that you can see them at a glance:

$$\text{Debt outstanding} = \$75 \text{ million}$$

$$r_D = 9\%$$

Equity outstanding = 2 million shares at $42 per share

r_E = Use the dividend growth model assuming:

$$D_0 = \$5$$

$$P_0 = \$37.14$$

$$g = 4\%$$

Tax rate = 35%

In this example, first calculate the return on equity by using the dividend growth model. After plugging these numbers into that equation, a return on equity of 18 percent is determined. Then plug that 18 percent into the weighted average cost of capital. Take 1 minus the tax rate of 35 percent and multiply it by the return on debt of 9 percent, which is then multiplied by the ratio of debt to the overall capital structure of 47 percent. This was solved by looking at the firm's capital structure. It has $75 million of debt and $84 million of equity, which is 2 million times $42 per share. Thus, the debt component of that is 47 percent. We then add that to the return on equity that was derived, 18 percent, multiplied by the ratio of equity to the overall capital structure of 53 percent. Finally, multiply this by the return on equity of 18 percent and then solve the equation to come up with 12.29 percent, the weighted average cost of capital. That is the discount rate that would be used to discount the future cash flows for this company.

$$r_E = \$5.2/\$37.14 + 0.04$$

$$= 0.14 + 0.04$$

$$= 0.18, \text{ or } 18\%$$

$$r_{WACC} = (1 - 0.35)(0.09)(0.47) + (0.18)(0.53)$$

$$= 0.12289, \text{ or } 12.29\%$$

In Chapter 9, you will see just how important the cost of capital is in valuing companies.

9

VALUATION

One of my first lessons on Wall Street was that to get ahead, you have to be creative. What I noticed was that successful investment bankers had a real knack for making something out of nothing. For example, when numbers didn't look just right, a good banker could always tweak them a bit. No matter what a client desired—a higher selling price, a lower purchase price, stronger margins, lower capital costs—the banker could produce the numbers. A really good banker would earn the title "numerical masseuse," and if you could send a masseuse to value a company, watch out!

The principles covered in this section apply not only to large corporate transactions but also to simple personal finance dealings. These principles lead to methodologies for valuing companies and opportunities. There are numerous ways to value a company, including adjusted net assets, capitalization of earnings, dividend-paying capacity, excess earnings return on assets, and specific industry formulas. In fact, I could furnish you with a list of 40 or 50 such methods, and indeed, most have some relevance in certain situations. However, only a few have proved to be credible, and those are the ones explained in this book.

Back in the mid-1990s, there was a strong movement to value Internet and software companies. The problem was that those companies were losing money and had very little prospect of ever making money. Nonetheless, many Wall Street analysts sought to formulate some method of valuation for them. Eventually, several clever equity analysts developed a hybrid form of ratio analysis by using price-to-sales ratios. The problem with those ratios is that the fact that a company is generating sales does not necessarily mean that it is generating profits, and a company that does not generate profits will not be around very long. Hence, most of those methodologies proved problematic and therefore are no longer around, much like the companies for which they were developed.

Among the myriad ways to value a company, only a handful have withstood the test of time and proved credible across industries. This chapter will discuss the following:

- Valuation basics
- Methods of valuation
- Net present value

VALUATION BASICS

You might recall the following facts from grade school:

- The island of Manhattan was purchased from the Manhattes Indians for $24 worth of trinkets in 1626.
- The Louisiana Territory was purchased from the French for $11 million in 1803.
- Alaska was purchased from the Russians for $7.2 million in 1867.

What do all these facts have in common? If you answered that each represents an effective use of economic imperialism as a means to emerge as a formidable competitor to the established European hegemony, well, you get an A in political science. Unfortunately, this is finance, and so you fail. You should have said that each purchase was a good deal for the acquiring government. Or was it? That would depend on what rate those amounts could have earned in competing investments. For example, $24 invested at a rate of 4 percent in 1626 would be worth about $70 million today. However, the same amount invested in 1626 at a rate of 8 percent would be worth over $100 trillion. The point of all this is that money spent yesterday has a different value today and will have a different value tomorrow. These values can change drastically, depending on the numbers used in calculating them. This is a fundamental principle in finance.

Time Value of Money

Before examining methods of valuation, it is essential to review a fundamental concept in finance known as the *time value of money*. The time value of money states that $1 received today has a different value from $1 received a year ago or $1 received a year from now. For example, a firm receives a $100 payment on January 1. It deposits the payment in an interest-bearing account that pays 5 percent. On December 31 that account is worth $105. It has earned 5 percent interest, or $5.

Now take that a step further. Suppose the firm was owed $100 on January 1 but was not paid until December 31. The value of that expected receipt is now less because of the forgone interest. In the course of that year, the expected receipt has diminished in value. How much less or what that new value is can be calculated by using the present value formula.

Present Value

Present value is the concept that money spent tomorrow must be worth less today because of the time value of money. The present value amount is calculated by using the formula

$$PV = CF/(1 + r)^n$$

where

PV = present value
CF = cash flow for the period
r = discount rate
n = period

If you are like me and the majority of my students, this can be somewhat daunting at first glance. What this formula shows is the value of something paid tomorrow in today's values. As noted, CF stands for cash flow for the period, or the payment that is expected in the future. That payment is divided by $1 + r$ raised to the n power, with r standing for the discount rate and n representing the future period. In valuing cash flows received one year from now, $n = 1$. In valuing cash flows five years from now, $n = 5$. The discount rate in this context is based on the cost of capital, which was covered in Chapter 8.

In the last example, the firm is owed $100 on January 1 but is not paid until December 31. If the discount rate (r) is 5 percent and the period (n) is one year, calculate the present value of the $100:

$$PV = CF/(1 + r)^n$$

$$= \$100/(1 + 5\%)^1$$

$$= \$100/1.05$$

$$= \$95.24$$

Thus, the present value of that $100 payment is only $95.24. If the firm had received $95.24 on January 1 and deposited it into an interest-bearing account, it would have $100 on December 31.

METHODS OF VALUATION

If there is one thing that years of work in the field of valuation has taught me, it is that valuation is far more of an art than a science. In fact, I would go so far as to say that it is far more three-card monte than science. Don't get me wrong. I've spent the better part of my career working to "value" projects, but at the same time, I'm the first to admit that there is only one true value of a company: what the buyer and seller agree on.

When you spot what appears to be framed smears of finger paint on your friend's wall and wonder, "Wow, I can't believe he spent $1 million on something a child could do," you may not be alone in your thinking. However, art collectors like your friend have created a market for such paintings and, more specifically, have set their value. Regardless of your opinion, the value of that work is $1 million because that is what the buyer and seller agreed on.

The world of finance takes this principle fairly seriously. However, often some dialogue first needs to be generated between prospective buyers and sellers. These methods of valuation enable this to occur. With detailed valuation models, the key factors that drove a company in the past, along with those that will continue to drive it in the future, can be examined. Both sides are able to form a better picture of the potential as well as the risks associated with this company. Through this process of dialogue, they hope to be able to build a consensus. Then, with a little luck, they just might close a sale. This process can be engaged in when one is buying companies outright, investing in them, restructuring them, and so on. In fact, there are numerous uses for valuation. A few of the more common ones are:

- Venture capital
- Initial public offerings
- Mergers and acquisitions
- Leveraged buyouts
- Estate and tax settlements
- Divorce settlements
- Capital raising
- Partnerships
- Restructurings
- Real estate
- Joint ventures
- Project finance

Even if you have no dealings in these types of transactions and, more specifically, no interest in them, it is important to have at least a basic understanding of the underlying principles and techniques of valuation. Why? Because so much of what we do and so much of what governs our personal lives is driven by these principles. The simple decision to lease or buy a car is driven by valuation. The decision to own or rent an apartment is driven by valuation. Changes in the stock market that might affect your job are a function of valuation. Get the picture? It is important that each one of us understand the basics of valuation because we no longer can rely on the experts on Wall Street, in corporate America, and at the big accounting firms. We have seen what can happen when we place absolute trust in them. In fact, it is easy to point fingers at these institutions for the financial catastrophes that have occurred throughout history. Ultimately, though, we all bear some responsibility because we were the ones who failed to educate ourselves. This is our chance. We are ready to dive headfirst into the financial abyss (or pool, depending on our objectives) by working with these various methods of valuation.

Replacement Method

The replacement method of valuation tends to be the simplest to explain but the most time-consuming to produce. It is based on a target company or asset that is valued by estimating the cost to create an exact duplicate. In other words, it seeks an answer to the question, What would this cost to build from scratch? To explore the answer, let's return to our favorite hardware store.

In the case of Cunningham Hardware, this method would measure all the costs involved in creating a duplicate store. Those costs might include

- Land
- Buildings
- Machinery
- Equipment
- Working capital

These costs are summed and then used as a proxy for fair value of the asset or business. Major drawbacks include difficulty in gathering complete information and, more important, difficulty valuing intangibles such as brand name, intellectual property, and perhaps customer loyalty.

In the case of Cunningham Hardware, suppose the following costs are needed to create a comparable store:

Land	$150,000
Building	$280,000
Computers and computer systems	$ 40,000
Inventory	$ 60,000
Hiring and training costs	$ 10,000
Legal costs	$ 5,000
Additional start-up costs	$ 8,000

Once these costs are totaled, a fair value of $553,000 is determined. Of course, this fails to consider the name that Cunningham has built, its reputation, its loyal customers, and so forth. Presumably, someone who spent this amount to create a similar hardware store would have to invest significant time to develop a comparable customer base.

Capitalization of Earnings

One of the more common and relatively straightforward methods of valuation is the capitalization of earnings method. Essentially, this method uses a risk rate to assess the value needed to generate the same amount of income as the business being valued.

Consider the following in the case of Cunningham Hardware. Suppose it is expected to generate exactly $10,000 each year in income indefinitely. Therefore, if the owner is trying to sell the store, the buyer would expect to receive this amount in annual income. Because the store is expected to generate this income level consistently, it should not lose its value. If the buyer can earn a guaranteed rate of interest of 5 percent elsewhere, what amount of investment would be needed to generate $10,000 each year in income?

Investment × 5% = $10,000

$10,000/5% = $200,000

Thus, an investment of $200,000 would earn $10,000 in interest each year, meaning the hardware store has a value of $200,000.

Unfortunately, such risk-free situations rarely exist. The owner of a hardware store undoubtedly assumes risks in day-to-day business dealings. Thus, with increased risk, a higher capitalization rate would have to be assessed to estimate fair value. These rates vary, and some might argue that they are entirely arbitrary. It is possible to use one of the cost of capital measures discussed in Chapter 8 or to consider rates used in comparable businesses. Regardless of the methodology, the result will prove highly sensitive to this rate. As a result, many analysts believe the capitalization of earnings method is problematic.

Excess Earning Method

A variation on the capitalization of earnings method is the excess earning method. The major difference is that this method separates return on assets from the excess earnings. Supposing Cunningham Hardware has assets of $28,000 and earns $10,000 per year. Suppose the reasonable return on assets in this industry is 10 percent, which indicates expected earnings of $2,800 from assets ($28,000 × 10 percent = $2,800). The remaining $7,200 ($10,000 − $2,800 = $7,200) represents the excess earnings. This excess earnings number is multiplied by a factor that incorporates risk, growth potential, and competitiveness. The factor is part estimation and part comparison. If the factor in this case is 3, fair value is estimated to be $21,600 ($7,200 × 3 = $21,600). This type of methodology works for smaller companies with substantial tangible assets such as PP&E, inventory, receivables, and cash. Wall Street analysts tend to place little emphasis on this method, and so you probably just wasted your time learning it.

Discounted Cash Flow Valuation

The discounted cash flow (DCF) method of valuation is one of the most commonly used methods. Most investment bankers know this method better than they know their own spouses, which probably explains a lot. Normally, the mere utterance of the term

DCF (the more insidious banker term) sends first-year financial analysts running for cover. A good DCF model can take several weeks to prepare, and this translates into many long nights spent at the office. The reason DCF models tend to be so complicated and time-intensive has little to do with the actual DCF calculations and much more to do with the research involved in creating projections. The reality is that a DCF model is far simpler than the investment banks would like you to believe.

In fact, the entire process can be condensed into four steps:

1. Calculate projections for future cash flows.
2. Calculate the cost of capital, or as it's referred to here, the *discount rate.*
3. Calculate the present value for each year's cash flow.
4. Finally, take the total of those present value cash flows.

Completing these four steps provides a very close estimate of the valuation for the company. The sum of these discounted cash flows is the company's valuation . . . well, almost.

Example

Here are Cunningham Hardware's five-year cash flow projections. Note that step 1—*calculate projections for future cash flows*—already has been done. In looking at this company, notice that in year 1 it has cash flows of $25,000; in year 2 its cash flow projections are $23,000; in year 3 cash flow projections are $30,000; in year 4 they are $33,000; and in year 5 they are $45,000.

CUNNINGHAM HARDWARE PROJECTIONS					
YEAR	1	2	3	4	5
Cash flow	$25,000	$23,000	$30,000	$33,000	$45,000

Discount rate (WACC) = 9 percent

These projections were given by the company. Of course, the company probably spent several weeks preparing them, because in any cash flow projection model there are a lot of assumptions and a lot of variables. In fact, the backup to this could be several hundred pages long. However, the primary concern here is the output, which is simply the cash flow projections themselves.

Start with these cash flow projections and work on your own to calculate the present value for each of the five years. Fire up that calculator and compute the present values by using the formula that is shown here. Remember, r represents the discount rate of 9 percent, which was calculated by using the weighted average cost of capital (WACC), and n is the period for which present value is being determined. No peeking!

$$PV = CF/(1 + r)^n$$

At this point, you have calculated the present values. Compare your answers with the solutions shown here. Depending on how you chose to round or how your calculator was set to round, you should have come up with something approximately equal to these numbers:

CUNNINGHAM HARDWARE PROJECTIONS

YEAR	1	2	3	4	5
Cash flow	$25,000	$23,000	$30,000	$33,000	$45,000

Discount rate (WACC) = 9 percent

$$\frac{CF}{(1+r)^n} = \frac{\$25,000}{(1+0.09)^1} + \frac{\$23,000}{(1+0.09)^2} + \frac{\$30,000}{(1+0.09)^3} + \frac{\$33,000}{(1+0.09)^4} + \frac{\$45,000}{(1+0.09)^5}$$

$$PV = \$22,936 + \$19,359 + \$23,166 + \$23,378 + \$29,247$$

In the first year, take the cash flow of $25,000 and divide it by 1 plus the discount rate. The discount rate in this case is given at 9 percent. In year 2, take $23,000 and divide it by 1 plus the discount rate raised to the second power. In year 3, divide the cash flow of $30,000 by 1 plus the discount rate raised to the third power. In year 4, take the cash flow payment of $33,000 and divide it by 1 plus the discount rate raised to the fourth power. Finally, in year 5, take the cash flow of $45,000 divided by 1 plus the discount rate raised to the fifth power. In total, the present values of Cunning-ham's future cash flows approximately equal $118,085.

Is this the value of the company? You took present values for each of these five-year cash flows. Next, you summed those present values and came up with a number around $118,000. In certain instances, you might conclude your analysis at this point. Those instances occur when, at the end of five years, the company simply dissolves, meaning there is no residual value. More often than not, however, the company continues to operate long after those projections end.

How do analysts account for what happens after the projections end? They use what is called *terminal value*. Terminal value is a concept used to calculate the value of an asset that continues after the projections end, or into perpetuity. There are a number of ways to calculate terminal value. A simple way is to multiply the last year's cash flow by some industry average multiple. This amount is added to the five-year discounted cash flows. This practice is based on loose estimates, and for that reason it often is perceived to lack credibility. A better method involves using the present value of a perpetuity. A perpetuity is an instrument that makes payments year after year without end. You can use the formula to calculate a perpetuity that assumes growth or a simpler formula to calculate one without growth. The two formulas are given here:

$$\text{Perpetuity without growth} = CF/r$$

$$\text{Perpetuity with growth} = CF/(r - g)$$

where

CF = cash flow
r = discount rate
g = growth rate

In this case, the next step is to go back to the company and ask for a year 6 cash flow estimate. Once that cash flow is obtained, assume it stays constant each year after that. Suppose the company wants to assume a year 6 cash flow of $50,000 and each year after that, cash flows remain constant at $50,000. Apply that $50,000 to the perpetuity calculation, which is $50,000 divided by the discount rate of 9 percent. This results in a perpetuity value of $555,556. Is that the final value? Can this simply be added to the present value and proposed to a client? No. There's something very important missing here.

Think about this: Cunningham's perpetuity value is $555,556. The total of the first year's cash flows, or first five years of cash flows, is $118,000. What's missing here is the present value of that perpetuity, because that $555,556 essentially is treated as the value at the beginning of year 6. When those cash flow payments after year 5 were projected, they were done so from year 6. When a total value for all of them was calculated, the value at the beginning of year 6 was determined. What needs to be done next is a calculation of the value of that perpetuity in today's dollars by discounting it back five years by using the present value formula. The present value of that perpetuity should equal approximately $361,073.

Now the numbers are in place to finalize a value. As a last step, add the present value of perpetuity to the total discounted cash flows for the first five years, $118,085. That results in a company valuation of $479,158. At this point, the analysis of this company has concluded. A very detailed analysis has been formulated that can lend a great deal of credibility to the overall analysis of the company.

Comparable Multiple Valuation

The final method of valuation is the most commonly used and probably the easiest to use as well. For this reason, it is widely regarded as the quick and dirty method of valuation by Wall Street bankers. It is based on benchmarking one company against an industry-average multiple such as the price-to-earnings ratio. For example, an analyst will take the price of a company's stock and divide it by the company's earnings. This also could be applied to other variations on this multiple, such as price to EBIT or price to EBITDA. The following example keeps it simple and uses the basic price-to-earnings (P/E) ratio.

Generally speaking, if a company's price-to-earnings ratio is greater than the industry average, it is fair to say that the company is overvalued. If the company's P/E ratio is less than the industry average, it is fair to say that the company is undervalued. However, I always caution myself when I state this because, as is the case in most of finance and accounting, no rules are without exception. As you saw in Chapter 6, many companies are seemingly undervalued, but for good reason. For example, a company might be a party in a pending lawsuit, and so the market has undervalued the company because it is unclear what the ruling will be.

In instances like that, investors will not necessarily scramble to acquire shares of the company even when they know that based on any type of valuation methodology, the company is undervalued. The comparable multiple method of valuation forms at least a starting point for making some basic assumptions about a company's value.

Take a look at the sample comparable multiple valuation model in Figure 9-1. The four companies listed constitute a sample peer group for which a price-to-earnings multiple will be calculated and applied to the target company (Cunningham Hardware). The first company has a share price of $36 per share. It has earnings per share of $2, and you can divide $36 per share by $2 earnings per share to come up with a P/E multiple of 18. The second company has a share price of $72 per share. It has earnings per share of $3. Divide that $72 by $3 to come up with a P/E multiple of 24. The third company has a share price of $64 per share and earnings per share of $4, which yields a P/E ratio of 16. Finally, the fourth company has a share price of $36 per share and earnings per share of $2, which yields a P/E ratio of 18.

To get the industry average, take a straight average of these four P/E ratios—18, 24, 16, and 18. Add them up, divide by 4, and the resulting industry average P/E is 19. Now it is possible to apply that industry average of 19 to the target company whose earnings are $4 per share. On the basis of this average, what do you think the share price or the perceived value of this company would be? If you calculated $76, you're absolutely right. This is calculated on a per-share

FIGURE 9-1 Comparable Multiple Valuation

Prices on a per-share basis

	Share Price	Earnings/Share	P/E
Beta Hardware	$36	$2	18
Gamma Hardware	$72	$3	24
Theta Hardware	$64	$4	16
Sigma Hardware	$36	$2	18
Industry average			19
Cunningham Hardware	?	$4	

By using the industry average P/E ratio, we calculate a fair value for Cunningham Hardware:

Industry P/E × company earnings = company fair value

19 × $4 = $76 per share

$76 × 1,600 shares = $121,600

basis; to find the value of the company, multiply the share price by the total number of shares outstanding. If it is assumed that the company has 1,600 shares outstanding, the total company market value is $121,600. That is the expected market capitalization, or the value of this company. This is the same company that was valued earlier by using the discounted cash flow method, which revealed a value of $479,000. One method reveals a value of $479,000, whereas another reveals a value of $121,600. Is this a problem? Yes, indeed. If you are an analyst and this company is your client, you have a mild crisis when your two valuations do not coincide.

This reminds me of one of my first experiences in investment banking. Years ago, I received a call late one evening from a senior banker in my group. He began with, "Guess what? We just secured the right to represent a large corporation on a sell-side transaction. I need your team to help me produce a valuation for this company, and to do that, I'd like two valuation models. First, I'd like a discounted cash flow model and, second, a comparable multiple model. Oh, and whatever happens, I need you to make sure that the values on each come out to $100 million."

More often than not, investment bankers have their value in mind long before they plunge into the models. The goal with any financial model is to justify that value. Valuation models are simply mechanisms for engendering dialogue and building credibility. When they use two valuation models, analysts often seek to ensure that those models converge on the same number. To do that, they come back to one of the two numbers, usually the lower of the two, $121,600 in this example, and look at ways to increase it. Perhaps they might eliminate one of the multiples that bring the average down. The third company here has a relatively low P/E number. They might exclude that for one reason or another. They might look at a slightly different way of calculating P/E. Perhaps right now they are using projected earnings. They might instead use historical earnings that potentially would yield a higher industry average P/E. And through some clever adjustments, they might boost the industry average P/E ratio, which in turn would boost the expected share price, which in turn would boost the company's valuation. In doing that, they would converge on that original discounted cash flow valuation number. Finally, they would have two different methods of analysis that reveal roughly the same valuation, and that is something they could bring to their client. Again, the only true value of a company is what the buyer and seller agree on.

> **Riddle:** *What do you call a company with negative historical cash flows and positive projected cash flows?*
>
> **Answer:** *You call it an Internet company.*

You cannot calculate a meaningful P/E ratio without positive earnings, and the market's failure to acknowledge this is essentially what drove the rise and subsequent fall of the Internet economy.

Lose Customers, Lose Value—Equifax

Nowadays, collecting customer data is just as important to a business as selling products to its customers. After all, knowledge is power, and power is value. Unfortunately, with this power comes great responsibility, and when not handled well, disaster can result. This is what happened to Equifax in 2017. One of the largest credit reporting agencies in the world, Equifax collected data on its millions of customers. Over several months in 2017, a group of hackers manage to exploit a website vulnerability and steal the data of tens of millions of customers. A company whose primary business revolves around collecting sensitive data to help customers obtain credit now created a credit nightmare for many of its valued customers.

News of the breach caused Equifax's stock to collapse. The reputational harm was significant, and the ensuing scrutiny from legislators was even worse. Customers had entrusted the company with some of their most guarded personal information. When that trust was breached, customer confidence was lost. Who wants to provide a social security number or bank account information when there's a chance it will be stolen?

The moral to this story: for a business, your customer information is your most valuable asset. Lose it and you can lose your business. A loss of business means a loss of profit. And a loss of profit means a loss of value. This is what investors were thinking as they scrambled to assess the damage and estimate the loss of future profits. In a matter of days, the verdict was in. The stock fell 35 percent, wiping away $6 billion market value. The market deemed the expected loss of business plus potential litigation to be worth $6 billion.

NET PRESENT VALUE

A common measure that often is used in the world of investment banking is net present value (NPV). Investment bankers use this term quite frequently in their discussions with clients. For the most part, it is a useful concept. NPV is derived from basic principles of discounting future returns. If you recall, a company can be valued by forecasting future returns (cash flow, income, EBITDA, etc.) and discounting them on the basis of some discount rate. From there, the present values of future returns can be summed and a fair value can be assessed for the company. What happens if the initial investment needed to launch that company is subtracted out? Net present value is left. Assume that $100,000 is needed to start the hardware store, which will generate present values of future cash flows that in total amount to $120,000. Once the initial investment is subtracted, $20,000 remains: the NPV.

NPV is calculated by using this simple formula:

$$\text{NPV} = \text{present value of future returns} - \text{investment}$$

When NPV is positive, the entrepreneur probably will move forward with the company. If NPV is negative, it will not make sense to move forward. Bankers like this measure because it reveals a return in cash and factors in risk based on a discount rate. Ultimately, bankers want to see that a deal makes money because they can always extract a fee from it. Investors such as venture capitalists, by contrast, tend to look at the internal rate of return (IRR).

IRR, according to most textbooks, is the maximum rate of interest that could be paid for capital employed over the life of an investment in order for it to break even. This definition takes an already complicated concept and makes it more complicated. I prefer a more informal definition of IRR, which is the discount rate at which the sum of present values of future cash flows equals the initial investment. This is still a bit confusing, but take a look at the example in Figure 9-2.

FIGURE 9-2 Internal Rate of Return

Example: Cunningham Hardware Co.

	Investment	Projections				
Year	0	1	2	3	4	5
Cash flow (CF)	$(118,085)	$25,000	$23,000	$30,000	$33,000	$45,000

$$\frac{CF}{(1+r)^n} = \frac{\$25,000}{(1+0.09)^1} + \frac{\$23,000}{(1+0.09)^2} + \frac{\$30,000}{(1+0.09)^3} + \frac{\$33,000}{(1+0.09)^4} + \frac{\$45,000}{(1+0.09)^5}$$

$22,936	$19,359	$23,166	$23,378	$29,247

PV of cash flows = $118,085
Initial investment = $118,085
IRR = 9%

9% is the discount rate at which the present values of future cash flows equal the initial investment.

In this case, we projected future cash flows. Suppose the company dissolves at the end of year 5 and assume that the amount needed to get this company up and running is around $118,000. Based on this, the discount rate that would cause the present value of these future returns to equal the initial investment is 9 percent. It is the breakeven discount rate, or the IRR. The IRR is useful in preference decisions. For example, a venture capitalist might review hundreds of proposals per month but may determine that only the ones with an IRR exceeding the firm's hurdle rate are worth investing in. If the firm has on average returned 20 percent per year, it is highly probable that it would designate this as its hurdle rate. Thus, projects with an IRR higher than 20 percent probably would receive a closer look than ones with an IRR lower than 20 percent. Again, no decision should be based exclusively on IRR or any other single performance measure, but IRRs do provide a reasonable starting point. Before you go on to Chapter 10, take a look at Figure 9-3. It offers a brief comparison of NPV and IRR in evaluating projects.

FIGURE 9-3 NPV Versus IRR—Evaluating Projects

Method	Accept	Reject	Indifferent
NPV	> 0	< 0	= 0
IRR	> k	< k	= k

Note: k denotes the required rate of return or cost of capital.

10

WALL STREET BASICS: STOCKS AND BONDS

When I finished college, I was up to my ears in debt and somewhat envious of my former classmates who had had their education paid for by their parents. My envy turned to sympathy when a friend explained to me that those who received parental funding faced the burdens of managing their primary equity investors: their parents. Their personal and professional pursuits would be subject to the approval of their board of directors, which was composed exclusively of Mom and Dad. Those of us who went the debt route would be beholden only to our creditors: the banks. The banks only demand repayment of principal in a timely manner; other than that, they issue few demands. Therefore, we suffer no equity dilution and maintain complete voting power in all decisions. Of course, that sounded nice until I tried to exercise my newly realized autonomy with a postcollege European adventure only to learn the hard way that parents function more like a third-world dictatorship in which any business is subject to the whims of the government.

The balance sheet helps us understand the overall financial health of a company. A major factor in determining financial health is the company's underlying capital structure. A question that arises in many discussions about the balance sheet is,

What is the best way to capitalize a company? Is it equity or debt? The answer is that it depends, as both debt and equity have their advantages.

Debt offers the following advantages. First, lenders have no direct claim on future earnings, and so debt can be issued without worries about a claim on earnings. As long as the interest is paid, the company is fine. Second, the interest paid on debt can be deducted for tax purposes. Third, most payments, whether they are interest or principal payments, are usually predictable, and so a company can plan ahead and budget for them. Fourth, debt does not dilute the owner's interest, and so an owner can issue debt and not worry about a reduced equity stake. Fifth, interest rates are usually lower than the expected return. If they are not, a change in management can be expected soon.

Debt securities can take a number of different forms, the most common being bonds. Bonds are obligations secured by a mortgage on company property. Bonds tend to be safer from the investors' standpoint and therefore pay lower interest. Debentures, in contrast, are unsecured and are issued on the strength of the company's reputation, projected earnings, or growth potential. Debentures, being far riskier, tend to pay more interest than do their more secure counterparts.

Equity has the following advantages. First, equity does not raise a company's breakeven point, and so a company can issue equity and not have to worry about achieving performance benchmarks to fund the equity. Of course, any company that issues equity has to meet certain investor expectations, but the breakeven point of the company is not adjusted as a result of an equity issuance. Second, equity does not increase the risk of insolvency, and so a company can issue equity and not have to worry about any subsequent payments to service that equity. Equity is essentially capital with unlimited life, and so a company can issue equity and not have to worry about when it comes due. Third, there is no need to pledge assets or offer any personal guarantees when equity is issued.

Equity can take a number of different forms. A simple form of equity is common stock. This type of stock offers no limits on the rate of return and can continue to rise in price indefinitely. There are no fixed terms; the stock is issued, and the holder bears the stock. Preferred stock entitles the holders to receive dividends at a fixed or adjustable rate of return and ranks higher than common stock in a liquidation. In fact, preferred stock may have antidilution rights so that in a subsequent stock offering, preferred stockholders may maintain the same equity stake. Nowadays, we're seeing the issuance of more and more convertible securities. These securities are highly structured in nature and are based on certain parameters; also, as the word *convertible* indicates, they may convert into other securities. Among the most common are warrants and options. Warrants and options stand for the right to buy a stated number of shares of common or preferred stock at a specified time for a specified price. There are also convertible notes and preferred stock, which refer to the right to convert these notes to some common stock when the conversion price is more favorable than the current rate of return.

These highly structured securities can be very problematic. This reminds me of a story about a transaction I worked on years ago during my days on Wall Street. At the time, we came up with a clever offering for a large oil company. The offering was structured around a form of preferred stock that could be called by the company at any time and that at maturity had to be redeemed into either cash or common shares. The entire offering was predicated on very detailed statistical analysis, the kind that even the most sophisticated fund managers had difficulty grasping. When the offering was marketed to the large fund managers, most of them left the room entirely perplexed. As a result, the offering wasn't nearly as successful as the investment bankers had hoped. Needless to say, our closing dinner was canceled and the deal was never mentioned again.

This chapter will discuss the following:

- Bonds
- Stocks
- Short selling

BONDS

Much of Wall Street and the US economy as a whole is driven by the debt markets. When the Federal Reserve raises interest rates, it affects every one of us in some way. The strategies that corporations employ to manage their debt can drive a company's overall performance. Bonds, or what generally are referred to as *secured debts*, have a number of distinguishing features. Here is a brief explanation of each one:

- *Amount (of issue):* how much was raised from the offering
- *Date (of issue):* the day of sale
- *Maturity:* when the principal will be repaid
- *Face value:* denomination of the bond
- *Offer price:* the percentage of the face value
- *Coupon:* the percentage of interest paid to bondholders (usually stated in annual terms)
- *Coupon payment dates:* dates of interest payments
- *Call provision:* whether the company retains the right to repay the bond before maturity
- *Call price:* if there is a call provision, the price at which the company can buy the bond back (usually above the bond's value, thus offering a premium for early repayment)

Types of Bonds: Corporate and Government

Among the broader classifications of bonds are corporate and government, with payment structures of zero coupon, fixed rate, and floating rate. Of course, there are variations on these bonds and numerous exotic bonds, but these classifications generally encompass the extensive universe of bonds.

Corporate Bonds

Corporate bonds can take many forms, but for the most part, an issuance of long-term debt to the public by a company is considered a corporate bond offering. A corporate bond will list most, if not all, of the features just described in its prospectus and will be traded in the open market, both on and off the major exchanges.

Most of these bonds will be rated by one of the major rating agencies, such as Standard & Poor's or Moody's. Those ratings will be based on the creditworthiness of the issuer, which will factor in a number of variables used to determine the probability of default. The higher the likelihood of default, the lower the rating. The bond prices, as you will see later in this chapter, are highly sensitive to these ratings. However, the prices also are sensitive to changes in interest rates, although that will not be factored into the ratings. The ratings range from AAA (S&P) and Aaa (Moody's) to D (S&P) and C (Moody's). A bond's ratings will affect its pricing. When a company falls to a rating of BB (S&P) or Ba (Moody's), it is called *junk* (known as *high yield* in more refined circles), meaning it is highly speculative and prone to risk of default.

Government Bonds

Most countries around the globe finance a portion of their activities through the issuance of bonds. In many of these countries, though, payback will never happen. However, the United States has a pretty good track record with this. In fact, the largest debtor in the world is the US government, and so we should all hope that this trend continues. The US government issues Treasury bills, notes, and bonds to finance its activities, with maturities on the latter two ranging from 2 to 30 years. Treasuries are considered risk-free (at least for now) and are exempt from state taxes. Most of them are simple coupon bonds.

Like the federal government, state and local governments issue municipal (muni) bonds. These bonds can have higher levels of risk and often are related to a specific project, such as the construction of a dam. Furthermore, they are usually callable. The most appealing quality of these bonds to the investor is the fact that they are exempt from federal tax. Because of the tax benefit of these bonds, their yields tend to be significantly lower than those of corporate bonds.

Consider the following: You decide to invest in one of two bonds. One, a corporate bond, pays 7 percent and is taxable, and the other, a muni, pays 5 percent and is exempt from federal tax. If you are in a 30 percent tax bracket, which would you choose?

On the taxable corporate bond, after tax you would earn 7 percent × (1 – 30 percent) = 4.9 percent. On the tax-exempt muni, you would earn 5 percent.

Types of Bonds: Zero Coupon, Fixed Rate, and Floating Rate

Zero Coupon Bonds
Zero coupon bonds are priced at a discount to par, with the difference accounting for the interest that will be paid. For example, a five-year zero coupon bond priced at $750 will pay $250 in interest ($1,000 – $750 = $250). The $250 accounts for the difference between the $1,000 par value and the initial price. Presumably, one-fifth of that $250, or $50, would count as interest for each year. In some cases, these bonds pay no coupons for a period of time and then commence coupon payments, thus functioning as a type of convertible instrument.

Fixed- and Floating-Rate Bonds
Aside from the zero coupon bonds, most bonds make some sort of coupon or interest payment. Fixed-rate bonds make a payment that is based on a fixed rate of interest. If that rate is 5 percent, a $1,000 bond will pay $50 per year. Floating-rate bonds, by contrast, make payments that are based on a variable rate of interest that usually is tied to an interest index such as Treasury rates or LIBOR (London Interbank Offering Rate). These indexes adjust periodically on the basis of various economic factors as well as those influenced by governmental monetary policy. When they adjust, so do the floating-rate coupons.

Bond Pricing and Valuation
Now comes the tricky part: bond pricing. Here is a bond quote for the company Car-E-Oki as it would appear in the newspaper:

BOND	CURRENT	YIELD	CLOSE	CHANGE
CEO	8½ 20	8.6	98.35	−0.42

This bond pays 8.5 percent of its face value in interest and matures in 2020. With a face value of $1,000, the bond will pay $85 in interest per year. This bond closed at 98.35, or 98.35 percent of its face value of $1,000, which would be $983.50. The closing price dropped 0.42 percent, or $4.20, since yesterday's close. The current yield, probably the most important component of the quote, shows what would be earned on the basis of the current price and coupon. Divide the coupon by the closing price to calculate this (8.5 percent/98.35 percent = 8.6 percent). Additional information, such as volume numbers, might show up in a more detailed quote.

What drives that bond price and, correspondingly, the yield? In other words, how are these bonds valued? A number of factors influence this. Among them are the following:

- Interest rates
- Inflation
- Credit risk
- Liquidity

Inflation and interest tend to work in tandem. If an outlook of high inflation is prevalent, interest rates will increase to compensate for it. Credit risk has to do with the creditworthiness of a company. In the case of Treasuries, this would not factor in because Treasuries are considered to be risk-free. Liquidity will influence prices, as investors typically prefer more liquid assets to less liquid ones. Therefore, some liquidity premium will have to be offered to entice investors when a bond is less liquid.

Junk Bonds

A long time ago in a city far, far away (Beverly Hills), there came a time of revolution when corporate America fell prey to bold promises and great parties. During that time, corporations raised billions of dollars and corporate managers, investment bankers, and traders bilked the public out of billions of dollars. They did so through the skillful use of junk bonds.

Junk bonds grew in popularity as corporations experienced a drop in credit quality resulting from a change in business or financing conditions. As more statisticians and financial analysts began to study the returns on junk bond portfolios, they soon determined that the risk-adjusted returns on a portfolio of junk bonds were higher than the risk assumed. Pioneers in that market, such as Michael Milken and his firm, Drexel Burnham Lambert, were successful in perpetuating this theory, which led to billions of dollars in fees for the underwriters and according to many people helped fuel the explosive economic growth of the 1980s. For the first time, large amounts of capital were made available to risky ventures, and that resulted in the expansion of industries such as cable television, telecommunications, and home building. Although Milken was not the originator of the junk bond, he is credited with bringing those bonds to the masses. Through his massive network of money managers, he was able to place junk bonds with funds all over the United States.

Milken's early career was marked by long hours in Drexel's bond group, working on "fallen angels," bonds of once great corporations that had been downgraded to junk by the rating agencies. His role was to determine whether the risk of default was outweighed by the interest premium paid. What he discovered was revolutionary. Milken's challenge to convention began with the rating agencies. He saw that those agencies offered investment-grade ratings to the top several hundred corporations in America. Those were established companies with large market capitalizations and proven performance. However, tens of thousands of other corporations were excluded from traditional Wall Street debt underwriting because of their limited size and histories. Such companies could borrow from commercial lenders or insurance companies only at unpredictable short-term rates and under restrictive covenants.

Milken felt this system was inherently flawed because top-rated companies could easily see a drop in their bond prices as a result of a bankruptcy or industry slowdown, leading to credit downgrades. Because of this, he felt that the rating agencies focused too much on the past, namely, the balance sheet, and not nearly enough on the future, namely, cash flows. Milken initiated a new paradigm that linked bonds to future cash flows. Soon he was underwriting debt that behaved more like equity. Not long afterward corporate raiders and leverage buyout kings such as Ron Perlman, T. Boone Pickens, and Henry Kravis were lining up to secure funding through Milken.

Milken became a buyer, seller, market maker, and underwriter of those bonds, a combination that probably led to his undoing. By assuming that much control over a single market, he raised scrutiny of his activities to a new level. The fact that he was making over half a billion dollars per year did not help matters either. Eventually, an insider trading scandal brought down Drexel Burnham and put Milken in jail.

STOCKS

Just as important as bond valuation is stock valuation. The interesting thing about stocks is that with detailed formulas and models, you might think you have it all figured out. However, we will soon see that none of this really matters, because the markets are inherently irrational.

Despite all the emphasis placed on valuing common stock, ultimately the process of valuation is wrought with uncertainty and controversy. For example, little is known about a company's future cash flows; more important, a stock does not have a maturity date like a bond, and so its life is forever. Nonetheless, equity research analysts, fund managers, and speculators devote most of their waking hours to this practice. Take a look at how stocks are valued through the use of some of the valuation principles that have been covered in this book.

Discounted Cash Flows

As was shown in Chapter 9, the value of a company can be assessed on the basis of the sum of the present value of future cash flows. Therefore, an equity analyst will build out these detailed cash flow models, come up with a discount rate, take the present value of these projected cash flows, and add them all up. The final step, barring any adjustments, is to divide the company value by the number of shares outstanding to determine a value on a per-share basis. This will form the basis of the price target assessed by the analyst.

Dividend Method

Another method of assessing stock values is to project a stream of dividends and discount them to present value. The idea is that dividends represent the return on a stock. Thus, these dividends can be treated the same way projected cash flows would be treated. If the dividend is assumed to grow at a constant rate, the stock price would be modeled as follows:

$$P = D_1/(1+r)^1 + D_2/(1+r)^2 + D_3/(1+r)^3 + D_4/(1+r)^4 + D_5/(1+r)^5 + D_6/(1+r)^6 + D_7/(1+r)^7 \ldots$$

In theory, the sum of the present values will yield a stock price. But where does it all end? Do these dividend projections stop? How can the dividend be forecast for each future year? Why am I even doing this?

Attempting to answer these questions would just complicate matters further. However, that has never stopped us before. Thus, in theory, the stream of dividends does not end. In this case, a perpetuity value would be assigned to one of the projected dividends and discounted back to present value. Again, the same principles used in discounted cash flow valuation are applied.

As far as forecasting the dividend goes, there are a number of ways to do this. The simplest, of course, is to assume that it does not change. In that case, a simple perpetuity calculation could be used, which would look something like this:

$$P = D/r$$

Also, assume that the dividend grows at a constant rate using the formula for a perpetuity with growth. In this case, a dividend would be used instead of a cash flow:

$$P = D/(r - g)$$

So there you have it. The value of a stock is the sum of the present values of future dividends. What happens, though, when a company does not pay dividends? Then you're back to good old-fashioned comparables. As was seen in Chapter 9, companies often are valued relative to industry-average multiples such as the price-to-earnings ratio. In fact, most publicly traded companies are valued this way. What happens if there are few comparables against which to value a company? Well, then you're on your own. I suggest you read a real finance book such as Brealey and Myers's *Principles of Corporate Finance* and get back to me when you've done so. I'd love to hear what they have to say.

SHORT SELLING

The beauty of the stock market is that someone always makes money. In fact, some people make money even when almost everyone else loses money. Short sellers make a bet that the price of a company's stock will fall. To do that, they borrow shares of a traded stock (usually held by a brokerage house) and sell it with the intent of buying it back at a lower price. When the price drops, the short seller can buy the stock back and earn a profit on the difference between the sale price and the purchase price. Of course, if the price of the stock goes up, the short seller may have to close the position by buying shares of the stock to replace the borrowed shares at a higher price, thus recognizing a loss. For example, a short seller sells shares of a company short at $4 per share. When the share drops to $0.10 after the company declares bankruptcy, the short seller buys the shares to replace the borrowed ones at $0.10, earning a $3.90 profit. Of course, if the stock had gone up to, say, $10, the short seller could close the position by purchasing the shares at that price, suffering a $6 loss.

Short sellers are as much a part of an efficient market as are the people who buy and hold shares of stock for an extended period. Many believe, however, that short sellers can push a stock to unprecedented lows in a very short period. Opponents of short selling argue that a lack of regulation allows short sellers essentially to gang up and beat a stock down to nothing. Unfortunately, a falling stock price, though a technical problem, can easily become a fundamental problem when a drop in stock price triggers concerns about a company's solvency. If these issues are not checked, a complete collapse of a company can occur.

What is the upside of short selling? When market sentiment reverses course, all the short sellers who borrowed shares of stock have to replace their borrowed shares as stock prices continue to climb. To do that, they must buy shares on the open market and replace the ones they borrowed. With everyone scrambling to buy those shares in haste, there are dramatic upward movements in stock pricing, which can send a stock into the stratosphere in a short period. This is a short seller's worst nightmare. Consider the following scenario. A company's stock is trading at $20 per share. It is about to release its earnings, and in light of the dismal performance of other companies in its sector, there is mounting concern that the company will fall short of expectations. Wall Street analysts are expecting the company to earn $2 per share, although with its competitors missing their expected earnings numbers, many believe that this company will do the same thing. As a result, short sellers begin to sell the stock short before the market closes. For example, Investor A sells 100 shares short at the price of $20 per share. In other words, he borrows 100 shares and sells them. In theory, he now has $2,000 in his account. The market closes, and the company announces earnings. As it turns out, the company earned only $1 per share. Investors are disappointed, to say the least, and the next morning the stock opens at $12 per share. Investor A can cover by purchasing shares of the company at $12 and replace the borrowed ones. Investor A earned $8 per share, or $800. Not bad for a night's work.

Suppose the company announced earnings of $3 per share. Clearly, investors will rejoice, and the next morning the stock opens at $25 per share. Investor A probably will cover, meaning he will purchase shares to replace the borrowed ones, knowing that the stock quite likely will continue to rise, creating additional losses. If Investor A is able to purchase the shares at the open and obtain the price of $25, his total loss will be $7 per share, or $700. Now imagine what happens when every short seller in the market is trying to cover a position while the stock continues to rise.

This will create additional buy orders, which will only serve to push the price higher and higher. A stock that would have opened at $25 per share is moving fast to $26, $27, $28 as short sellers scramble to cover.

This type of situation is known as a short squeeze. Just as short sellers can push a stock's price down through momentum, they can contribute to a stock's meteoric rise in a short squeeze.

11

WALL STREET PART DEUX: ARBITRAGE, DERIVATIVES, AND HEDGE FUNDS

Years ago, a colleague of mine and I would frequent an Indian restaurant near our office in Manhattan. As each of us was on a fairly tight budget, we applied our skills in finance to optimize our food consumption while minimizing the cost. The chicken tikka plate, which came with six pieces of chicken and a bowl of rice, was priced at $11.95. The chicken tikka appetizer, which came with three pieces of chicken, was priced at $3.95. A bowl of rice was $1.95. What do you think we did? As pioneers in the chicken tikka arbitrage market, we figured that by ordering from the appetizer menu, we were able to consume six pieces of chicken and a bowl of rice for $9.85, saving $2.10 by not ordering from the dinner menu. In fact, if we had been more sophisticated arbitrageurs, we might have considered selling our meal to the table next to us for $10.95, earning us just over a dollar and saving that table a dollar. However, I'm sure that if we had done this, the market would have corrected and we would have been shown the door.

This chapter will discuss the following:

- Arbitrage
- Derivatives
- Forwards
- Futures
- Derivative disasters
- Hedge funds

ARBITRAGE

Arbitrage, technically speaking, is the simultaneous purchase and sale of an asset or security to capitalize on the price differentials that exist between different marketplaces or exchanges. In other words, it is an opportunity to earn a return on a transaction without assuming any risk. For example, suppose the spot price for gold in the United States is $400 per ounce. In the United Kingdom, it should trade at the same price. However, because of fluctuations in the currency exchange rate, at this very moment it is selling for $401 per ounce. With some sophisticated software and rapid-fire decision-making skills, the gold can be purchased in the United States and, within a second, sold in the United Kingdom for a $1 profit, representing the momentary difference. Granted, the return is only 0.25 percent, but a big player in this market might have made a $100 million trade leading to a $250,000 profit for a second of work. Not bad.

Obviously, such trades are few and far between, and they are rarely this simple. Moreover, a number of costs were incurred in the process of finding such a trade. It is quite likely that this kind of trade occurs only once every few years. Among the other trades that were attempted, most ended up losing when the market corrected at the time of sale. Thus, a person may try several trades but see a return on only one. Plus, there is always the risk that the price may fall when one is selling, causing a monetary loss. This type of arbitrage is risky, and the process of finding such opportunities can be time-consuming.

Currency Arbitrage

Currency arbitrage is one of the most profitable forms of arbitrage. Suppose the exchange rate between British pounds (GBP) and US dollars (USD) is 2, and so one could trade £5 for $10. The USD-to-GBP rate would be 0.5. However, what happens if the USD-to-GBP rate is 0.6 for a moment? One then could trade $10 for £6. In this process, £1 is earned. In theory, the market will correct soon, but for a fleeting moment, a class of arbitrageurs has done its best to exploit this difference.

A more complex form of such a trade is one in which three currencies are traded simultaneously. For example, suppose GBP to USD is 2 and USD to Canadian dollars (CAD) is 3. To figure out the appropriate exchange rate of GBP to CAD, multiply as follows:

GBP to CAD = (GBP to USD) × (USD to CAD)

The rate would be 6, and likewise, the CAD to GBP would be 1/6. What happens, however, if it is 1/5 for a brief moment? Again, there is an arbitrage opportunity. One could take £5, swap it for $10 US, and then take the $10 US and exchange it for $30 Canadian. Finally, if the CAD-to-GBP rate is 1/5, one could trade the $30 Canadian for £6. In aggregate, one extra British pound would be earned.

In many cases of arbitrage, hefty transaction costs preclude traders from executing the transaction. As a result, currency arbitrage tends to be more common than other types as a result of the lower transaction costs. Currency arbitrage is discussed in more detail in Chapter 13. Some other types of arbitrage are detailed in this chapter.

Merger Arbitrage

Merger arbitrage is the simultaneous purchase and sale of two companies involved in a proposed merger. A merger arbitrageur analyzes the probability of the merger not closing within the stated time frame or at all. Because of this uncertainty, the target company's stock price trades at a slight discount to the acquirer's offer price. Therefore, the merger arbitrageur might assess that there is a high probability that the deal will close and try to profit from the price differential. Remember a guy named Ivan Boesky? He helped make merger arbitrage part of the mainstream finance vernacular. In the mid-1980s, Boesky amassed a fortune of some $200 million and established himself as one of the best arbitrageurs the world had known. What investors and regulators failed to see for quite some time was that his massive stock purchases occurred only days before a corporation announced a takeover. Boesky was relying on tips from his pal Michael Milken and using the information to make lucrative stock trades. Boesky became an icon of Wall Street bravado, going so far as to tell a room full of college students in 1986, "I think greed is healthy. You can be greedy and still feel good about yourself," a line that inspired Michael Douglas's speech in the movie *Wall Street*. Eventually, SEC investigators got wind of Mr. Boesky's dealings and sent him to prison for two years.

Index Arbitrage

Sometimes stock traders find minor discrepancies in the pricing of index funds and the individual stocks that compose them. In such instances, traders may buy the index and simultaneously short the individual stocks. These trades tend to be more complex and often involve dealing with several dozen or more individual stocks.

Convertible-Debt Arbitrage

With these instruments, you might have the option to convert your debt to common stock at a certain price. In rare instances, you might be able to convert at one price and then sell at a different market price.

Barings Bank

One of the greatest tales of arbitrage gone awry involves Barings Bank. Barings had a long history as one of the most respected banks in the United Kingdom. In early 1995, the bank was bankrupted by $1 billion in trading losses attributed to a trader by the name of Nick Leeson. Leeson, who made a name for himself on Wall Street, was appointed general manager of Barings Futures in Singapore. In that position, he had responsibilities in both trading and administration, and that created an opportunity for him to hide unauthorized trading activities.

Over the next several years, Leeson took sizable positions in an effort to capitalize on arbitrage opportunities between the Singapore International Monetary Exchange (SIMEX) and the Osaka Securities Exchange. However, the senior managers at Barings, who were merchant bankers and not seasoned traders, believed that these were evenly matched positions. The positions were assumed to be low-risk, low-profit positions. In reality, Leeson was trading derivatives on the two exchanges that in some cases were mismatched in size. For example, he would create a straddle (simultaneously selling a put and a call) with the hope that the markets would remain relatively flat. If this happened, the options would expire, and he would have profited from the premiums received through their sale. If the markets were volatile, such positions could result in large losses.

Leeson maintained an error account to conceal his losses. He hoped that through subsequent gains, those losses would be wiped out and the account would be reduced to a zero balance. As losses mounted, he took on larger positions with the hope of recouping those losses sooner rather than later. The need to emerge from that hole fueled his intensity in taking risks and disguising losses. Leeson's story unraveled when the Nikkei 225 fell 1,000 points after a major earthquake hit Japan in early 1995. That unforeseen occurrence caused Leeson to suffer inordinate losses and raised questions about the legitimacy of his accounts. Two months later, Barings, unable to craft a realistic plan to emerge from financial catastrophe, was sold to the Dutch bank ING for 1 pound sterling. Thus, the tale of this once prestigious European boutique that helped the United States finance the Louisiana Purchase over a century earlier came to an end.

DERIVATIVES

I once knew a young woman who dated unemployed men with multiple degrees from prestigious schools. I respected the fact that she was drawn to their intellect but never quite understood the appeal of unemployment. In fact, most of them lived with their mothers and spent the majority of their days playing online games or watching one of the sci-fi channels. I one day mustered the courage to discuss this somewhat unconventional practice with her and asked, "Why are you consistently attracted to this type of guy?" She readily responded, "Some people buy the over-priced stock; I buy the call option. You see, these guys do not demand much up front, show a lot of promise, and may someday be worth quite a bit. So if even one makes it big, I'm set. I've created a risk-weighted portfolio of call options."

Sadly, she was hoping one of those guys would become the next Bill Gates, but like many of the high-risk tech companies in the late 1990s . . . well, let's just say they still live with Mommy and the options expired.

Derivative securities are securities based on the movement of an underlying security or index. This might include stocks, bonds, commodities, currencies, or even indexes. Derivatives were created to hedge against market risk, and today there is an abundance of such instruments. The more common ones include options, warrants, and swaps.

Options

An ordinary option grants the holder the right to buy or sell something at a specified price within a specified period. The most basic forms of options are calls and puts.

Call Options

With a call, the option holder is able to purchase a security (for example, a stock) at a certain price. Suppose you have your eye on the company that just invented Car-E-Oki—the karaoke machine for the car. The company, which trades under the ticker CEO, is offered at $10 per share. You have $1,000 to invest, which would get you 100 shares of CEO. CEO is about to announce the release of its new machine, which is made exclusively for pickup trucks. Now everyone will be able to enjoy live country music on America's highways, something you believe will cause the stock to appreciate nicely. If you buy 100 shares of CEO and the stock doubles this year, you will have made $1,000. Not a bad return.

However, you are extremely confident that the stock will double and are seeking to get the highest returns possible from your investment. Rather than buy the stock, you buy the call option. That option gives you the right to buy the stock at a specific price within a fixed period. In this case, the January 10 call options trade at $1, and so you could buy the right to purchase one share of stock before next January at the price of $10 per share. In fact, with $1,000, you could buy the right to purchase 1,000 shares. Assuming you do this and the stock price doubles between now and next January, how much have you made?

You bought 1,000 options, each representing the right to buy one share. If you were to exercise these options, meaning purchase the shares at the strike price of $10, you would own $10,000 worth of the stock. If the stock goes to $20 per share, effectively doubling in value, your position would now be worth $20,000. In total, you would recognize a gain of $10,000, minus the $1,000 to purchase the options initially, for a net gain of $9,000. This is considerably more than the $1,000 you would have made by simply buying 100 shares of stock in the first place. What happens if you do not have the funds to purchase those 1,000 shares of stock? No problem. Before the expiration date, you need not exercise the option. Rather, the option will appreciate in value as the stock price appreciates. With a $1,000 investment, you have net $9,000. Not bad. But if the stock price falls below $10, you lose your entire investment.

Put Options

Consider another scenario. Suppose you are not willing to lose your $1,000 investment if you buy the call options and the stock drops below $10 at the time of expiration. Furthermore, you are interested in protecting your investment, in other words, purchasing some sort of insurance on it. In this case, you might consider buying the stock outright and then purchasing put options to hedge against any drop in price. You might purchase 100 shares at $10 each for a total of $1,000. You also might purchase January 10 puts at a price of $1. With these, you have the right to sell your shares at $10 even if the price falls below $10. In total, it costs you $100 for this right. If the stock goes up, you lose the full $100 that you spent on the puts. You hope, though, that the stock will appreciate more than that $1, providing you with some profit. If the stock falls, the most you will lose is $1 per share. Thus, paying $1 per option, or a total of $100, buys some insurance.

Put options can be pricey. You will see how they are valued next. Giving up 10 percent of your stock value can be considerable, especially when few stocks earn more than this. Furthermore, the stock price may remain flat throughout the life of the option and then fall after the option expires. Not only do you lose the option premium, you are left exposed to the drop. Buying longer-dated options, though, is more expensive.

Option Valuation

Option valuation is a tricky business. There are a number of ways to value these options, but most option models consistently factor in the following:

- Strike price
- Expected option life
- Current stock price
- Expected dividends
- Volatility
- Risk-free rate

The most commonly used method is the Black-Scholes model. Back in the early 1970s, two guys by the names of Fischer Black and Myron Scholes wrote a paper in which they detailed a mathematical model that could be used to value options. The model incorporates each of the factors mentioned in our list and, through some sophisticated mathematical maneuvering, generates a number reflective of an option's fair value. The model is used so widely that most option traders regard it as the most important tool of the trade. At the same time, the Black-Scholes model often is criticized for a number of shortcomings. First, the model is driven heavily by historical movements of a stock, which may not depict expected future developments accurately. Second, the model is mathematically complex, and aside from the occasional

PhD in finance, few are comfortable using it. Third, long-term, nontraded stock options would not be covered by such a model.

Although alternatives to Black-Scholes exist, most financial managers prefer this method. The binomial lattice model (also known as *Cox, Ross, Rubinstein*) uses more inputs and thus is seen as more accurate. Nonetheless, Black-Scholes remains the preferred method because of its long history and, more than anything else, concern over changing internal controls. Most CFOs would be reluctant to adopt a new standard because of the time and cost associated with development and training.

Option Arbitrage

As we saw earlier in this chapter, arbitrage can be an effective way to profit from pricing discrepancies. Sometimes options create such opportunities. Suppose you notice that Company ABC is trading at $50 per share. The call option to buy one share of ABC at $30 is trading at $10. You can buy the option for $10, exercise the call for $30, and sell the stock that you now own for $50. You have paid $10 for the option plus $30 for the stock for a total cost of $40, and so you walk away with a $10 return. Such instances are extremely rare, although it is possible for an active options trader to pick up a discrepancy of a few basis points on a similar trade. If you are trading millions of dollars, this can amount to a nice return.

Warrants

Warrants are similar to options, with the largest differences stemming from duration. Aside from that, the differences are minor, as you can see here:

WARRANTS	OPTIONS
Usually dated between three and five years	Usually dated less than nine months
Involve new shares being issued	No new shares issued
Issued by companies for investors	Contracts between investors
Traded on the stock market	Traded on an options exchange

Swaps

Swaps are a type of derivative in which two parties enter into an agreement to exchange their streams of cash flows. One of the more common types of these is interest rate swaps. Often, a company that pays a fixed rate of interest on corporate debt seeks to protect these payments from a fall in interest rates. These simple swaps are known as *vanilla interest swaps*. Typically, such an arrangement will involve two loans of the same denomination that pay interest on the same dates. One loan pays a fixed rate, and the other pays a floating rate. Let's go back to the CEO example. Suppose you were just named CEO of CEO or, better yet, CFO of CEO. Your first order of business is to protect that new corporate debt issuance. The company issued $100 of corporate debt that pays 5 percent interest annually. Suppose you would prefer to service that debt by using a floating rate. You could swap your fixed payments for floating payments. The difference between the two rates would be paid to you or paid out by you, depending on the fluctuations of the floating rate. Figure 11-1 shows this.

FIGURE 11-1 Swap Structures

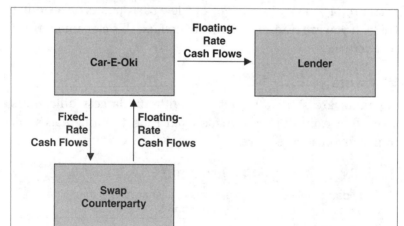

Normally, vanilla interest rate swaps are quoted on the basis of the fixed rate, and so the difference between the fixed rate and the corresponding floating rate (US Treasuries, LIBOR) will be quoted as the swap rate. Swaps are used not only by financial managers but by bond traders as well. A trader betting on a rise in interest rates might enter into a pay-fixed swap.

FORWARDS

A forward contract is an obligation to transfer an asset at a specific price on a specific date. It is an effective hedge, especially in the commodities markets, which can be quite volatile and subject to forces outside the market. The party that will sell the asset is called the *short* party, and the party that buys it is called the *long* party. When the deal is structured, no funds actually change hands.

One thing about the Car-E-Oki machine that was not mentioned earlier is its innovative design. The speaker box has a silver lining that further amplifies high-pitched singing. In fact, most of the cost of production is tied to this silver component. You recently received a large order from one of the major automakers to outfit all its new cars with Car-E-Oki machines. Production begins in about a month, and for that reason, you will need to oversee the purchase of materials. One of your biggest concerns right now is the price of silver, as that will constitute a large portion of your cost. You approach your supplier of silver and mention that you need a large delivery in one month. You are concerned that silver prices are rising and want to lock in a price today. To do that, you enter into a forward contract with the supplier.

One month has passed, and you take delivery of the silver at the price that was agreed on. At this time, the current (spot) price of silver has increased considerably. You still pay the price agreed on in the forward contract and breathe a sigh of relief that you entered into it in the first place. Your supplier is clearly disappointed, knowing that he has lost out on substantial gains. Nonetheless, he entered into the agreement initially to lock the sale in place. For him, it was a way to protect the sale. Thus, in the end, you got a fair price for the silver and your supplier got to lock in a sale. Both sides were able to manage risk effectively.

FUTURES

Futures are contracts to buy or sell an underlying asset on a particular date. Futures generally are traded for commodities such as oil, gold, wool, and frozen concentrated orange juice. When one buys a future contract, one is agreeing to buy a certain commodity or index on a certain date, and when one sells a future contract, one agrees to sell the underlying commodity or index on a certain date. The cash settlement that occurs on that date is based on the movement in price of the underlying commodity or index.

Futures can be used to do the following:

- Hedge a portfolio position to protect it in the event of a market downturn.
- Achieve leveraged returns with a small investment, potentially leading to sizable returns.
- Capitalize on market declines; if the market should turn south, an investment could be protected and recognize sizable gains through the use of futures.

Futures and Valuation

Futures are valued on the basis of market demand rather than a fixed or predetermined price. Futures traders do their best to assess a fair value by using a calculation that is loosely equal to the underlying asset plus a premium, referred to as the *cost of carry*. The cost of carry pertains to any expenses incurred while holding that position. Consider the following example:

- The NASDAQ is currently at 2,000.
- Interest rates are at 4 percent.

- There are 180 days until maturity for this futures contract.
- The average dividend yield on stocks in this index is 2 percent.

To calculate the fair value, use the following formula:

Fair value = current level of **NASDAQ** + cost of carry

$$= 2{,}000 + [2{,}000 \times (4\% - 2\%) \times 180/365]$$

$$= 2{,}019.73$$

As with options, this premium will decrease as the maturity date approaches.

DERIVATIVE DISASTERS

Orange County

Before Orange County, California, was known for its ability to churn out quality television story lines, it was a hotbed of financial mismanagement. In the mid-1990s, the treasurer of the county made a bet that interest rates would remain low. He was not alone in his thinking, as many economic experts at the time held the same view. Unfortunately, the move cost the county $1.6 billion.

At the time, Robert Citron was among the most respected county treasurers in the country. Overseeing a pool of funds in excess of $7 billion, he crafted a strategy to invest those funds in a leveraged portfolio that primarily consisted of interest-based securities. The strategy was predicated on the expectation that short-term interest rates would remain low relative to medium-term rates. As the Fed began a strategy of raising rates, the Orange County portfolio began to lose value. By the end of 1994, mounting demands from government investors and Wall Street bankers created an insurmountable liquidity crunch for Citron. Eventually, the investors reached a settlement in bankruptcy court, receiving $0.77 per $1.00 invested, and Citron was sentenced to one year under house arrest plus a $100,000 fine. Meanwhile, the firm most responsible for advising Citron, Merrill Lynch, reached a $400 million settlement with Orange County in 1998 amid allegations that it had provided poor advice.

What happened? Ultimately, Citron used the following techniques to leverage a $7.5 billion fund into $20 billion in assets:

- *Reverse repurchase agreements.* By using securities already in the pool as collateral, he was able to leverage his position further. However, if the market value of those securities fell, they exposed him to margin calls.
- *Structured notes.* These derivatives included inverse floaters, index-amortizing notes, and collateralized mortgage obligations. Such instruments were highly structured and easily veiled in the reporting process, making it difficult for experts and analysts to discern the holdings in these structures.

All was fine provided that short-term interest rates remained low, as was the case during the early 1990s. However, in February 1994, the Fed began a series of rate hikes that in total amounted to more than a 2 percent increase in rates by the end of 1994. Such a movement can be catastrophic to a multibillion-dollar fund, especially one that is highly leveraged and invested in highly sensitive derivatives.

Bear Stearns

Bear Stearns was one of world's largest global investment banks and securities trading companies. In 2007, it was damaged by the global credit crisis when it was disclosed that two of its funds had lost nearly all their value as a result of declines in the mortgage market. One year later, JPMorgan Chase and the Federal Reserve Bank provided a 28-day emergency loan to Bear Stearns to prevent a complete market crash. The belief was that if Bear collapsed, other banks would soon follow. Imagine that. Shortly thereafter, Bear Stearns signed a merger agreement with JPMorgan Chase in a stock swap worth $2 per share (a price that later was increased to $10 per share). The sale price highlighted just how far the company had fallen. Just a year earlier, its stock had traded as high as $172 per share.

What happened? In June 2007, news surfaced that the two Bear funds were heavily invested in something called collateralized debt obligations (CDOs). These complex financial instruments are massive bundles of debt that at the time were bought and sold by financial institutions. Bear's CDOs were backed primarily by risky mortgages, and as signs of trouble emerged in the housing market, down went the CDOs. Bear pledged a collateralized loan of over $3 billion to save one fund and negotiated with other banks to lend money to the other fund. CDOs were determined to be worth less than the financial analysts thought, and they quickly collapsed. As other banks scrambled to seize the underlying collateral, panic set in when the collateral was auctioned for pennies on the dollar. Soon bankers, traders, and government officials had a revelation: if Bear liquidated its CDOs, the mark-to-market value of similar holdings at other financial institutions would collapse, and a collapse of those values would send a shock wave across global markets. Bear failed to secure capital, and in early March 2008, clients closed accounts while the stock price plummeted. Bear, a mere shadow of its former self, was swallowed up by JPMorgan Chase.

AIG

AIG, one of the largest global insurance companies, was brought down by its involvement with a type of derivative known as a credit default swap (CDS). Although the math behind CDSs can be complex, they are essentially insurance policies on debt default. Suppose a bank buys bonds from a major corporation. Concerned that the corporation is facing major financial challenges, the bank purchases CDSs as a hedge or form of insurance. If the corporation defaults on its debt, the bank is covered for the amount of the bond since it purchased the CDSs.

In light of AIG's involvement in the insurance market, entering the CDS market seemed to make sense. It was a chance to take insurance to the next level and develop a reputation as a financial innovator. Unfortunately, AIG applied methods of assessing pay-out probabilities on the CDSs that were similar to the ones it used for auto insurance. Furthermore, it failed to consider the possibility of a global credit crisis and what that would mean for CDSs. As trouble emerged across these markets, AIG's liabilities were called into question. As credit markets continued to deteriorate and AIG's obligations soared, its ability to raise capital on short notice became nonexistent. The only option was a bailout from the US government. Thanks to AIG's CDSs, the American people became the proud owners of AIG.

AIG failed for many reasons, but ultimately it was its heavy involvement in the CDS market that did it in. But how could the global financial system allow something like this to happen? Although CDSs were designed as insurance on bad debt, they soon became a profitable instrument for speculators. More important, those speculators further complicated things through a process known as netting. Suppose Bank A believes Corporation X will soon be on the verge of financial collapse. Bank A purchases CDSs from AIG on Corporation X's debt at a cost of $10 million per year. This payment is not unlike an annual insurance premium. If Corporation X fails, Bank A receives a $100 million payout from AIG. Now suppose Bank A sells its own CDSs to Bank B for $20 million per year. Bank B is willing to pay more because Corporation X looks more likely to fail. If it does indeed fail, Bank A pays Bank B $100 million, which won't be a problem because it will collect $100 million from AIG. Thus, Bank A neither gains nor loses from Corporation X's failure. However, it collects $10 million per year based on the difference between what it pays for its CDSs and the price at which it sells other CDSs to Bank B. This system works well and is highly profitable, but what happens if one link in the chain breaks? The entire system breaks down if one company fails, and this is precisely why the failure of AIG could have spelled disaster for the global financial system.

The VIX

In early 2018, global stock markets were roiled by excessive volatility. Much speculation surrounded the source of the market swings, but few could argue against the fact that complex volatility tracking instruments played a role in the market swings. The basis for these instruments was the CBOE (Chicago Board of Options Exchange) Volatility Index (VIX), which is an indication of the expected volatility in the market. Based on a portfolio of S&P 500 index options, the VIX is often termed "the fear gauge." When volatility spikes, investors are presumed to be fearful.

The VIX has spawned numerous trading instruments that allow investors to buy or sell "fear" as a hedging and trading mechanism. For example, someone sensing that investors are growing increasingly nervous about market valuations may opt to buy the VIX. If the market drops, the investor may offset losses based on a rise in the VIX. At the same time, someone who believes that the market may soon stabilize and fears will subside may choose to either short the VIX or purchase an inverse VIX fund. An inverse VIX fund increases in value when the VIX drops.

Here is the problem: very few investors understand the mechanics of these funds, and in times of extreme volatility, investor losses can accrue rapidly. This is what happened in February of 2018. At one point, the VIX spiked more than 80 percent in one day as the stock market was in free fall. Fears of inflation and a rise in interest rates fueled panic selling and caused a surge in the VIX. This was great for investors who had positions in VIX tracking instruments but bad for people who bought reverse tracking VIX instruments. This was so bad that one instrument in particular lost nearly 90 percent of its value in a matter of hours, prompting the bank that issued the instrument, an ETN (Exchange Traded Note), to issue a press release stating that the security would be permanently halted in a matter of weeks to prevent further acceleration of market volatility. The lesson in all of this: tracking fear can add to fear. Know the risks.

HEDGE FUNDS

With exotic securities and innovative investing strategies on the rise, hedge funds are a popular means of achieving strong returns

THE WALL STREET MBA

for high-net-worth individuals. These funds are formed through a managed portfolio that takes aggressive positions in what are often highly speculative opportunities. Most of these funds are limited to a small pool of individual investors, usually no more than 100. Hedge funds are generally unregulated, because it is assumed that the people investing in them are sophisticated investors. Investing strategies might involve derivatives, swaps, arbitrage, leverage, and short selling (selling a security that you don't own and then buying it at a lower price to fulfill the order and earn a nice profit). The problem is, however, that hedge funds do little in terms of hedging. In fact, they often take exceptionally large amounts of risk in an effort to produce astronomical returns. Most hedge fund managers will argue that they diversify against stock market risk by taking on complex positions. Whether this is true is a great source of debate. Nonetheless, hedge fund returns can be impressive, but once in a while, the results are disastrous.

12

MERGERS AND ACQUISITIONS

My first foray into the world of mergers and acquisitions (M&A) began years ago when I crafted a merger scenario between two major oil companies. It was a hypothetical scenario but one that nonetheless revealed tremendous potential. In my analysis, I assumed cost savings by eliminating certain operating expenses, bringing about regional diversification (one company had major holdings in Colorado, the other in Texas), and creating production efficiencies resulting from better supply chain management. Despite those foreseeable benefits, I concluded that the merger would not work because of inevitable management conflicts. The Ewings and the Carringtons would never get along.

M&A continues to be a driving force behind the global economy. Corporations seeking to fuel growth, boost profits, and increase shareholder value are constantly on the lookout for merger opportunities. Despite the flurry of multibillion-dollar mergers that dominate business headlines these days, we still face the reality that many of those mergers fail to return what was promised to investors. To understand why this occurs, we will examine the reasons for mergers along with some well-known historical cases. This chapter will discuss the following:

- History of M&A
- Types of mergers
- Why merge?
- Valuation
- Defenses
- Merger obstacles
- Mergers gone wild
- Leveraged buyouts

HISTORY OF M&A

The first major corporate mergers took place in the early nineteenth century when a trend toward consolidation swept the railroad industry. Within a few years, the merger wave began in earnest, as William Procter and James Gamble merged their candle and soap companies. The second half of the nineteenth century was characterized by several noteworthy M&A trends, including the Singer Company's "roll-up" of the sewing machine industry as it sought to buy out most of its competitors. General Mills was formed through the consolidation of several milling companies, and General Electric was created through a merger between Edison General Electric and Thomson-Houston Electric. This early merger wave was without boundaries, and concerns arose about the power those corporations wielded over the consumer. Eventually, the merger trend led to trusts, in which equity holders placed the voting rights of their shares in the hands of a small committee of administrators. Trusts were formed in the steel, tobacco, sugar, and copper industries. They soon morphed into monopolies, which eventually were dismantled by the trust-buster himself, President Theodore Roosevelt.

The boom years of the 1920s brought about numerous mergers aimed at vertical integration. From the Depression through the decade after World War II, M&A activity was relatively quiet. In the 1960s, however, merger mania revived when stock swaps became an easy source of funding. By the 1980s, high-yield debt and easy access to it became a driving force behind large corporate mergers. That was followed by globalization and a booming stock market working in tandem to propel mergers in the 1990s. The new millennium has brought forth mergers between some of the world's largest corporations, with each new announcement eclipsing the last.

TYPES OF MERGERS

Generally speaking, most mergers fall into three categories.

Horizontal Merger

This occurs between two companies in the same industry. For example, two oil companies may decide to merge because they believe they can create efficiencies within the company and thus eliminate costs and improve profitability. This inevitably causes valuation to increase because profitability is a key driver of valuation. In doing this, the two companies have achieved some synergy, and this type of horizontal merger makes sense.

Vertical Merger

This occurs between two companies involved in different stages of production. Suppose two companies in the media production industry decide to merge. One produces content, and the other owns a network with vast distribution capabilities. This results in the perfect formula for a successful vertical merger, with content and delivery now offered by one company. Ultimately, the different stages of production delivery combine to create more efficiency, more productivity, more profitability, and, of course, more value.

Conglomerate Merger

This occurs between companies in often unrelated industries that seek to create a diversified portfolio of companies intended to hedge against risk. This type of merger can create some operating efficiencies resulting from the combination of redundant departments.

WHY MERGE?

Mergers ultimately are driven by the quest for improved valuation. This goal manifests itself through the frequently used, and more often misunderstood, concept of synergy. Synergy in its purest form is based on a simple formula: Company A, when added to Company B, becomes Company AB, whose value or productivity exceeds that of the two individual parts treated as separate entities. In other words, 1 plus 1 equals 3.

For example, suppose Company A is valued at $20 billion and Company B is valued at $15 billion. The managers of the two companies believe that if they merge to create Company AB, they will achieve the following:

- Reduced operating expenses
- Better purchasing power with suppliers
- Tax benefits
- Lower costs of financing
- Stronger brand awareness
- Cross-promotional opportunities

If all goes according to plan, these changes should lead to increased profits, stronger growth, and ultimately better value for shareholders. In fact, if the market believes that this will be achieved, the combined market value of the merged entity may be substantially more than the $35 billion it would be if the two companies stayed separate. Thus, when two companies combine, they seek to create synergy that justifies the need to merge.

The goal of any merger is ultimately to create additional value for shareholders. Some of the specific opportunities that might lead to this are detailed here.

Utilize Surplus Funds

Cash-rich firms may use cash to fund acquisitions in an effort to generate long-term growth. It is a means by which they can rid themselves of excess cash while creating additional growth opportunities. For example, an oil service company may acquire a technologically strong logistics company with significant upside potential. The oil service company is working with a good deal of surplus cash, and by acquiring the logistics company, it improves its operating efficiency.

At the same time, cash-rich firms often become targets of takeovers from larger firms that are seeking to build steady, consistent cash flows. For example, a mining company may acquire a construction company with a steady cash flow to hedge against risky mining projects. The mining company is accustomed to significant ups and downs within the industry, and so to maintain steady reserves of cash, it may decide to acquire a construction company whose business is more predictable from a cash standpoint.

Eliminate Management Inefficiencies

The need or the decision to merge often stems from the goal of eliminating management inefficiencies. Acquisition often creates opportunities to eliminate certain management teams and replace them with new ones. In doing this, the expectation is that bringing on new management with fresh ideas will eliminate old inefficiencies. Quite often, the simple public relations impact of such a move is enough to create additional value for publicly traded companies.

Increase Revenues

Increases in revenue can arise from a number of sources, including better distribution, a diversified product mix, access to new markets, and access to new sales channels. Ultimately, anything resulting in a boost to the top line can be justification for a merger.

Decrease Costs and Expenses

A decrease in costs and expenses is the goal of virtually any type of merger. The decreases result from the greater efficiencies that occur through the consolidation of certain services. In many cases, the efficiencies arise from the consolidation of back-office operations such as office management, accounting, public relations, and marketing. By combining entities, companies very often eliminate inefficiencies and decrease overhead.

Create Production Efficiencies

Companies often seek a competitive advantage by optimizing the production process, and a merger is frequently the best way to achieve this. This can be facilitated through the efficient coordination of the administration or delivery of a certain business product or business unit. For example, a shipping company that leases ships may look to purchase or acquire a company that already owns those ships. This might eliminate some of the inefficiencies involved with the delivery of the leasing process.

Realize Tax Benefits

Of course, tax benefits often result from mergers. Tax gains provide powerful incentives, especially for multibillion-dollar corporations. Firms with net tax losses can be attractive targets for an acquirer with a significant tax burden. These tax losses or even tax credits can be used to offset the tax burden of the acquirer. Also, a firm with unused debt capacity can be an attractive takeover target because of the tax savings that result from additional debt financing. Also, sometimes there is an opportunity to write up certain depreciable assets. As was shown earlier in this book, tax deductions often are generated through additional depreciation.

Reduce Capital Expenditures

Mergers can reduce combined capital expenditure. If Firm A needs new manufacturing facilities and Firm B has excess manufacturing capacity, a merger may eliminate Firm A's capital requirements to build or expand. Mergers also can create working capital efficiencies for both firms. The merger may create more liquidity that could be used to pay off short-term debt or invest in much-needed infrastructure. Such moves could create additional value.

Lower Financing Costs

Mergers can lead to lower financing costs. When a company with a strong credit rating is acquired, the credit rating of the new entity will be better than that of the acquirer company. Therefore, this will help lower the overall cost of financing.

VALUATION

The reasons to merge outlined here may make strategic sense, and all it takes is a smooth-talking CEO with a minor in drama to impress the masses. However, convincing Wall Street is another story. Enter the bean counters. When cost savings and revenue enhancements resulting from a merger are projected, a detailed financial model can make the case for the merger. For example, in determining whether there is a justifiable reason to merge, the bean counters would look at present values for the proposed merged entity. The first step would be to forecast cash flows for the merged entity. If the present value of the merged entity's cash flow exceeds the current market values for the individual companies, they've got a good case for a merger.

Another way to assess the viability of a merger from a financial standpoint is to take the projected additional cash flows that would result from the merger and discount them to present value. The sum of those discounted cash flows is subtracted from the investment amount needed for the acquisition. This is a standard net present value calculation that was covered in Chapter 9. If the net present value is greater than zero, the merger makes sense. If it is less than zero, well ...

This can all be problematic if companies simply rely on this one type of analysis to justify their case. Many other assumptions are involved, some that are quantifiable and others that are not, such as management's ability to deliver the expected benefits.

Example

Suppose Firm A and Firm B are competitors. Both have after-tax cash flows of $100 per year and a cost of capital of 10 percent. Firm A decides to acquire Firm B with the expectation that the after-tax cash flows of the newly combined entity will be $210 per year. Does this merger make sense? In this example, analysts can see that the cash flows from the merged entity are $210 per year, whereas the combined cash flows of the separate firms equaled $200 a year. There is an incremental gain in cash flow of $10. The value of the merged firm, assuming that these cash flows stay constant and applying the perpetuity formula to value them, would be $2,100. If each part was valued separately, the combined value would be $2,000. Thus, when the firms are merged, an additional $100 in value is created. That value captures the synergy that was reflected in the incremental cash flow gain.

These are some of the types of analyses that would be used to determine whether this merger makes sense. Indeed, this is a somewhat simplistic look at merger analysis, but it sets forth the basic principles needed to determine financial viability.

DEFENSES

Any discussion of mergers and acquisitions requires some mention of the many defensive tactics that companies use to avoid being acquired. First, consider why a company's management might consider such defensive options. For starters, it might seek to extract a higher price from the acquiring company. At the same time, it could want to preserve jobs that would be lost if the merger went through. Or perhaps it simply is concerned with preserving the foundation and purpose of the company.

Company managers often consider the following options in crafting a defensive strategy.

Poison Pills

Poison pills work when existing shareholders are issued rights to purchase additional shares of stock in a company at a bargain price during a takeover attempt. This effectively creates a dilutive impact on the number of shares outstanding and makes it difficult for the acquiring company to take over the target company at a reasonable price.

Poison Puts

Poison puts occur when bondholders demand repayment if there is a change of control as a result of a hostile takeover. This effectively raises the overall price of the acquisition.

Golden Parachutes

Golden parachute payouts offer hefty compensation packages to corporate managers. This can dissuade a cost-conscious acquirer.

Supermajority

Supermajority provisions push a simple majority requirement for merger approval to upward of 80 percent of outstanding voting rights to approve a merger.

Pac-Man

The Pac-Man defense is modeled after the famous video game. A target company turns and acquires its would-be buyer.

Pac-Man Defense and Bendix

The best example of a Pac-Man defense in M&A history was the attempted hostile takeover of Martin Marietta by Bendix Corporation in 1982. At the time, Martin Marietta was a diversified corporate giant with holdings in aerospace, electronics, and cement, and Bendix was a leader in air navigation systems. In response to Bendix's hostile overtures, Martin Marietta started buying Bendix stock with the intention of assuming control over the company. Bendix simultaneously persuaded Allied Corporation to act as a white knight, and the company was sold to Allied the same year.

Greenmail and Mesa

In 1982, Mesa Petroleum, owned by Texas wildcat T. Boone Pickens, started acquiring shares of Cities Petroleum. To dissuade Pickens, Cities issued more shares of stock to dilute the current pool, making it more difficult for him to acquire control. Mesa then upped its bid for shares of Cities. Meanwhile, Cities decided to take the offensive and responded by making a bid for Mesa. In the end, Mesa pulled its bid for Cities and agreed not to make another bid for at least five years. Cities agreed to purchase the shares that Mesa originally acquired, earning Mesa an $80 million profit. Mesa went on to bid for Gulf and Phillips, each time losing but also earning sizable profits through buyback agreements. In total,

T. Boone Pickens made nearly $1 billion through failed takeover attempts and earned a reputation as the world's best greenmailer (someone who profits from a more refined form of blackmail).

MERGER OBSTACLES

Invariably, mergers face a number of obstacles, including compliance with regulatory bodies and the overriding difficulties of integrating distinct business cultures.

Legal Issues

One of the biggest impediments to an effective merger is the web of legal issues that can slow, if not halt, the entire merger process. Among other things, corporations must address the following issues when engaged in a merger:

- *Compliance with federal, state, or local statutes regarding antitrust issues.* In the United States, the Clayton Act prohibits a corporation from acquiring the assets of another company if that substantially "lessens competition or tends to create a monopoly." For example, acquiring suppliers or customers may close the market to competition or create an interindustry behemoth that eliminates new entrants. Similar principles are observed in larger overseas markets, and in fact, the European Union has blocked a number of high-profile mergers for these reasons.
- *Compliance with the DOJ and FTC.* Both the Department of Justice and the Federal Trade Commission can take an active role in determining whether a proposed merger could lead to issues of anticompetitiveness. The review process can be exhaustive and ultimately costly to all the parties involved.
- *SEC filings.* All proper documentation must be filed with the SEC in order for publicly traded companies to complete a merger or acquisition.

- *Employee benefits*. Because employee benefits often are altered in a merger or acquisition, the proper legal protocol must be observed to ensure that employees receive their granted benefits. Oversights in this area can lead to costly lawsuits.
- *Foreign ownership*. Federal law restricts ownership of certain assets by non-US entities. In particular, certain aircraft manufacturers, telecom facilities, newspapers, nuclear power plants, and defense businesses are subject to this regulation.

Integration Issues

Integrating a merger often creates insurmountable problems. Integration issues, in fact, have contributed to the failure of several large corporate mergers. It is not uncommon for a new merged entity to exhibit the following:

- Clashes among managers
- Loss of key employees
- Unforeseen costs
- Drop in employee morale
- Difficulty with systems integration

MERGERS GONE WILD

AOL–Time Warner:
Biggest Merger = Biggest Failure?

We do believe we're on the path of building what may be the most valuable company and most respected company in the world someday, and we're going to continue to focus on making that happen.

—Steve Case, former CEO, AOL–Time Warner, January 12, 2000

The largest corporate merger in history is becoming widely regarded as the biggest corporate failure in history—funny how that works. In 2001, AOL merged with Time Warner in a deal worth approximately $350 billion. The new company, AOL–Time Warner, brought forth the convergence of media, entertainment, and the Internet. Through the merger, AOL would gain access to Time Warner's broadband content delivery as well as content from magazines, movies, music, and television. Time Warner, after several failed Internet initiatives, would have access to AOL's 28 million subscribers. The story culminated in the eventual write-down of nearly $100 billion in goodwill, a painful reminder of how corporate mergers are all too often overvalued.

What happened? Among other things, the enormous size and scope of AOL–Time Warner (90,000 employees) proved difficult to manage. Specifically, the size of the new company proved unwieldy in responding to the characteristically rapid changes that occur in the Internet market. Additionally, merging a high-tech company with a media conglomerate created cultural issues, and failure to achieve economies of scope (i.e., cross-promotional marketing) proved costly. A number of analytical oversights that caused further problems included a poor assessment of Time Warner's broadband systems, which proved to be geographically limited, thus hampering AOL's expansion plans. Finally, both companies were overvalued during the tech bubble, and both suffered as a result of stock market correction.

Citi + Wachovia + Wells Fargo = Lovers' Triangle

One of the best lessons anyone can learn when entering the working world is to get everything in writing. In October 2008, the bank Wachovia was on the verge of becoming the next casualty of the global financial crisis. Overexposed to the mortgage-backed securities market, Wachovia was about to meet the same fate as many of its banking counterparts. Citigroup offered a deal to Wachovia that involved the US government and would guarantee a large portion of Wachovia's distressed assets. Citi's management and Wachovia's management seemed relieved that yet another crisis was being averted. A few days later, Wells Fargo surprised everyone when it announced that it had entered into a definitive merger agreement to acquire Wachovia at a much higher price than Citi's and with no government involvement. Both Wachovia's and Wells Fargo's stock prices rallied on the news, a clear indicator that the market was thrilled by the announcement. Citi, however, was not. It threatened to block the transaction but soon learned a very important lesson: even multibillion-dollar M&A deals need more than a handshake.

LEVERAGED BUYOUTS

Leveraged buyouts (LBOs) are essentially an extension of mergers and acquisitions, with the difference being that LBOs are acquisitions that are heavily financed through large amounts of debt. They gained prominence in the 1980s when companies issued heavy amounts of debt to acquire assets of seemingly undervalued companies. The goal of such transactions was that through an LBO, the target company could achieve some cost benefit or some level of efficiency. This strategy evolved over time to the point where the goal of an LBO became simply to achieve the highest return on investment in the shortest period. Nowadays, large private equity firms, or LBO shops, acquire distressed assets through the issuance of heavy amounts of debt with the intention of either revitalizing these assets or, quite often, selling them off piece by piece for higher returns at some point in the future.

LBOs traditionally were financed with high-yield (junk) bonds, which were at the time an easy source of financing, albeit a costly one. Typically, LBOs are financed with more than 50 percent senior bank debt, with a lesser portion of public debt and an even lesser portion of equity. In most LBOs, management not only takes an active interest in the structuring of the deal but often is involved in the ongoing management of the company.

The LBO Model
The LBO financial model involves some of the following inputs, among which is the purchase price of the overall asset. This is a key driver of the distribution between debt and equity. Unlike any other type of financial model, the actual split between debt and

equity becomes increasingly important because it dictates how much is returned to the investors.

The acquiring company also looks at the projected income statement and the balance sheet for the target company to see how the returns will affect the overall financial health of the company. Aside from the general returns, the overall financial impact on the balance sheet can affect the future sale price.

The LBO model is used to address the following questions:

- How much is a reasonable price to offer for the business?
- What percentage of the deal makes sense for the buyer?
- How sensitive are returns to performance targets?
- How will negative performance affect bank deals?
- If the business plateaus, how will this affect the overall returns?

In the next example, assume that a company has the opportunity to acquire a new store. This store costs $100 million. It is expected that this investment will generate cash flows of $8 million a year for the next five years. Further assume that this real estate value is expected to increase in value at a rate of 3 percent per year for each of the next five years. Finally, assume a discount rate of 10 percent. Based on these assumptions, what is the net present value (NPV) of this opportunity? Figure 12-1 shows the calculation.

FIGURE 12-1 Calculation of Net Present Value in the LBO Financial Model

NPV Calculation*

Year	0	1	2	3	4	5
Cash flows ($)	−100	8	8	8	8	124 (8 plus value of real estate after 5 years)
Present value ($)	−100.0	7.3	6.6	6.0	5.5	76.9
NPV ($)	2					
Discount rate	10%					

*Cash flow and NPV in millions.

In calculating NPV, first observe the cash flows in Figure 12-1. The acquiring company has a negative cash flow of $100 million in the current year. This is the amount of its initial investment. In subsequent years, there is the $8 million in cash flow achieved in years 1 through 5, plus the projected value of the store in year 5, which yields a total cash flow in year 5 of $124 million. A present value calculation can be based on a discount rate of 10 percent. In doing this, the resulting year 1 cash flow in present value terms is $7.3 million; year 2, $6.6 million; year 3, $6.0 million; year 4, $5.5 million; and year 5, the $8 million in cash flow plus the sale price of that real estate, which works out to a present value of $76.9 million. When these present value cash flows are added and the difference between the initial investment and these cash flows is taken, the net present value is $2 million.

Once the third variable, leverage, is introduced, the model is complete. What happens now if the acquirer can borrow 80 percent of the purchase price at an interest rate of 5 percent? Figure 12-2 shows the numbers. After that debt has been serviced, the net cash flow is reduced to $4 million per year. However, the initial investment is now only $20 million. Thus, the net present

---

FIGURE 12-2 Calculation of Net Present Value, Showing Leverage Variable, in the LBO Financial Model

- **Our net cash flows reduce to $4 million, but our initial investment is only $20 million.**
- **The opportunity reveals the power of leverage.**

NPV Calculation*

Year	0	1	2	3	4	5	
Cash flows ($)	−20	4	4	4	4	40	(4 plus value of real estate after 5 years less debt outstanding)
Present value ($)	−20.0	3.6	3.3	3.0	2.7	24.8	
NPV ($)	17						

Discount rate   10%
Of the $100 million purchase price, the company borrowed $80 million.
Cost of borrowing 5%.
Now, a $20 million investment becomes more compelling.

*Cash flow and NPV in millions.

value increases to $17 million. This reflects the power of leverage, which is a key driver in such transactions.

RJR Nabisco LBO

Perhaps the most famous leveraged buyout in history was the takeover of RJR Nabisco. In 1988, the RJR board revealed that F. Ross Johnson, the company's CEO, had formed an investor group that was seeking to acquire company stock for $75 per share. Johnson's group was backed by Shearson Lehman, which at the time was a subsidiary of American Express. Upon this announcement, RJR's stock price moved from $56 to $75, giving shareholders a 36 percent gain over its last stock price. Once the company was in play, a number of other investors arrived. In fact, that initial bid of $75 was trumped by KKR's offer of $90, which included $79 in cash plus $11 in preferred stock. One month later, bidding closed. At that time, KKR had raised its bid to $109—$81 of which was based on cash, another $10 of which was based on convertible subordinate debentures, and $18 of which was pre-ferred stock. Johnson's group offered more, $112 in cash and securities.

Yet the RJR board eventually chose KKR. Why? The board believed that Johnson's valuations were softer and used loose assumptions. Furthermore, KKR's asset sales were less severe. What KKR had projected, as is the case in many leveraged buy-outs, was the sale of certain assets to boost cash flows and pay down debt. Furthermore, KKR's operational plan tended to be more efficient. Finally, the board believed that Johnson's manage-ment compensation was overly generous.

How could this move from $56 per share just before the first announcement to $109 per share be justified? KKR and other investors were betting on the benefits from certain interest tax shields, lower capital expenditure, and the sale of certain assets. In fact, the asset sales were expected to generate some $5 billion alone, and some of this included the sale of the corporate jets, affectionately termed the "RJR Air Force."

Amazon and Whole Foods Merger

2017 was the year of Amazon. The company made global conquest look easy. And investors responded favorably. Amazon's stock price continued to plow higher making Amazon shareholders and its founder very happy. But was this increase in valuation justified? It depends on how you measure valuation.

Amazon's purchase of Whole Foods is a good example of how Amazon created synergy through cross-platform sales. Amazon's massive online marketplace would be able to sell Whole Foods' products, while shoppers would be able to make purchases online and pick them up in a Whole Foods store. Amazon's online/in-store combo approach to grocery shopping disrupts the traditional notions around the grocery shopping experience. But does it create value?

As we discussed, the value of a company is based on the sum of the present value of future cash flows. For the Amazon–Whole Foods deal to create lasting value, Amazon will need to create stronger sales, higher margins, and greater profits. Most of all the result of such a deal should produce strong cash flows that grow significantly for years to come. If Amazon is able to demonstrate success in these areas, the company will be able to justify its lofty value based on nearly any valuation methodology.

13

CURRENCY

In my younger days, I experienced the complexities of international currency exchange through intensive research and practical application. I eventually learned not only how to manage currency fluctuations but also how to profit from them. For example, I learned that nearly identical products sold in different countries can have major price differences when currency exchange is factored into the equation. Furthermore, I realized that directional shifts in currency exchange rates could allow one to hedge against, or even profit from, those shifts. My extensive study of those markets led me to achieve the ultimate currency arbitrage when I scored a better deal buying the CD *ABBA Oro* with pesos than buying the CD *ABBA Gold* with dollars. Of course, I had to hire someone to translate the lyrics for me, which effectively wiped out any gains from the currency play.

Throughout this book we have discussed various accounting concepts, asset classes, and valuation methodologies, yet we have hardly touched on a concept that affects nearly every aspect of finance. In a global economy, currency plays a pivotal role in the way transactions are structured. From investment banking to corporate management, currency is involved in nearly all international financial decisions. As the global economy becomes more complex, currency issues will continue to evolve.

This chapter will discuss the following:

- Currency exchange rates
- Exchange rate systems
- Currency trading

CURRENCY EXCHANGE RATES

The country of Sweden is known for its amazing contributions to global consumer markets, including fine automobiles, do-it-yourself furniture, and meatballs. Through massive distribution networks and efficient transfers of capital, the country ranks among the world's best in export-led growth. With the advantages of selling to the world come the challenges of managing global finance. Specifically, currency plays a prominent role in the way Swedish businesses conduct their business and to whom they sell. Swedish financial managers must develop currency strategies to manage their receivables and payables. For example, if the krona drops, it could hurt a Swedish company whose receivables are denominated in kronor. If the krona increases in value, it could raise the company's manufacturing costs and perhaps cause management to consider moving its manufacturing facilities abroad. Shifts in currency exchange rates can affect how much a company ultimately earns; therefore, a solid understanding of currency will allow management to craft an effective strategy to address unexpected shifts.

Determining the Exchange Rate

The exchange rate of any currency is its price. In other words, it indicates how much of one currency is needed to buy one unit of another currency. Suppose you are planning to take a trip to Japan. You currently reside in the United States and therefore need to exchange your US dollars for Japanese yen. You must consider how many yen a dollar will purchase. Suppose it takes 1 dollar to purchase 80 yen. The value of 1 dollar would be 80 yen. The value of one yen in dollars therefore would be 0.0125 dollar (1 dollar/80 yen). The trillion-dollar question is, How is this value determined? In other words, what causes that 1 dollar to equal

80 yen and 1 yen to equal 0.0125 dollar? To answer this, think of a unit of currency as an asset.

For example, to determine the exchange rate between US dollars and Japanese yen, it might be helpful to consider the price of a US dollar if you bought it with yen. The price depends on the intersection between the supply curve and the demand curve for a particular currency. I know, you thought this was a finance book, not an economics book. I'll do my best to keep you awake during this part, but unfortunately, currency is no different from anything else that is bought or sold, and therefore economic principles determine its price. A currency's price is based on the price at which demand for that currency equals supply of that currency. This is known as the equilibrium exchange rate. Simply put, supply and demand curves determine this, and where supply meets demand is where we find the equilibrium exchange rate.

For any given price of yen quoted in dollars, there is an associated supply of yen and an associated demand for yen. As you might imagine, changes in supply and demand affect the exchange rate. In Figure 13-1, you will notice the upward-sloping supply curve. This tells us that holders of yen are more likely to supply yen to the market because of the favorable exchange rate. Of course, when the value of the yen is weak, holders of yen are less likely to supply yen to the market. Someone holding yen would prefer to

FIGURE 13-1 Currency Supply and Demand

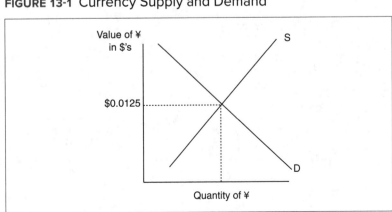

offer the yen to the market at a higher value than at a lower value. Thus, the supply of the currency increases when the value of the currency is strong. This incentivizes Japanese consumers and corporations to supply more yen to the market as they are interested in exchanging the yen for dollars. When the yen is strong, they can buy more American products for the same amount of yen and are therefore more likely to exchange yen for dollars to fund those purchases.

The demand curve for the currency is downward-sloping, meaning that buyers tend to demand more of something when its price is lower. In other words, when the value of yen is lower, buyers of yen demand more, and when the value of yen is higher, buyers should demand less. For example, Americans would be more likely to exchange their dollars for yen when the value of the yen is lower. This enables American consumers and corporations to buy more Japanese products at a lower price. Of course, when the value of yen is higher, demand for yen will be lower as Americans are less likely to exchange their dollars for yen as Japanese products are now more expensive.

Currency Quotes

Currency exchange rates are quoted in terms of a bid price and an ask price.

USD/JPY
Last Trade: 80.1
Change: 0.1800 (0.22 percent)
Bid: 80.0100
Ask: 80.2200
Previous close: 79.92000
Open: 80.3300
Day's range: 79.9650–80.4050
52-week range: 76.5700–91.6254

The quote in this box lists the following:

- *Last trade:* the most recent trade price
- *Change in price:* the increase or decrease from the prior day's close
- *Bid:* the highest price the buyer is willing to pay to purchase the currency
- *Ask:* the lowest price the seller is willing to accept for the currency
- *Previous closing price:* yesterday's closing price
- *Open price:* today's open price
- *Day range:* high and low prices for the day
- *52-week range:* high and low prices for the year

Cross Exchange Rates

Most exchange rate tables quote prices against a base currency. For example, a dollar-based table would quote rates in terms of dollar-euro, dollar–Swiss franc, and so on. Suppose you ran a business in Japan and expected to receive payments from your customers in yen. Each yen-denominated payment would be deposited in a Swiss bank account. To decide whether such an arrangement makes sense, you would consider the cross exchange rate for yen to Swiss francs. Consider the following:

$$1 \text{ USD} = 80 \text{ JPY or } 1 \text{ JPY} = 0.0125 \text{ USD}$$

$$1 \text{ USD} = 0.82 \text{ CHF (Swiss franc) or } 1 \text{ CHF} = 1.22 \text{ USD}$$

In this particular example, the cross exchange rate would be

$$\text{(Value of 1 JPY in USD) (Value of 1 CHF in USD)} =$$
$$\$0.0125/\$1.22 = 0.01 \text{ JPY to } 1 \text{ CHF}$$

Although cross exchange rate calculations can seem tedious, exchange rate tables simplify them.

Factors That Affect Currency Exchange Rates

The following factors have a direct impact on exchange rates.

Relative Inflation

Consider what might happen if the United States experiences higher inflation relative to Japan. US goods become more costly than Japanese goods, and as a result, American consumers will demand Japanese substitutes. This will increase the demand for Japanese yen needed to purchase Japanese products. At the same time, the supply of yen for sale probably will decrease as Japanese holders of yen are less likely to buy American products, which are now more expensive. The increased demand for yen and the decreased supply of yen will push the price of yen higher.

Interest Rates

If US interest rates rise relative to Japanese interest rates, the supply of yen for sale will increase as more holders of yen will want to purchase dollars to earn more interest in dollars. As a result, the value of yen will decrease. Furthermore, the demand for yen should decrease because investors would rather deposit their money in American banks and therefore will demand dollars more than yen. The decrease in demand combined with the increase in supply will cause a drop in the value of yen as a result of rising interest rates in the United States.

Income

If income levels in the United States increase while income levels in Japan remain unchanged, demand for Japanese goods should increase along with yen. The shift in relative income is not likely to affect the supply of yen as a change in US income levels will do little to incentivize Japanese yen holders to exchange more yen for dollars. The increase in demand therefore should raise the exchange rate as American consumers probably will buy more Japanese products overall.

Speculation

Speculators can cause dramatic movements in currency prices. They may base their trades on economic predictions or in some cases on expectations of what other high-volume traders will do next. As more market participants move in tandem, currency values are often driven less by economic fundamentals and more by momentum traders.

Government

By imposing trade barriers and foreign exchange barriers, governments can affect currency values indirectly. They do this by making it more difficult for foreign businesses to engage in import and export activity, which in turn will affect supply and demand for currency. At the same time, a government can buy or sell its country's currency, which will affect its supply and ultimately its value. Government policy changes, however, may not achieve the desired outcome when it pertains to currency...or anything else for that matter.

Interaction of Factors

Any combination of these factors can affect currency in unpredictable ways. I wish I could give you a better explanation, but if I could predict precisely how a combination of factors will affect currency values, I would be busy trading currency from my private island instead of writing books.

EXCHANGE RATE SYSTEMS

The factors discussed so far in this chapter clearly affect the movement of exchange rates, but they are largely dependent on the type of exchange rate system that is in place. Consumers, business managers, and governments depend on these systems and must recognize the risks inherent in each one.

Floating Exchange Rate System

A floating exchange rate system is based on the notion that market forces, as opposed to government policy, determine currency exchange. Buyers and sellers of a currency determine the price, with the bid price being the price at which the currency can be sold and the ask price being the price at which it can be purchased. Buyers and sellers can include traders, fund managers, banks, multinational corporations, and governments.

Although a floating system leaves the process of determining exchange rates to market forces, those forces can force a currency to collapse. If a major fund assumes a short position in a particular currency, it can push that currency, and in turn the underlying economy, to the verge of collapse. Suppose a major hedge fund decides to take a multibillion-dollar short position on the Costa Rican colón. It does this through a series of large trades distributed over several days. Other traders sense economic doom on the horizon as they witness these trades and decide that they too must unload positions in the colón. The colón drops 1 percent, 3 percent, 5 percent. Now businesses based in Costa Rica are forced to contend with decreased buying power as a result of the declining colón. If a corporation based in Costa Rica is buying component parts from the United States, those parts just became a heck of a lot more expensive thanks to currency speculators. The currency drop continues, and soon everyone is panicking. Before long, major corporations and individuals must cut spending as foreign-produced items are more expensive than before. This can prove disruptive and in extreme cases disastrous. Such examples are far from regular occurrences, and in many countries, including Costa Rica, government-imposed exchange limits will prevent a complete currency collapse caused by speculation. Nonetheless, this example illustrates what could happen when currency speculation takes on a life of its own in a floating system.

Fixed Exchange Rate System

A fixed rate currency system is one in which exchange rates are static or move within a very tight range. To facilitate this, the central bank of a country must adjust monetary policy frequently to prevent major shifts in its currency's value. In extreme cases, the central bank may revalue or devalue (increase or decrease the value of) the currency. The advantages of a fixed system include the fact that it minimizes speculation and enables businesses conducting transactions in that currency to do so without the risk of major fluctuations. Importers and exporters can structure transactions with foreign counterparts without fear of currency fluctuations undermining the economics of the transaction. Investors allocating funds to a foreign country need not worry about their returns eroding because of currency fluctuations. Overall, the theory behind the fixed rate system is that it stimulates economic activity by minimizing the risk of significant fluctuations in exchange rates.

With the good comes the bad. A major problem with a fixed system is that it may not reflect the real value of a currency relative to another currency accurately. This can cause economic problems to spread. If inflation runs rampant in a country where the currency exchange rate is fixed against another country's currency, major economic disruptions can occur. For example, if the United States and Japan are locked in a fixed rate system and the United States experiences high inflation, American consumers will buy more Japanese goods, which are priced relatively lower than American goods. With excess demand for Japan's goods, prices could move higher, causing inflation in Japan. In essence, the US inflation could spread to Japan. Eventually, the fixed system could collapse. The Japanese would have inherited problems from a weak American economy. For holders of the yen, such a move could prove disastrous. Imagine waking up one morning to find that all the money you tucked away safely in the bank is now worth half as much as it was the night before. Although this type of occurrence is rare, it can happen in a fixed currency system.

Other Systems

The fixed and floating currency systems generally explain the broader framework of currency exchange. However, modified systems also exist. For example, a pegged system is based on fixing the home currency value to another currency or an index of currencies. A managed float system is a floating system that allows for occasional government intervention. In other words, it's a "have your cake and eat it too" system. Of course, the simplest system is the dollarized one in which the dollar replaces the local currency. This system allows a country to outsource the currency management process to the United States of America.

CURRENCY TRADING

Currency can be traded much like securities or as derivatives. The purposes for trading vary but generally can be distilled down to either speculation or hedging.

Currency Speculation

Currency speculation can be a lucrative pursuit for skilled traders. By analyzing macroeconomic variables such as inflation, interest rates, income levels, and governmental policies, currency traders can place bets on a currency with the hope of profiting from them. Currency speculation can be complicated by the combination of market forces, the outcome of which can be difficult to predict. Suppose Trader Joe decides he wants to bet on the euro because he believes the European Central Bank will raise interest rates. At the same time, countries across the European Union are reporting substantial increases in inflation. Now Trader Joe learns that one of the largest currency hedge funds is selling its position in the euro. The moral to this story: currency trading is complicated.

There is no foolproof algorithm for predicting what will happen to a particular currency as a result of movements in influential variables. Although some traders have a fairly good idea of what might happen, and their compensation generally reflects this, no one can predict the direction currency will take 100 percent of the time. And if someone does have that ability, please get in touch with me as I would be delighted to work for him or her as an unpaid intern.

Currency Hedging

Currency hedging is a practice that can be employed by anyone taking a relatively large speculative position in a currency or by a business seeking to manage risk. Suppose Car-E-Oki starts buying parts from a supplier in Europe. Part payments are made in euros and are due 30 days after receipt of the parts. The euro seems to be rising against the dollar, which leaves Car-E-Oki rather vulnerable. In fact, if the euro rises significantly by the time payment is due, it could wipe out a good portion of Car-E-Oki's expected profits. What can the company do? Several protective hedging strategies discussed in Chapter 11 present themselves:

1. *Options.* Buy calls on euros. If the euro rises, the call becomes worth more, offsetting the increased payment amount owed to the supplier. The downside of this strategy is that calls come at a price.
2. *Forwards.* Car-E-Oki can structure a forward contract to lock in a specific exchange rate, thus hedging from any exchange rate fluctuations. The forward rate would be the specified exchange rate at which the currency will be exchanged.
3. *Futures.* Car-E-Oki can purchase a currency future requiring a standard amount of currency to be exchanged at a specific exchange rate on a specific settlement date. Car-E-Oki could purchase the future on an exchange, enabling the company to sell the future if rates hold or reverse.

Now suppose Car-E-Oki sells its products in Europe and payments are made in euros. The company stopped buying parts from Europe and now merely exports its products to Europe. Sales are often credit-based, leaving the company with hefty accounts receivable. What happens if these credit payments are owed 30 days after the customer takes possession? If the euro fell against the dollar, the company would see its profits erode. Hedging strategies can be employed by using the tools mentioned previously:

1. *Options.* Buy puts on euros. If the euro falls, the puts become worth more, offsetting the decreased payment amount owed to the company by its customers.
2. *Forwards.* Just as before, Car-E-Oki could create a forward contract to lock in the rate received from its customers.
3. *Futures.* Car-E-Oki could purchase dollar futures. If the euro declines against the dollar, the dollar future will increase, offsetting any loss of value on the receivable.

Currency Arbitrage

Chapter 11 introduced the topic of arbitrage, which allows an investor or trader to capitalize on pricing discrepancies. Arbitrage is used widely in the currency markets and usually takes on the following forms.

Locational Arbitrage

Locational arbitrage is based on the idea that one can buy currency at one location and sell it immediately at another location, instantaneously locking in a profit. In other words, a pricing discrepancy in the market allows for this. Consider the following:

Dollar to pound exchange rate: $1.5 to £1

You can buy pounds for $1.52 at Bank A, where the bid is $1.51 and the ask is $1.52. You can sell pounds at Bank B, where the bid is $1.53 and the ask is $1.54. With minimal effort and cost, you should be able to earn $0.01 by buying pounds at A and then selling them at B (paying the ask of $1.52 and receiving the bid of $1.53). What's the catch? As was discussed in Chapter 11, arbitrage opportunities are generally short-lived, so you have to act fast, and usually the market corrects itself quickly.

Triangular Arbitrage

Things become more interesting with triangular arbitrage. What if you could buy dollars with pounds, exchange the dollars for euros, and then exchange the euros back to dollars, earning a tidy profit during this round trip? Not bad.

Suppose the bank quotes you the following:

- Dollar to pound: £0.61
- Dollar to euro: €0.70
- Pound to euro: €1.15

To determine whether a triangular arbitrage opportunity exists, you first would determine the cross exchange rate by dividing the USD-to-euro rate by the USD-to-GBP rate. This would give you a cross exchange rate, GBP to euro, of €1.14, as shown in Figure 13-2. This tells you that the bank is offering too many euros for pounds, which means the arbitrage opportunity does indeed exist. For example, on the basis of the quoted rates, you could do the following:

FIGURE 13-2 Cross Exchange Rate Table

	USD	GBP	EURO
USD	1.00	0.61	0.70
GBP	1.64	1.00	1.15
Euro	1.43	0.87	1.00

1. Use $1,000 to purchase €610 ($1,000 × 0.61).
2. Buy £701.5 with your €610 (€610 × 1.15).
3. Convert £701.5 back to $1,002.14 (£701.5/.70).

In this transaction, you earned a profit of $2.14 because the bank overstated the cross exchange rate. You were able to capitalize on this and earned a profit in the process.

There you have it: Currency 101. Although it's not rocket science, it can feel like it at times. Perhaps the biggest problem currency market players face is not understanding why currency exchange rates move in a particular direction when the factors affecting currency indicate something else. Unfortunately, the driving forces behind currency do not always indicate a definitive outcome; that is why currency trading is not for the faint of heart.

14

REAL ESTATE

My first experience with real estate placed me at the epicenter of high-powered deal making. I recall being seated at the head of the deal table, negotiating the sale of a property to an aggressive buyer. The buyer was keenly focused on developing the property by building first houses and then hotels. Negotiations were heated, and things got ugly when he realized financing was not an option, a problem compounded by the fact that his other properties were plagued by low rents. Compromise was not an option as it became clear that this was a winner-take-all scenario. Things reached a breaking point when he walked away from the deal, leaving me with Park Place (he kept Boardwalk).

This chapter will discuss the following:

- Real estate valuation
- Calculating real estate returns
- REITs
- Mortgage-backed securities
- Lehman

REAL ESTATE VALUATION

Real estate is one of the broadest areas of investing, incorporating elements from many other areas of finance. It distills finance down to its most basic components, which in the aggregate can be highly complex. Whether it's residential or commercial, rental or development, real estate affects Main Street and Wall Street alike. To understand what drives real estate finance, it's important to consider the ways to value real estate. As we learned earlier in this book, market value ultimately boils down to what someone is willing to pay for something. This certainly holds true in real estate. As is the case with most assets, the question becomes: How does one arrive at the point of agreement? Real estate valuation is similar in many aspects to most other areas of valuation.

Cost Method

The cost method of valuing real estate is very similar to the cost method used in valuing any asset. It seeks an answer to the question, What would it cost me to build this from scratch? In real estate, one might consider the cost of land, construction labor, materials, and so on to determine the overall project cost. This method falls short because it fails to consider what the market might perceive the value to be. Clearly, the completed project is worth more than the sum of its parts. This method, however, can be helpful in determining a project's breakeven point. In other words, if the total cost of a project is $1 million, a developer probably will consider how long it would take to return that amount to investors on the basis of what the project is expected to earn.

Comparable Multiple Method

Perhaps the fastest way to gauge the value of a property is to consider what similar properties sell for. If you decide to sell your home, the first step in determining an offer price is to consider what your neighbor just sold her home for. Careful attention must be paid to building a truly comparable list. Including luxury high-rises in the mix along with student housing doesn't build a case for a credible multiple or provide a buyer or seller with an objective price estimate. To build a solid set of comparables, items such as location, size, and amenities should be consistent within the mix.

Sales Comparison Approach

Recent sales within a neighborhood can form a useful valuation proxy. For example, suppose three buildings on one block were sold recently. In Figure 14-1, we calculate the average price per square foot in the three sales, which works out to $163. If the target property has 1,800 square feet, an appropriate price would be:

FIGURE 14-1 Sales Comparison Table

SALE PRICE	SQUARE FOOTAGE	PRICE/SQUARE FOOT
$300,000	2,000	$150
$275,000	1,500	$183
$340,000	2,200	$155
	Avg. Price/Sq. Ft.	$163

$$163/\text{sq. ft.} \times 1,800 \text{ sq. ft.} = \$293,400$$

This may not be the price you want to pay if you are buying the property or the price you want to accept if you are selling the property, but it gives you a reasonable starting point to consider.

Income Capitalization Approach

This is one of the most popular methods for valuing income-generating properties. The most important variable in this model is what is called the capitalization rate (cap rate), which is net operating income (NOI) divided by property value. NOI in real estate is like operating income in any business. It generally is based on a property's income before interest and taxes. Income-generating properties can be measured on the basis of multiples of NOI. For example, suppose NOI is on average approximately 10 percent of recent sale prices in a particular neighborhood (similar properties report NOI that amounts to 10 percent of their value). To put it another way, the cap rate gives us the expected rate of return on our property. If the annual NOI on a target property is $20,000, its value would be $200,000 ($2,000/0.10).

Discounted Cash Flow Method

The discounted cash flow (DCF) method in real estate is based on the idea that to value a piece of property, you must calculate the present value of future cash flows. Think back to the valuation examples in Chapter 9, where we learned that the value of any asset is the sum of the present values of future cash flows. This principle applies to property values as well. If we consider an apartment building that generates rental income, we can value it on the basis of projected NOI. To form those projections, we might consider variables such as monthly rents, occupancy rates, and expenses, to name a few. We also might assume a sale of the property at some point in the future. The assumptions will form projections that ultimately will produce a NOI number for each year. This number will be discounted to present value by using the present value formula:

$$PV = NOI/(1 + r)^n$$

The sum of these present values is the value of the building. Consider the following example: You are interested in purchasing Building A, which has the following attributes:

- Monthly rent: $1,000 (with a 3 percent annual increase)
- Number of units: 25
- Average yearly occupancy: 75 percent
- Operating expenses: 40 percent of gross rents
- Required rate of return/discount rate: 7 percent
- Terminal value: year 5 NOI/cap rate (assumes you sell the property at the price determined by this multiple)

Using these assumptions, we will project five years of NOI. In the fifth year, we will assume that the building is sold on the basis of the projected cap rate. Each year's NOI number, along with the sale amount, is discounted to present value, and the sum of the present values offers a good indication of the building's value.

There are a number of problems associated with this method, such as the following:

1. Real estate is cyclical, and projecting rent increases can be problematic.
2. The discount rate often is based on market rates at times when market conditions shift.
3. It can be difficult to form projections because unforeseen capital improvements invariably arise.

Nonetheless, this method is helpful in that it provides another means of price comparison. If nothing else, it can create dialogue between buyer and seller at the deal table and allow them to reach an agreement (see Figure 14-2).

FIGURE 14-2 Discounted Cash Flow Model

	YEAR 1	YEAR 2	YEAR 3	YEAR 4	YEAR 5	TERMINAL VALUE
Monthly Rent/Unit	$1,000	$1,030	$1,061	$1,093	$1,126	
Annual Rent/Unit	$12,000	$2,360	$12,732	$13,116	$13,512	
Number of Units	25	25	25	25	25	
Avg. Occupancy	75%	75%	75%	75%	75%	
Total Rent	$225,000	$231,750	$238,725	$245,925	$253,350	
Expenses (40% of Rent)	$90,000	$92,700	$95,490	$98,370	$101,340	
Total Operating Expenses	$90,000	$92,700	$95,490	$98,370	$101,340	
Pretax Cash Flow/NOI	$135,000	$139,050	$143,235	$147,555	$152,010	$1,689,000
Present Value	$126,168	$121,452	$116,922	$112,569	$108,381	$1,204,234
Sum of PV Cash Flows	$1,789,726					
Terminal Value Cap Rate Year 5	9%					
Discount Rate/ Required Rate of Return	7%					

CALCULATING REAL ESTATE RETURNS

Although understanding whether a property is fairly priced is important, understanding the expected returns on the property is just as important. In real estate, there are several ways to do this.

Cash on Cash

Cash on cash returns assess the return on investment on the basis of the amount of cash invested to purchase the property. It usually is based on the following formula:

Cash on cash ROI = pretax cash flow/cash investment

Pretax cash flow in real estate can be based on NOI minus the mortgage payment, although some real estate analysts may use a variation of this. The cash invested is the amount of cash invested to purchase the property (not including the amount financed).

Consider the following: We purchase a property for $1,000,000. Our cash investment is $200,000, and our mortgage is $800,000. Suppose our annual NOI is $135,000 and our annual mortgage payment (principal and interest) is around $40,000. This number will be sensitive to the duration of the mortgage, the monthly payments, and the interest rate. Keep in mind that the interest portion decreases gradually as the principal is paid each month; in turn, the principal portion increases. In most conventional mortgages, the monthly payment remains constant. In our example, we would subtract the $40,000 principal and interest from the NOI, which would give us our pretax cash flow of $95,000. Since we invested $200,000, our cash on cash ROI would be as follows: cash on cash ROI = $95,000/$200,000 = 47.5 percent.

Total Return on Investment

Total ROI offers a more comprehensive overview of what a property returns by incorporating not only pretax cash flows but proceeds from the property sale as well.

The formula is:

$$\text{Total ROI} = (\text{pretax cash flow} + \text{sales proceeds} - \text{initial cash investment})/\text{initial cash investment}$$

Building on this example, let's assume that we sold the property for $1,200,000 three years from now. At that point, our mortgage balance would be around $762,000. Our selling expenses, including taxes and broker fees, would amount to about 8 percent of the sale price, or $96,000. Our net sales proceeds would be $1,200,000 (sale price) − $762,000 (mortgage balance) − $96,000 (selling expenses) = $342,000 (sales proceeds).

Finally, let's assume that total pretax cash flow for the three years is $285,000 ($95,000 NOI/year × 3 years). Our Total ROI would be the following: total ROI = [$285,000 (pretax cash flow) + $342,000 (sales proceeds) − $200,000 (initial investment)]/$200,000 = 213.5 percent. Not a bad return for three years. Keep in mind that several aspects of this deal proved favorable. First, the appreciation over three years was substantial. Second, NOI was relatively stable. Third, the cost of financing was low. All in all, this proved to be a lucrative deal and the type that most real estate investors dream of. The reality, however, is that any number of factors can hurt the total ROI.

REITS

A corporation generates profit and pays its taxes on the profit, and what is left over is divided between retained earnings (investment back into the company) and dividends paid to the shareholders. The dividends paid to the shareholders are now subject to individual taxes. Real estate investment trusts (REITs) are real estate investment vehicles designed to avoid double taxation. Generally, REITs are investment funds that purchase income-producing properties. Each year, a REIT must distribute a substantial percentage of its taxable income to shareholders in the form of a dividend. This structure reduces or eliminates corporate income taxes. The shareholder pays tax on the distribution, and the REIT itself pays little to no tax and therefore maximizes returns.

REITs are similar in nature to mutual funds, with the primary difference being that mutual funds invest in stocks and REITs invest in real estate. In Figure 14-3, we can review the performance of a REIT at three points in time based on the following performance metrics:

FIGURE 14-3 REIT Analysis

	YEAR 1	YEAR 3	YEAR 5
Assets			
Gross Assets	$10,000,000	$10,000,000	$10,000,000
Less Accumulated Depreciation	$ –	$1,500,000	$2,500,000
Net Assets	**$10,000,000**	**$8,500,000**	**$7,500,000**
Revenues	**$2,000,000**	**$2,000,000**	**$2,000,000**
Operating Expenses	$800,000	$800,000	$800,000
Interest Expense	$300,000	$300,000	$300,000
Depreciation Expense	$500,000	$500,000	$500,000
Total Operating Expenses	**$1,600,000**	**$1,600,000**	**$1,600,000**
Net Income	**$400,000**	**$400,000**	**$400,000**
FFO (NI + Depreciation – Gain on Property Sales)			
NI	$400,000	$400,000	$400,000
Depreciation	$500,000	$500,000	$500,000
Gain on Property Sales	$ –	$ –	$ –
FFO	**$900,000**	**$900,000**	**$900,000**

NAV ANALYSIS		
FFO	$900,000	NI + depreciation – gain on property sales
NOI	$1,200,000	FFO + interest
Cap Rate	8%	Based on market averages of NOI/Property Value
Market Value	$15,000,000	Capitalize NOI based on cap rate
Less Debt	$5,000,000	Mortgage principal outstanding
NAV	$10,000,000	Market value less debt
No Shares	1,000,000	Number shares outstanding
Capital Expenditures	200,000	
CAD	700,000	

- *Net asset value (NAV).* NAV is based on the notion that the book value will not necessarily reflect market value in real estate. As a result, NAV seeks to capture the market value by first dividing the NOI by the cap rate. From there, any debt outstanding is subtracted to come up with NAV. NAV then can be divided by the total number of shares outstanding to come up with the fair value of the common shares (the actual share price should be close to this).

- *Funds from operations (FFO).* FFO is calculated by taking net income and adding back depreciation and subtracting any gains on the sale of property. In real estate, depreciation is included in various income calculations, but when it comes to FFO, the belief is that property rarely loses value. Whether you believe this is up to you, but as it stands, FFO is the primary performance measure when it comes to REITs.
- *Cash available for distribution (CAD).* CAD is based on FFO minus any recurring capital expenditures. This forms a general approximation of cash on hand and could be distributed to shareholders in the form of a dividend.

MORTGAGE-BACKED SECURITIES

It's no secret that the financial world developed elaborate ways to profit from a booming global real estate market. The advent of mortgage-backed securities proved an effective way to capitalize on that boom. Investment bankers around the world were eager to structure complex financial instruments backed by pools of mortgages. Those instruments, as was discussed in Chapter 11, sometimes were termed collateralized debt obligations (CDOs) and were traded across the financial world. When they were actively traded, assigning a value to them was easy to do as they generally were based on the most recent purchase price. However, when signs of a housing collapse emerged, the appetite for CDOs dissipated, leaving far fewer buyers than sellers. At that point, valuing them became more a function of bold assumptions used in financial models and less a function of what the market believed those instruments were worth.

LEHMAN

In 1844, Henry Lehman opened a dry goods store in Alabama. A few years later, the German émigré was joined by his brothers, and Lehman Brothers was formed. As the brothers often accepted payments in cotton, they amassed significant enough stockpiles of the commodity to form a secondary market for it. The business was relocated to New York City to be closer to the cotton exchange. At that point, Lehman officially had become a commodities trading firm. In the early twentieth century, the company underwrote several major initial public offerings (IPOs) and began making venture capital investments in early-stage companies. Throughout the twentieth century, Lehman continued to expand its domain in financial services. The firm would merge with another investment company before being sold to American Express, which took it public in 1994. By the start of the new millennium, Lehman was a global financial powerhouse with particular strengths in fixed income investments.

The Lehman story began to unravel when the company got involved with the subprime mortgage market. Subprime mortgages were offered to individuals with poor credit, and those individuals were considered to be high-risk borrowers. The mortgages, backed by residential and commercial real estate, were bundled into CDOs. As the market for those instruments started to collapse, Lehman was forced to write down the values of those assets. Investors grew wary of Lehman stock as they watched the company's balance sheet weaken. As the year progressed, it became clear that Lehman was headed for disaster. In August 2008, the Korea Development Bank contemplated a bid for the company but eventually passed. Investor confidence in Lehman continued to erode, and after other banks chose to pass on Lehman, its fate was sealed. On September 14, 2008, the International Swaps and Derivatives Association offered an extra trading session to allow traders to structure trades to manage the risks associated with a Lehman bankruptcy. In the early morning of September 15, it was announced that Lehman would file for Chapter 11 bankruptcy.

The implications of the Lehman bankruptcy were significant. At the very least, it unleashed a spell of fear and uncertainty, causing the financial markets to decline significantly in the coming months. It raised the question: If Lehman failed, who would be next? More important, it raised questions about Lehman's accounting procedures and what that meant in terms of investor disclosure. Specifically, Lehman listed a technique as Repo 105, allowing it to exchange $50 billion worth of assets for cash just before finalizing its quarterly financials. This allowed the company to overstate its cash and in essence create a misleading level of liquidity. Additionally, the company's use of mark-to-market accounting allowed it to value a significant portion of its assets on the basis of fair market value. When the market for those assets nearly froze, valuing them became a challenge.

What Happened?

Lehman's overexposure to subprime mortgages and the catastrophic decline in values of the securities based on those instruments caused a severe weakening of Lehman's financial statements. As individual home ownership and mortgage issuances reached all-time highs, banks such as Lehman sought to capitalize on that growth through the purchase of CDOs. As the CDOs possessed varying risk levels, some of them were more prone to default. Of course, the riskier ones offered higher rates of return (the greater the risk, the greater the reward). One can imagine the CDOs as a massive debt-based portfolio valued off future cash flows generated from interest payments.

The problem, however, was the fact that default rates were unrealistically low. Few considered the fact that many of the higher-risk mortgages were adjustable-rate mortgages, meaning that they offered low teaser rates that later increased. Because of this, default rates increased. On top of it all, firms such as Lehman purchased CDOs with borrowed funds, in some cases leveraging their position 30 to 1. In other words, every $1 paid purchased $30 of CDOs. All would have been fine if real estate prices had continued to increase. When real estate values are on the rise, even high-risk borrowers can refinance their adjustable-rate mortgages. Unfortunately, what goes up must come down.

As the real estate market weakened, more and more people defaulted on their mortgages. The cash flows expected from those mortgages ceased, and the CDOs plummeted in value. Firms such as Lehman, with their high leverage ratios, were stuck holding CDOs that were declining in value while their debt remained intact. In essence, the inability to service the hefty debt associated with the CDOs rendered them insolvent. Eventually, this became too much to bear, and it was determined that no amount of government intervention could save Lehman.

15

COMMODITIES

Each day, the Chicago Mercantile Exchange facilitates millions of trades in commodities that range from lean hogs to lumber. This exchange serves as a central clearing point for various commodities, but more active exchanges are found in urban and rural centers around the globe. In each one, just about anything can be traded. The information is disseminated fairly, and the markets are always liquid. Derivatives rarely displace physical items, and the market is as efficient as a market can be. Unfortunately, trades can go awry when someone delivers a spoiled shipment of milk or fails to pay. In such cases, the regulatory authority will blow her whistle, grab the culprit by the ear, and drag him to the principal's office. Now, if we could only recruit these market players to solve our global financial problems.

Commodities are the world's oldest instruments of financial exchange. The ancient Romans traded salt on the street, and although that was a far cry from the modern commodity exchange, the principles governing these markets are timeless. This chapter will discuss the following:

- Commodity types
- Commodity trading
- Oil
- Gold

- Corn
- Commodities and the financial markets

COMMODITY TYPES

Modern commodities fall into broad categories, including energy, metals, and food. Although these categories account for much of the commodities world, plenty of others exist. Some of the more obscure traded commodities are

- Cotton
- Wood pulp
- Dry milk
- Whey
- Dirt

Okay, I made up the last one, but who knows? Perhaps this suggestion just might inspire some clever Wall Street neophyte to develop a marketplace for dirt. Until then, the most widely traded commodities are those listed here:

- Energy
    Gas
    Oil
- Metals
    Aluminum
    Copper
    Gold
    Lead
    Nickel
    Palladium
    Platinum
    Silver
    Tin
    Zinc

- Agricultural
    Cattle
    Cocoa
    Coffee
    Corn
    Cotton
    Hogs
    Soybeans
    Sugar
    Wheat

COMMODITY TRADING

Commodities are traded on and off exchanges in a similar way to the other asset classes that were discussed earlier in this book. The exchanges provide for a better flow of information and give commodity market participants an efficient means of determining market pricing. Additionally, these exchanges provide a set of regulations that encourage fair practices as well as a system to settle disputes. The largest commodity exchanges in the world are the following:

- United States
    Chicago Mercantile Exchange (CME) Group
    NYSE Euronext
- Japan
    Tokyo Commodity Exchange
- China
    Dalian Commodities Exchange
- India
    Multi Commodity Exchange
- United States, Canada, China, United Kingdom
    Intercontinental Exchange

Spot Market

The spot market, also called the cash market, implies that the actual commodity is delivered immediately after the completion of the transaction and the current market price of the commodity becomes the transaction price. Historically, a physical inspection of the actual item was required to complete the transaction, but nowadays, agreed-on terms prevail and therefore inspection is not required. Think eBay on steroids.

Forward Market

We have discussed forwards several times in various forms throughout the book, but nowhere are forwards more relevant than in the commodities markets. Two parties can agree on the delivery amount and price for a particular commodity on a future date. This allows both parties to avoid the painful possibility of a price disruption if something changes between the current date and the delivery date. Recall that in Chapter 11 we discussed a situation in which Car-E-Oki wanted to lock in the price of silver. Both the buyer (Car-E-Oki) and the seller (the supplier) shared the goal of hedging against pricing movements of silver. The forward contract allows them to achieve these goals by locking in a sale price in spite of what might happen to the spot price over time. One party may miss out on gains if the spot price moves in its favor, but such is life in the forward market.

Futures

Futures, which also were introduced in Chapter 11, offer similar advantages, with the primary difference from forwards being that futures are traded on exchanges. There is no need to bother with tedious negotiations over deal terms. Just buy the futures! When it comes to commodities, futures offer an efficient means of trade. A future is ultimately a legally binding contract that specifies the price, amount, and delivery date for a particular commodity. There is no immediate transfer of the commodity involved, thus minimizing transaction costs. Anyone can trade commodities without ever possessing them. A standard futures contract for most commodity types usually lists some, if not all, of the following:

- *Ticker symbol:* symbol referencing the commodity type
- *Contract quality:* describes the grade of the commodity; after all, you need to know whether you are buying ground chuck or top sirloin
- *Exchange:* notes the exchange where the commodity is traded
- *Trading hours:* lists the hours of operation for the exchange
- *Units:* specifies the unit of measure for the commodity
- *Contract size:* specifies the size of the contract based on the standard commodity unit
- *Contract months:* lists the delivery months for the commodity
- *Price change minimum:* lists minimum price movement for purchase or sale of a futures contract
- *Daily trading limit:* notes the amount the exchange has set to prevent major price changes

Futures Movements

A standard futures curve begins with the spot rate and then slopes upward or downward, depending on the future price. If you take a long position one year out, you agree to pay that price in a year. If the curve were inverted, the futures price would be less than the spot price. The curve may invert if there was some benefit in holding on to it. When the futures price is trading above the spot price, it is called *contango*. This probably would be due to costs associated with the commodity such as insurance and storage. In other words, the spot price is lower than the future price because if you purchased the commodity today, you would incur additional future costs, including storage, insurance, and interest. Contango also may occur if traders believe that future demand will exceed supply, meaning that prices could trend higher. As a result, they would be willing to pay a premium for the future price over the spot price. If the spot price is $20 and the future price is $30, contango exists. Backwardation occurs when the future price is lower than the spot price. If the spot price is $20 and the future price is $10, backwardation exists. This may occur if the prevailing belief is that the future supply of a commodity may be restricted, and so one would rather have it today.

OIL

Oil, whether we like it or not, is one of the most important commodities in the world. Fortunes are made in it, wars are fought over it, and ecosystems can be destroyed by it. Oil prices are a major force in the economy; that is why understanding the factors that affect them is as important as understanding any set of variables in global finance.

Factors That Affect the Price of Oil

Supply

The supply of oil plays a major role in determining its price. One of the most important organizations that determine this is the Organization of Petroleum Exporting Countries (OPEC). OPEC sets a quota for oil and regulates the output of oil (see the following sections).

Weather

Winter storms, hurricanes, and other natural disasters are just a few of my least favorite things. Not only can they take a catastrophic toll on humanity, they can affect the price of oil through supply disruptions.

The Economy

Economic booms and busts affect how much people spend on travel, which will affect the demand for oil.

Geopolitical Forces

Anytime the threat of war surfaces within oil-producing nations, fears of oil supply disruptions abound.

OPEC

OPEC was formed in 1960 by several oil-producing countries to form an alliance aimed at regulating the supply and ultimately the price of oil. Today, representatives from its 12 member countries (Algeria, Ecuador, Indonesia, Iran, Iraq, Kuwait, Libya, Nigeria, Qatar, Saudi Arabia, United Arab Emirates, and Venezuela) meet regularly to determine oil output, and this has a direct impact on supply and, to a large degree, price. OPEC faces the challenge of maximizing pricing without lowering demand. If oil prices reach lofty heights, it may affect consumer demand, which could prove costly to these countries. Higher prices can incentivize oil-consuming nations to seek out other sources of oil and, over the long run, alternative energy sources. The United States stores nearly a billion barrels of oil in the Strategic Petroleum Reserve, which is tapped when there is extreme demand for oil, such as after a natural disaster or when the threat of political upheaval in OPEC nations presents itself.

Measuring Oil

The price of oil generally is based on the spot, or current, price and measured off WTI/light crude traded on the New York Mercantile Exchange (NYMEX) or Brent crude futures traded on the Intercontinental Exchange (ICE). Oil is quoted in terms of barrels, with a barrel holding 42 US gallons or 159 liters. The price of oil reflects its price per barrel (i.e., $80/bbl). BPD stands for barrels per day and measures output or consumption. For example, a country might consume 1 million BPD and a field might produce 10,000 BPD.

Trading Oil

We've discussed futures many times throughout this book, and they are highly relevant in the case of oil trading. Oil traders seek to profit from anticipated movements in oil prices by bidding on futures. Projected supply and demand clearly play a role in the price of futures. Herein lies the oil futures paradox: if traders bid up the price of oil futures, oil will become more expensive and speculation becomes reality. Many believe the oil asset bubble that peaked in 2008 was a product of such rampant speculation. At the time, oil prices hit $147 a barrel.

GOLD

Gold is unlike any other commodity. It can be a store of value, an economic indicator, or an adornment worn by your friend from the Jersey Shore. It can bring a nation to its knees and a bride-to-be to tears. Despite its complexity and cross functionality, it becomes the lowest common denominator in times of economic crisis.

Factors That Affect the Price of Gold

Overall, three primary factors can affect the price of gold:

1. *Demand for the physical commodity.* Whether it's jewelry or industrial parts, gold will appreciate in value if people use it more.
2. *The value of the dollar.* Gold generally is priced in dollars, so if the value of the dollar decreases, the price of gold should increase. In other words, it will take more dollars to purchase the same amount of gold, thus reflecting a higher price in gold.
3. *Safe haven.* When there is a war or an economic melt-down, people turn to gold when panic sets in.

Reasons for Investing in Gold

There are many reasons to invest in gold, a few of which are listed here.

Hedge Against Dollar Drop

When the dollar declines, gold tends to appreciate. The dollar is the world's reserve currency, and a drop in its value can send investors and governments alike running for cover. Gold can hedge against this.

Hedge Against Inflation

As history has shown, when inflation rises, so do gold prices. Investors will bid up the price of gold as they see prices in general increasing. As a result, buying gold when inflationary pressures are mounting is a popular hedging strategy. If inflation takes shape, the increase in gold prices can offset the economic challenges associated with inflation.

Hedge Against Declining Stock Market

The stock market can decline for many reasons, but this generally results from fears about the economy or an actual economic slowdown. In some cases, these market downturns are short-lived and can be related to a correction in an overheated sector. Nonetheless, this will hurt stock market indexes and probably stimulate buying of gold as a hedge. When investors are scared, gold seems like the only safe port in the storm.

Hedge Against Geopolitical Uncertainty

Again, fear surfaces and gold seems like a safe bet. Geopolitical uncertainty, if nothing else, creates fear that can lead to panic selling. One thing is for certain: investors don't like uncertainty. When a global event threatens economic stability, gold becomes a popular investment option.

Store of Value

Currencies come and go, but as a means of financial exchange, gold is timeless. Need I say more?

CORN

Whether you choose to believe it or not, it is corn that makes the world go around. Corn is one of the most important food commodities in the world. In addition to being a source of food for much of the world's population, it is used in feed as well as ethanol, which is mixed with gasoline. Ethanol generally is considered the least expensive biofuel. Corn is measured by the bushel.

Factors That Affect the Price of Corn

Overall, four primary factors can affect the price of corn:

1. *Demand for the physical commodity.* Clearly, demand for corn and corn products will affect price. Population growth or a global trend toward more breakfast consumption could lead to an increase in price.
2. *Weather.* Weather extremes include too much rain, sun, snow, and so on. Those extremes certainly affect crop size and in turn the price of corn.
3. *Demand for biofuel.* When ethanol demand increases, it will affect the price of corn.
4. *The value of the dollar.* A weakening of the dollar against another major currency means American corn is priced relatively cheaper. This should increase demand for corn and push prices higher. This relationship between the dollar and corn prices is widely accepted, but it has been known to stir up a fair amount of debate. If you plan on trading corn, don't quote me on it.

Who Suffers When Corn Prices Are High?

- *Beverage companies.* Corn affects major beverage producers. When corn prices are high, beverage companies suffer as corn is used to make high-fructose corn syrup, a sweetener used in most soft drinks.
- *Livestock companies.* Corn is used in feed, and higher corn prices mean higher feed costs.
- *Snack food and cereal companies.* Crackers, chips, and breakfast cereals are made from corn. Rising corn prices means lower profits for these companies.
- *Consumers.* When commodity prices are high, any price increases are passed on to the consumers, whether they are purchasing gas or cereal.

Who Benefits When Corn Prices Are High?

- *Farmers.* Higher corn prices usually mean better profits. Of course, if prices become too high, demand could be affected.
- *Fertilizer companies.* Farmers use more fertilizer to yield more crops.

- *Corn seed companies.* Genetically engineered seeds produce quality ethanol, and farmers will purchase more as they seek to profit from higher corn prices.

COMMODITIES AND THE FINANCIAL MARKETS

Commodities have advanced to the point of becoming a leading indicator in global finance. Investors and consumers look to current and future commodities in an effort to gauge possible movements in other markets. Although it's fun to watch market "experts" defend their interpretations of commodity pricing movements, the consistent lack of consensus in those discussions points to a simple fact: we may never truly understand the commodities market. So good luck!

16

PORTFOLIO THEORY

A child's birthday party can be magical. Junk food, games, friends, and ... gifts! Everything a kid dreams of. I put a lot of thought into planning my own party as a kid, and, unbeknownst to my parents, employed my own version of portfolio theory. Careful thought was given to the invite list based on probabilities of obtaining the best gifts and weighing these probabilities against the ever-present backdrop of the midparty tantrum. I wanted to maximize my return in terms of quality gifts but minimize the risk of inviting someone who was likely to throw a fit if they didn't get to sit next to me. Ultimately, I had to craft a balanced invite list that, drawing on my limited understanding of portfolio theory, maximized gift return while minimizing tantrum risk.

Modern portfolio theory is based on the idea that investors expect the lowest possible risk for a target rate of return. A great deal of analysis is involved in this process. This chapter will discuss the following:

- Expected return
- Modern portfolio theory
- Risk management

EXPECTED RETURN

Expected return in a portfolio is based on the weighted average expected returns on individual assets within a portfolio. In other words, if one asset weighs heavily on the portfolio and is expected to produce outsized returns, the overall portfolio expected return would be higher than if the asset returns were more in line with those of the other assets. Assume a portfolio based on the following four education sector stocks:

Jimi's Experiential Learning Software	8 percent
Jerry's Psychedelic Enrichment Centers	5 percent
Grace's Petting Zoo Franchise	12 percent
Janis's Kozmic Space Camp	15 percent

To determine the expected return on the portfolio, a weighted average return is calculated. The total expected return formula can be written as:

$$E(R) = w_1 R_1 + w_2 R_2 \ldots + w_n R_n$$

In other words, we multiply individual expected returns for each portfolio asset by its weight within the portfolio. In our example, the total expected portfolio return, assuming equal weighting, would be:

$$(.25 \times .08) + (.25 \times .05) + (.25 \times .12) + (.25 \times .15) = 10\%$$

Assuming we purchased equal dollar amounts of each company, our expected return would be 10 percent. Keep in mind that the expected rate of return is anything but guaranteed. Nonetheless, it proves useful in forecasting.

MODERN PORTFOLIO THEORY

At the heart of modern portfolio theory is the idea that investors are risk averse and therefore prefer the highest return with the lowest risk. Intuitively, this makes sense. A few key points to keep in mind about modern portfolio theory include:

1. The goal is to maximize expected return for a given level of risk
2. Risk is based on variance
3. The risk pertaining to an individual asset should relate to how it impacts the overall portfolio

To put it plainly, if three different investment portfolios offer an expected rate of return of 10 percent, the investor will choose the one with the lowest risk.

Standard Deviation and Variance

Standard deviation and variation are popular concepts in statistics as well as finance. The basis for each is the mean of a set of data. Variance examines the extent to which each data point differs from the mean. Standard deviation, which is the square root of variance, is used to measure volatility and, in turn, risk. The lower the company's standard deviation, the less risky the company's stock. Let's look at how we calculate standard deviation for Jimi's Experiential Learning Software Company.

1. Calculate average return over 10 years.
2. Subtract each year's actual return from average return.
3. Square the resulting differences.
4. Calculate average of these squared differences, which is the variance
5. Calculate the square root of this average, which is the standard deviation.

Note: we assume that there are only nine years of total returns. If there were more years of return data, we would have to calculate our averages by subtracting 1 in the denominator based on the average of a sample set. We'll keep it simple so as not to turn this into a statistics book that will certainly put you to sleep (if this section hasn't done so already).

In the case of Jimi's Software, standard deviation is 3.77 percent. Assuming the company offers the same expected return as other companies in the industry but has a lower standard deviation than others, it would prove the better investment choice. Lower risk and comparable return is what one should aspire to in portfolio theory.

	Returns %	Yearly Return Less Average Return	Yearly Return Less Average Return Squared
Year 1	10	3.56	12.64
Year 2	4	(2.44)	5.98
Year 3	6	(0.44)	0.20
Year 4	8	1.56	2.42
Year 5	2	(4.44)	19.75
Year 6	12	5.56	30.86
Year 7	11	4.56	20.75
Year 8	4	(2.44)	5.98
Year 9	1	(5.44)	29.64
Average Return (Nine Year Ave.)	6.44	Variance	14.25
		Standard Deviation	3.77

Variance, like standard deviation, demonstrates how much a stock deviates from its mean. However, variance squares results, which enhances the effects of outliers. Additionally, it mitigates the effects of data points canceling each other out due to their relation to the mean, which could result in a variance of zero. Stocks with broader fluctuations will have a higher variance and therefore prove riskier. Consider two companies and their stock prices over time:

	Stock A	Difference from Mean	Squared Difference
End of Q1	$ 16	$ (5)	$ 25
End of Q2	$ 32	$ 11	$ 121
End of Q3	$ 26	$ 5	$ 25
End of Q4	$ 10	$ (11)	$ 121
Average (Mean)	$ 21	Variance	73.00
		Standard Deviation	8.54

	Stock B	Difference from Mean	Squared Difference
End of Q1	$ 18	$ (3)	$ 9
End of Q2	$ 20	$ (1)	$ 1
End of Q3	$ 22	$ 1	$ 1
End of Q4	$ 24	$ 3	$ 9
Average (Mean)	$ 21	Variance	5.00
		Standard Deviation	2.24

As you can see, variance helps us see how far data points deviate from the mean or average. For stock A, we see that the standard deviation is $8.54, meaning that movements away from the mean price are around $8.54. On the other hand, the standard deviation for Stock B is $2.24, which means that the movements away from the mean tend to be much smaller. Even though the two stocks have the same mean price, clearly Stock A is more volatile and, in turn, riskier.

The concept of variance can be applied to an entire portfolio. Things get a bit more complicated from here. Portfolio variance is based on the variance of the individual assets within the portfolio as well as the covariance between them.

Covariance

Covariance reveals the extent to which two assets in a portfolio move in tandem. A positive covariance means that the returns move in the same direction, and a negative covariance means the returns move in opposite directions. The reason this is important in modern portfolio theory is because it allows portfolio managers to reduce variance and, in turn, risk. By selecting assets with low or even negative covariance, risk can be reduced. In other words, reducing covariance can be achieved through . . . drum roll, please . . . diversification!

$$\frac{\sum(\text{Return Stock - Average Return Stocks}) * (\text{Return Bond - Average Return Bond})}{(\text{Sample Size - 1})}$$

In the example below, we calculate the average four-quarter return for a portfolio of stocks as well as a portfolio of bonds. As the formula states, we then take the individual quarterly return for the stock portfolio and subtract the average return for the stock portfolio. The result is multiplied by the difference between the individual quarterly return for the bond return and the average return for bonds. From there, we add the result using the same formula for the next quarter and so on. The overall result is divided by the sample group size of four quarters less one. The result is a covariance of –2.67.

Quarter	Stock Returns	Bond Returns
1	1 %	4 %
2	1 %	5 %
3	3 %	2 %
4	4 %	1 %
Average Return Stock	(1+1+3+4)/4 =	2.25 %
Average Return Bond	(4+5+3+1)/4 =	3.00 %

$$\frac{[1-2.25)*(4-3)]+[(1-2.25)*(5-3)]+[(3-2.25)*(2-3)]+[(4-2.25)*(1-3)]}{(4-1)}$$

Covariance	-2.67

Based on this covariance, we can observe that the stock portfolio and bond portfolio move in opposite directions.

Efficient Frontier

Portfolio managers can determine an optimal portfolio by plotting what is called the efficient frontier. The efficiency portfolio compares individual portfolios based on standard deviation and expected return. The goal of this nifty graph is to illustrate the highest expected return for a prescribed level of risk (or the lowest level of risk for a prescribed level of return). Suppose you walk into your financial planner's office and say, "I want to earn a 15 percent annual return!" Assuming your financial planner doesn't call the police, he just might walk you through the efficient frontier to find a set of options that lie on the frontier allowing you to minimize your risk while earning 15 percent. Of course, nothing is guaranteed, but your expected return would be 15 percent at the lowest charted level of risk.

The efficient frontier is curved, which is a product of diversification. Investment professionals make every effort to locate portfolios as close to the curve as possible. Consider Figure 16-1. As you can see, Portfolio A and Portfolio B have the same level of return although Portfolio B carries significantly more risk.

FIGURE 16-1 Efficient Frontier

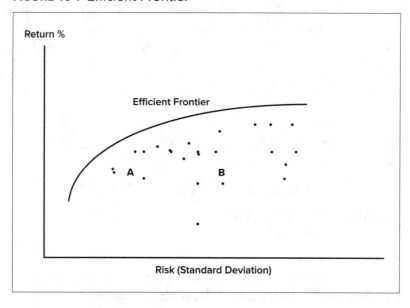

Alpha and Beta

No, this is not a section on college fraternity life. Rather, we'll touch on two of the most important variables in portfolio management: alpha and beta. We've already discussed beta in our cost of capital section in Chapter 8, so let's start with alpha. Alpha is a measure of performance relative to the market. If the S&P 500 returns 12 percent and your portfolio returns 16 percent, your alpha would be 4 percent. Alpha is the portion of your return that is not tied to market performance. Alpha performance is often driven by active portfolio strategies that affect the timing of investments and how funds are allocated. Nowadays, these types of decisions can be driven by a portfolio manager, an algorithm, or some combination of the two. Think about an alpha driven portfolio as a sports team with a coach and/or coaching plan.

Beta represents the extent to which an investment's returns move relative to the market. A passive investment strategy would involve analyzing these expected returns based on their beta. Active management, however, will look at alpha, which measures returns beyond the market return. Maximizing a portfolio's alpha requires a thoughtful approach to the selection of individual securities within the portfolio.

RISK MANAGEMENT

One of the fastest-growing sectors of finance today is risk management. Why? Risks can prove costly. And more important, avoiding losses is just as important and creating gains. Finance comes with high rewards, and as we learned earlier in the book, high rewards create high risks. Many of the greatest investment managers in the world have attributed their success to one factor above all others: managing risk. No matter how great an opportunity may appear to be or how significant its upside may be, risks always persist. To mitigate these risks, risk management tools have developed over the years. Let's examine some of these risks and how the financial community manages them.

Diversification

Diversification is one of the most important principles in all of finance. Portfolio diversification allows one to effectively manage risk. In other words, it's the "don't place all your eggs in one basket" theory of finance. For example, suppose most of your portfolio was based on oil company stocks. An investor would face serious risks if oil prices drop. To manage this risk, the investor might build a diversified portfolio of stocks from other industries that may benefit from a decline in oil prices such as airlines. To put it another way, the goal is to reduce overall portfolio risk while still maintaining the same expected return. Suppose that an investor places his or her life savings in one company with an expected return of 12 percent. If things go according to plan, then a 12 percent annual return seems decent. However, things do not always go according to plan, and expected returns are not guaranteed returns. That 12 percent gain could become a 12 percent loss should market conditions change. To manage this risk, it makes sense to diversify the portfolio such that overall expected returns are maintained but correlations may differ. In other words, the portfolio is somewhat insulated against movements affecting any one asset component.

Smart Beta

Smart beta combines the best of passive and active investing. Ultimately, it seeks to increase alpha by minimizing risk, maximizing returns, and minimizing costs. That's the goal of any investment strategy, right? Smart beta has created a focused movement around this novel idea and seeks to quantify it. Here's how it works. Smart beta seeks the efficiencies of passive investing while incorporating active investment strategies based on variables such as volatility, momentum, and fundamentals. Smart beta strategies will vary from manager to manager but afford one the opportunity to capitalize on mispricing or inefficiency. For example, a portfolio manager may recognize that small-cap and large-cap stocks behave differently. A simple industry or index exchange-traded fund (ETF) would give more weight to larger-cap companies than smaller-cap companies. A smart beta ETF might incorporate additional fundamental factors to assess weighting. For example, a small-cap company with a low PE multiple might weigh more heavily on the ETFs pricing than a large-cap company with a high PE multiple. In other words, smart beta ETFs incorporate additional variables into the construct and weighting of the fund, which hopefully translates to better performance and lower risk.

17

THE BUSINESS
OF FINANCE

When I was kid, I used to look forward to the holiday season every year. Sure, I liked the family time and the gifts, but the best part was watching the movie *It's a Wonderful Life*, which was broadcast about half a dozen times daily. While most view the timeless classic as a touching portrayal of a small town family man struggling to understand his purpose, I regard it as a colorful overview of the financial services industry. That's right. *It's a Wonderful Life* is one of the best finance films ever made! Ripe with themes of commercial banking, acquisitions, and insurance, the film is more than the typical holiday classic. In the film, the ruthless bank owner, Mr. Potter, attempts to acquire the Building and Loan, issues mortgages to the town's people, and encourages the protagonist, George Bailey, to cash in his life insurance policy. In essence, Mr. Potter was a full-service financial services operator.

The world of finance today looks quite different from the world of Mr. Potter's era. The core institutions remain intact, but the advent of new technologies has produced a financial world in which transactions occur in the blink of an eye.

This chapter will discuss the following:

- The sell side of finance
- The buy side of finance
- FinTech

THE SELL SIDE OF FINANCE

The term *banking* is as broad a finance term as you can imagine. It encompasses nearly every type of transaction. Much of what falls within the realm of banking involves selling services, which is why it's termed the "sell side" in the financial services world. In fact, the earlier distinctions between commercial banking and investment banking are no longer as defined as they once were. The most important lesson in studying the modern financial services industry is that the sector lines are blurred. Let's take a look at what defines each broad sector.

Commercial Banking

Commercial banks make their money by securing deposits and lending the money. As long as the rate of interest paid to depositors is lower than the rate of interest charged to the borrowers, the bank makes money. The lifeblood of the commercial banking industry in the United States is the federal funds rate. This is the rate at which banks and credit unions lend money overnight to other banks. The rate is determined by the Federal Reserve Bank's Federal Open Market Committee, which meets eight times per year and sets this rate. The banks are able to borrow at this rate and, in turn, lend to consumers and businesses at a higher rate. It's that simple. Easy money.

It gets better, though. Commercial banks charge all kinds of fees. ATM fees, account maintenance fees, and application fees are just a few. And don't forget the penalties. Whether it's a nominal penalty when your bank balance falls below a required level or a hefty one when you make a payment late or early (that's right, you can get slapped with a hefty penalty just for being responsible), the banks make large sums of money from penalties.

Investment Banking

Investment banking has been around almost as long as the idea that you should always invest with other people's money. Investment banks have mastered the fine art of making money, regardless of whether or not their clients make money.

Underwriting

One of the primary functions of the investment bank is to offer underwriting services to its clients. Suppose company XYZ needs capital to expand. The investment bank will gladly analyze the market to determine where the best opportunities lie to raise the most capital at the lowest cost. The bank will then look at the debt markets to gain a sense of what the cost of debt would be for a client with this credit rating. Additionally, the bank will consider interest rate trends and the debt market outlook for the coming years. Next, the bank will examine the equity markets to determine whether an equity offering might make more sense. Of course, selling shares of stock will dilute the existing shareholders, so the bank will have to make a determination as to whether the additional capital, without any direct financing cost, will outweigh the dilutive effects of the stock offering. The best part about all of this is that the investment bankers will make a hefty commission on the transaction.

Mergers and Acquisitions

Bankers often advise clients on buying and selling companies. Much of the banker's work revolves around valuation. Whether the banker values a company for sale or for purchase, valuation will form the cornerstone of the transaction. And as we learned earlier, valuation is more art than science. That being said, it's necessary nonetheless.

Sales and Trading

Many large investment banks have sales and trading groups. Traders will buy and sell securities in blocks and earn commissions on each trade. Since the traders are dealing with large allocations of securities, they will rely on salespeople to pitch the trade idea to large institutions. The trader can add value by finding the best price, which often entails parceling out individual blocks of the trade or dividing it into smaller portions. While it might be easy as an individual to buy 100 shares of a favorite stock, buying 10 million shares on behalf of an institutional client will require a complex interaction between the sales team, the trading floor, and other institutional investors. If the trade is executed in a timely manner and at a good price, the client will be happy.

While sales and trading desks are often segmented between equity and fixed income (or stocks and bonds for the sake of simplicity), other asset classes often have their own dedicated sales and trading teams. Currency, commodities, and derivatives are only a few additional asset classes where traders and salespeople will develop asset specific skills. Exceling in these areas requires a keen understanding of the marketplace as well as an outlook for price trends. Most of all, it requires key relationships with the right players in the space.

Equity Research

One of the most powerful influences in the world of finance is equity research. Equity research analysts will research entire industries as well as individual companies that form these industries. The goal of the research analyst is to provide value-added market insights that allow customers who subscribe to the research to make smart investment decisions. For example, a research analyst who covers consumer products will research the entire industry and articulate changes to key industry drivers. The equity research analyst will produce colorful reports that seek answers to questions such as:

- Where are key commodity prices headed, and how will they influence the cost of producing the products?
- What do demographic shifts mean for consumer buying trends?

- What do demographic shifts mean for the broader economy?
- Will trend shifts impact purchases in this space?
- Will a recession spark a slowdown or uptrend in this space?
- If I use a larger font in my report, will I increase my page count and make my boss happy? (Okay, I made this one up.)

Answering these questions allows the research analyst to form a solid, qualitative assessment of the industry.

The equity research analyst will also research individual companies and offer a buy, hold, or sell recommendation. Much of this will be driven by the macro overview offered in the industry report, with the remainder of the report focused on the individual factors driving the company itself. Questions addressed in a company-specific report would include:

- Is the company gaining market share?
- Is the company expanding to new markets?
- Is the company planning to acquire a competitor?
- Is the company facing cost increases that could affect profits?

Ultimately, the answers to these questions form the basis for the inputs that feed into a detailed valuation model. More often than not, the model is built off of valuation methodologies discussed in Chapter 9, including the comparable multiple method and the discounted cash flow method. The end result from this rather elaborate valuation mosaic will be a target price per share.

The best part about equity research is the economics. Top-tier research analysts charge a hefty sum for their reports. It's not unheard of for individual reports to sell for thousands of dollars each. It also allows the bank to offer these reports to marquis clients from whom the bank may generate millions of dollars in advisory and underwriting fees.

Retail Brokerage

One the oldest businesses in the finance world is retail brokerage. Retail brokers, or stockbrokers, are the good folks who bring Wall Street to Main Street. Many years ago, if you wanted to buy stock in a company, it meant that you needed to first set up an account with a stockbroker. Next, you had to call the broker with specific instructions including how many shares to buy and at what price. The broker would then place the order and, once executed, would call you back to let you know that your trade went through. Sometimes the hefty commissions on these orders would eclipse the actual purchase price of the shares! Great for the broker but not so great for the client.

Fast-forward to the early 1970s when a movement began to bring affordable stock trades to the masses. Brokerage fees dropped and new technology all but eliminated the need for human resources in the world of stock purchases. Later, the advent of the Internet brought about real-time information along with rapid-fire execution, which meant that individuals could execute trades for a fraction of what it once cost. Thank you Charles Schwab and E*Trade.

THE BUY SIDE

Where would we be without fund management? Perhaps, we would read *The Wall Street MBA* and try to manage our own investments. While this is unlikely to happen anytime soon, for now we rely on the myriad managed portfolio options available. By pooling funds from individual and institutional investors, fund managers are able to deploy capital in a manner that, in theory, produces strong returns. While stellar results are hard to achieve, it doesn't stop people from investing in the various fund options that exist.

Mutual Funds

A mutual fund is managed by a professional money manager who receives investments from many investors. The pool of funds formed from these investments is invested in various assets or securities of companies within an industry. Mutual funds afford the investor an opportunity to diversify while achieving economies of scale. For example, an investor could buy shares in 10 separate companies within an industry and create a mini mutual fund. This would prove costly given that transaction fees alone would add up and eat away at future returns. Additionally, the investor would need to actively manage the individual holdings by determining the right time to buy and sell each stock.

A mutual fund takes the hassle out of this process while minimizing the transaction fees. The downside, of course, is that mutual funds can charge relatively steep management fees when compared with other investment vehicles. But hey, what's 1 percent in fees if the fund returns 40 percent annually? (Note: not a realistic scenario, but one can dream, right?)

Exchange-Traded Funds

Exchange-traded funds (ETFs) are a nice alternative to mutual funds as they offer similar diversification and economies of scale at a fraction of the cost of mutual funds. ETFs are traded on an exchange, much like a stock, and often track an index. For example, one could buy an ETF that tracks a major stock, bond, or commodity index. Since an index fund is usually easy to manage (hint: you buy all the securities in the index), it involves little to no effort in selecting which securities to purchase. In fact, much of this can be done by a computer. As a result, ETF fees can be lower than 1 percent. And it goes without saying that saving on fees means returns will be greater.

An ETF is a low-cost way of buying a basket of individual assets such as stocks, bonds, or commodities. This could mean buying each of the major companies in a particular sector or perhaps buying an entire index. Suppose you wanted to buy the S&P 500 Index. It would cost you a pretty penny to buy all of the stocks in this index, and even if you had the funds to buy a share of each company, you would need to pay transaction costs for each share purchase. That could amount to a small fortune in transaction fees. Thankfully, the ETF was formed to address this economic challenge, and nowadays, owning a portfolio of stocks within an industry or a bundle of commodities is as simple as one low-cost transaction. Instead of buying gold bullion, one can simply buy the gold ETF. Interested in owning US Treasury bonds? Just buy the Treasury ETF. How about a basket of high-yield bonds? No problem. Buy the ETF.

Investing this way has made portfolio management and diversification a breeze. One can build a portfolio based on a mix of high-growth stocks, low-risk debt, commodities, real estate, and money market instruments. In other words, the cost of balancing the portfolio and diversifying risk is low. If stocks go up, bonds may go down. And if the financial system melts down as it did in 2008, at least the money market component should maintain its value. ETFs afford investors even more sophisticated options including derivative-based ETFs or inverse funds based on short selling and put option strategies. Perhaps you are heavily invested in stocks across industries but you believe that the market may be overheated. Purchasing shares in the S&P inverse ETF may prove an effective hedge should the market correct. While your individual stocks lose value, the value of your inverse ETF may increase, offsetting some of your losses.

Hedge Funds

Hedge funds are to money management what ski jumping is to the Olympics. We discussed hedge funds in Chapter 11 and learned, among other things, that hedge funds don't necessarily hedge. In fact, an idea that began many years ago with the hopes of investing while protecting capital through various hedging mechanisms has evolved into anything but that. Hedge funds are pools of money, usually from accredited investors and institutions. Hedge fund managers are given license to invest in just about anything, although they tend to stick with liquid assets such as stocks and bonds. In many cases, they will employ leverage by borrowing against their capital base. This allows them to earn outsized returns when things go well and, of course, suffer big losses when things don't go so well. The best part about hedge funds, at least for the managers, is the fee structure. Normally, hedge fund managers collect a 2 percent management fee based on assets under management (AUM) plus 20 percent of the returns. If a fund has one billion dollars in assets, the management fee alone is 20 million dollars per year. Now, if the fund returns 10 percent, the fund manager earns 20 percent of that 10 percent, which would be another 20 million dollars. Not bad. Does that seem fair? Well, no one said finance is fair, and the bottom line is that investors are willing to pay handsomely for the possibility of strong returns.

Private Equity Funds

Private equity funds invest in less liquid investments than their counterparts. They tend to buy large stakes in companies, actively manage these companies, and sell their stake several years later. Their fee structures vary but tend to mimic hedge fund economics. Additionally, private equity funds will rely heavily on debt to fund the acquisition of companies and in this manner utilize leverage to capture strong gains.

Venture Capital Funds

Let's suppose you just invented the time machine. That was the easy part. Now comes the hard part. You actually have to raise capital to build a business around your invention. Venture capitalists manage funds that invest in early stage companies. The typical private equity fund will buy an equity stake in your company with the hopes that through its capital and strategic guidance, your time machine invention will turn into a successful company with many customers and strong profits. Assuming your business continues to grow, at some point, perhaps years from now, the venture capital firm will sell its stake to another venture capital firm, a large corporation seeking to acquire your business, or cash out through an IPO. Of course, the venture capitalist will have to contend with customers traveling back in time to invent their own time machine before you did, which won't bode well for your company's valuation.

Pension Funds

Pension funds are built around the idea of providing retirement income to the individuals who have contributed to the funds. These funds can be extremely large and can take on various forms. For example, open pension funds offer unrestricted membership to all employees of an organization, whereas closed pension funds are only offered to certain employees of an organization. The most common pension plan is a defined benefit plan in which employees receive payments based on a percentage of their salary from their last years on the job. The amount is largely tied to how long the employee worked at the company. Pension fund fees can be hefty and may include setup charges, annual management charges, platform charges for individual discretion over what to buy, transaction fees, and exit fees. These charges can add up.

FINTECH

It's no secret that the world of finance and technology intersected many years ago. What is most intriguing, however, is that the two areas have formed a symbiotic relationship. Financial technologies, FinTech for short, has transformed the way financial service firms conduct transactions, afforded greater access to a broader base of customers, and increased the speed at which information is disseminated. All in all, it seems pretty exciting and continues to expand. Let's explore some of the areas that show the most promise when it comes to reshaping the world of twenty-first-century finance.

Crowdfunding

Only a few years back, raising capital to start a business meant going through the painful process of applying for a bank loan or asking Mom and Dad to cash in their retirement savings to help with start-up costs. Thanks to innovative technologies and movement toward the democratization of financial markets, this is no longer the case. Most any entrepreneur with a good idea and a solid business plan can turn to crowdfunding to raise seed capital. Crowdfunding allows entrepreneurs to access smaller investors en masse without some of the costs and restrictions associated with a traditional angel round of fund-raising.

Blockchain

Blockchain represents one of the most significant developments in the world of finance. In the financial world, blockchain is the technology that drives distributed ledgers. Distributed ledgers form a database that can be shared across networks or geographies. As the name implies, a chain of blocks is linked together and secured using something called cryptography. Cryptography uses a series of computer-based algorithms to ensure security. A blockchain stores data across a network, which means the data is decentralized and, more important, verified by others in the network

Blockchain technology is presenting numerous disruptive possibilities for the world of finance. Digital currencies allow for secure, low-cost transactions that eliminate the financial middleman. The transaction ledgers are open and verifiable, which lowers the risk of fraud. Real estate and other transactions will likely utilize blockchain technology for purposes of record verification and to minimize administrative costs.

Artificial Intelligence

In the good old days of finance, most any financial transaction would involve a few brokers, agents, or intermediaries to both execute the transaction and make key decisions to determine things like timing and pricing. Nowadays, however, machines are taking over the decision-making process. Artificial intelligence (AI) is reshaping everything from compliance to valuation. AI, by definition, is the use of technology systems to replace tasks normally managed by humans. An AI system can seamlessly parse the volumes of data in a nanosecond to determine with a high level of accuracy whether a bank is complying with a specific regulation. What percentage of borrowers is meeting specific loan requirements? How do these borrowers affect the bank's capital requirements? Thanks to artificial intelligence and data analytics, questions like these can be answered quickly. This information can allow a bank not only to draft a revised compliance strategy but to chart future trends in borrowing patterns. This can even impact how loans are priced! AI and data analytics have replaced an army of analysts and theoretically, can perform these tasks better.

AI and its offshoot, machine learning, are playing a major role in fraud detection. Credit card companies now use this technology to determine shopping patterns for individual users. When deviations from these patterns are determined, a fraud warning may be issued. If you often spend $10 on a cheeseburger for lunch but your card just revealed a charge for an $80 Kobe beef steak at a restaurant 200 miles from your office, you just might receive an automated message from your credit card company.

Banking Chatbots
One of the most intriguing developments in the realm of AI is the chatbot. Through the use of natural language processing and machine learning algorithms, chatbots help you manage your savings. They can do this by analyzing your spending and savings patterns to determine what, and when, you should be saving. Based on this, they even make deposits into your bank account when appropriate. In essence, they serve as your own personal money manager.

Algorithmic Trading
When I was a bright-eyed Wall Street analyst, I was taught that there were two ways to analyze a company's stock: fundamental analysis and technical analysis. Fundamental analysis involved reviewing a company's financial statements and measuring performance based on various financial ratios. From there, valuation models could be built.

Technical analysis was based on analyzing trading patterns around a company's stock. Often called a chartist, a technical analyst would review stock price movement over time to determine when it would be time to buy, hold, or sell a stock. For example, a stock that continues to achieve higher daily highs exhibits a bullish trading pattern that can signal a buy. Nowadays, AI does much of this for us and the possibilities are limitless. Imagine an algorithm that, based on millions of data points, draws a correlation between unusually cold weather and video streaming subscriptions. Harsh winter ahead? Time to buy Netflix stock.

Of course, this may be oversimplifying the value of algorithmic trading, but hopefully you get the point. Sophisticated programs can now determine when traders should buy, sell, or hold by parsing large amounts of data in an instant.

Big Data

Many of the FinTech initiatives described in this chapter are made possible through the advent of big data. Thanks in part to dramatic increases in data storage space and computing power, big data is nearly ubiquitous. You would be hard-pressed to find a new company that does not incorporate data analytics into its value proposition. If knowledge is power, big data is the switch that unleashes that power and does this on a massive scale. Gone are the days of manually entering numbers into a spreadsheet and using the sort function to determine data subsets and trends. Big data has increased the ability to parse data by orders of magnitude. Imagine the *Millennium Falcon* trudging through an asteroid field. That was old data. Now imagine jumping to light speed. That is big data.

CONCLUSION

So there you have it—the good, the bad, and the ugly of finance and accounting. Although you may not be quite ready to structure the Coke-Pepsi merger or audit Amazon's financial statements, you have, I hope, acquired a better understanding of what the so-called experts do. No longer will you wallow in ignorance when your favorite stock is downgraded, your company is acquired, or your boss is hauled off to jail for accounting fraud. Although you have gobbled up a number of complex concepts in a short period, don't be afraid to review them periodically or refer to them when needed. My goal was not to turn you into a financial wizard but to give you an insider's perspective on the world of accounting and finance. If you have come away with an appreciation for these concepts, great, and if you are skeptical, even better. It pays to question these concepts and the people who work with them. Take nothing for granted and be prepared to challenge them. Because we failed to do this before, we learned some important, albeit costly, lessons.

APPENDIX A

Case Study: Car-E-Oki, Inc.

Chapter 11 introduced you to Car-E-Oki, the up-and-coming company that is hoping to bring karaoke to automobiles and other vehicles. This appendix presents the typical documents you should study if you are thinking about investing in Car-E-Oki—or any other company.

SHRED & BURN, CPAS

Cayman Islands

The Board of Directors and Shareholders
Car-E-Oki, Inc.:

We have audited the accompanying consolidated balance sheets of Car-E-Oki, Inc., and subsidiaries as of December 31, 2017, and December 31, 2016, and the related consolidated statements of operations, shareholders' equity, and cash flows for each of the years in the two-year period ended December 31, 2017. These consolidated financial statements are the responsibility of the Company's management. Our responsibility is to express an opinion on these consolidated financial statements based on our audits.

We conducted our audits in accordance with the standards of the Public Company Accounting Oversight Board (United States). Those standards require that we plan and perform the audit to obtain reasonable assurance about whether the financial statements are free of material misstatement. An audit includes examining, on a test basis, evidence supporting the amounts and disclosures in the consolidated financial statements. An audit also includes assessing the accounting principles used and significant estimates made by management, as well as evaluating the overall financial statement presentation. We believe that our audits provide a reasonable basis for our opinion.

In our opinion, the consolidated financial statements referred to above present fairly, in all material respects, the financial position of Car-E-Oki, Inc., and subsidiaries as of December 31, 2017, and December 31, 2016, and the results of their operations and their cash flows for each of the years in the two-year period ended December 31, 2017, in conformity with U.S. generally accepted accounting principles.

Shred & Burn, CPAs

May 31, 2018

A sample auditor's report, like those prepared for most publicly traded companies.

CONSOLIDATED BALANCE SHEETS

All numbers in thousands except per-share amounts

Two fiscal years ended December 31st	2017	2016
ASSETS		
Current Assets:		
Cash	$887,851	$316,391
Accounts Receivable	38,048	13,736
Inventories	127,328	136,828
Prepaid Expenses & Other Assets	52,836	40,257
Total Current Assets	$1,106,063	$507,212
Fixed Assets:		
Motor Vehicles	115,601	101,605
Machinery & Equipment	23,143	21,343
Leasehold Improvements	19,619	19,619
Furniture & Fixtures	11,194	11,194
Total Fixed Assets	169,557	153,761
Accumulated Depreciation	(71,896)	(62,378)
Net Fixed Assets	97,661	91,383
Total Assets	$1,203,724	$598,595
LIABILITIES AND SHAREHOLDERS' EQUITY		
Current Liabilities:		
Bank Line of Credit	$ 59,050	$59,050
Notes Payable Bank	17,584	0
Notes Payable Other	11,782	15,410
Accounts Payable	105,035	89,107
Accrued Expenses and Other Liabilities	36,213	29,369
Total Current Liabilities	$229,664	$192,936
Notes Payable, Bank	27,232	10,000
Notes Payable, Other	24,546	27,516
Total Long-Term Debt	51,778	37,516
	$281,442	$230,452
Stockholders' Equity:		
Paid-in Capital	11,000	11,000
Retained Earnings	911,282	357,143
Total Stockholder Equity	922,282	368,143
Total Liabilities and Equity	$1,203,724	$598,595

A standard format balance sheet depicting two years of performance; this is useful in determining trends.

CONSOLIDATED INCOME STATEMENT

All numbers in thousands except per-share amounts

Two fiscal years ended December 31st	2017	2016
Net Sales	$2,171,451	$1,675,456
Cost of Goods Sold	654,325	543,604
Gross Profit	1,517,126	1,131,852
Selling, General, & Administrative Expenses	88,664	99,852
Total Operating Expenses	88,664	99,852
EBITDA	1,428,462	1,032,000
Depreciation	9,518	2,667
Earnings before Interest & Taxes	1,418,944	1,029,333
Interest Expense	14,758	10,654
Profit before Taxes	1,404,186	1,018,679
Income Taxes	505,507	366,724
Net Income	$898,679	$651,955
Average Shares Outstanding	2,000,000	2,000,000
Net Income/Share	$0.45	$0.33
NET INCOME	$898,679	$651,955
PLUS Beginning Retained Earnings	357,143	76,438
Distribution to Stockholders	(344,540)	(371,250)
Ending Retained Earnings	$911,282	$357,143

A standard income statement followed by a statement of retained earnings (last four lines), which captures the link between the balance sheet and the income statement.

CONSOLIDATED STATEMENTS OF CASH FLOWS

All numbers in thousands except per-share amounts

Two fiscal years ended December 31st	2017	2016
Cash Beginning of Period	316,391	9,781
Cash Flows from Operations:		
Net Income	$898,679	$651,955
Adjustments to Reconcile to Cash		
Provided (Used) in Operations		
Depreciation	9,518	2,667
Accounts Receivable	(24,312)	81,741
Inventory	9,500	(7,595)
Prepaid Expenses	(12,579)	(4,296)
Accounts Payable	15,928	8,202
Accrued Expenses and Other Liabilities	6,844	(12,056)
Net Cash Flow from Operations	903,578	720,618
Cash Flows from Investing:		
Purchase of Fixed Assets	(15,796)	(14,920)
Cash Flows from Financing:		
Borrowings (Repayment) of Bank Credit Line	$0	($14,200)
Borrowings (Repayment) of Notes Payable, Bank	34,816	0
Borrowings (Repayment) of Notes Payable, Other	(6,598)	(13,638)
Distribution to Stockholders	(344,540)	(371,250)
Cash Flows from Financing	(316,322)	(399,088)
NET Increase (Decrease) in Cash	571,460	306,610
Cash End of Period	**$887,851**	**$316,391**

A standard cash flow statement, which is used to document changes in cash position. The ending cash balance forms the link between the cash flow statement and the balance sheet.

Press Release Source: Car-E-Oki, Inc.

Car-E-Oki Reports Third Quarter Results

February 23, 2018 4:30 p.m. ET

Car-E-Oki Delivers Record Revenue & Earnings

CUPERTINO, Calif., February 23 /PRNewswire-FirstCall/ Car-E-Oki® today announced financial results for its fiscal year ended December 31, 2017, reporting the highest revenue and earnings in the Company's history. Car-E-Oki posted a net profit of $898 million, or $.45 per diluted share, and revenue of $2.17 billion. These results compare to a net profit of $651 million, or $.33 per diluted share, and revenue of $1.67 billion in the prior year, and represent revenue growth of 29 percent and net profit growth of 38 percent. Gross margin was 70 percent, up from 68 percent in the prior year. International sales accounted for 39 percent of the revenue.

Car-E-Oki shipped 11,182,000 iCroons units during the year, representing 35 percent growth over the prior year.

"We are delighted to report Car-E-Oki's best quarter ever in both revenue and earnings," said Cancion Fuerte, Car-E-Oki's CEO. "The launch of these new products has been a tremendous success, and we have more amazing new products in the pipeline. We're very pleased to report 29 percent revenue growth and a 38 percent increase in net income."

Car-E-Oki will provide live streaming of its 2017 financial results conference call. The live webcast will begin at 2:00 p.m. PDT on February 24, 2018, at http://www.Car-E-Oki.com.

This press release contains forward-looking statements about future products and the Company's estimated revenue and earnings for the fourth quarter of fiscal 2017. These statements involve risks and uncertainties, and actual results may differ. Potential risks and uncertainties include continued competitive pressures in the marketplace; the effect competitive and economic factors and the Company's reaction to them may have on consumer and business buying decisions with respect to the Company's products; the ability of the Company to make timely delivery of new products and successful technological innovations to the marketplace; the continued availability on acceptable terms of certain components and services essential to the Company's business currently obtained by the Company from sole or limited sources; the effect that the Company's dependency on manufacturing and logistics services provided by third parties may have on the quality, quantity, or cost of products manufactured or services rendered; the Company's reliance on the availability of third-party music content. More information on potential factors that could affect the Company's financial results is included from time to time in the Company's public reports filed with the SEC, including the Company's Form 10-K or the Company's Form 10-Q. The Company assumes no obligation to update any forward-looking statements or information, which speak as of their respective dates.

A quarterly earnings press release highlighting earnings per share and key growth drivers.

BULL-STEARNS

T. Jones
(555) 555-8546
tjones@bull.com

Equity Research
IT Hardware / Rated: Strong Buy
July 29, 2018

Car-E-Oki, Inc. (CEO-20.00) - Strong Buy
Another Big Upside for Mobile Music; Well Positioned for Future Growth

B. Smith
(555) 555-9208
bsmith@bull.com

Data

Target Price-Yr.End '18 $31   Current Market Cap (000s) $40,000,000   Shares Out (000s) **2,000,000**

Pro Forma Estimates

	Q1 Dec	Q2 Mar	Q3 Jun	Q4 Sep	Year	P/E Year
2012	$0.15	$0.23	$0.39	$0.52	$1.29	24
2013	$0.17	$0.25	$0.43	$0.57	$1.42	22
2014	$0.18	$0.28	$0.47	$0.63	$1.56	20

Decision Points
• This stock is a must own. Car-E-Oki in-dash system experiencing strong double-digit sales growth.
• New product launches include: Boat-E-Oki, Bike-E-Oki, Board-E-Oki (for skaters and surfers).
• Halo effect from flagship car brand will enhance sales of other products.
• Advent of Car-E-Oki casting will allow for on-road duets further fueling the phenomenon.
• Discussions in place with major airlines for Plane-E-Oki although pilots' unions demand right of first refusal on song collection.

Industry Outlook
Growth prospects abound with few new entrants in the market. Car-E-Oki's plan to expand to other verticals (i.e., boating, biking, boarding) should solidify its presence as a preeminent player in the global karaoke market. As one senior manager stated, "People around the world will be belting out their favorite tunes on Car-E-Oki machines, and in a few years, people will be singing in unison wherever you go."

Revenue Growth
We expect Car-E-Oki to continue to exhibit double-digit top-line growth due to the following markets initiatives:
• Expansion into new products (boating, biking, boarding).
• Expansion overseas—namely, the Asian markets were the earliest adopters of traditional karaoke machines. Rollouts to Japan, Korea, and China planned within the next two years.
• Expansion to new demographics targeting the lucrative under-four market with Toddler-Oki.

Reiterate Buy with Price Target
CEO is undervalued at current levels. We reiterate our strong buy rating with a price target of $31.

A sample Wall Street equity research report highlighting earnings forecasts, industry outlook, revenue drivers, and price target (based on valuation).

Comparable Multiple Valuation

Prices on a per-share basis

All numbers in thousands except per-share amounts

	Share Price	Earnings/Share	P/E
Musica Buena S.A.	$72	$2.00	36
Mr. Roboto Corp.	$48	$3.00	16
Vegas Sounds, Inc.	$64	$4.00	16
Canadian Idol Studios	$54	$2.00	27
Industry average			24
C.E.O.	?	$1.29	

Industry P/E × company earnings = company fair value

24 × $1.29 = $31

$31 × 2,000,000 shares = $62,000,000

A sample valuation model used to determine the price target on an equity research report.

INCOME STATEMENT PROJECTIONS

All numbers in thousands, except per-share amounts

Three fiscal years ended December 31st	2018	2019	2020
Net Sales	$9,258,118	$10,183,930	$11,202,323
Cost of Goods Sold	4,681,408	5,150,163	5,710,176
Gross Profit	$4,576,710	$5,033,767	$5,492,147
Selling, General, & Administrative Expenses	$518,450	$587,834	$601,238
Operating Income	$4,058,260	$4,445,933	$4,890,909
Depreciation	10,500	10,500	10,500
Earnings before Interest & Taxes	$4,047,760	$4,435,433	$4,880,409
Interest Expense	9,980	9,980	9,980
Profit before Taxes	$4,037,780	$4,425,453	$4,870,429
Income Taxes	1,453,601	1,593,163	1,753,354
Net Income	$2,584,179	$2,832,290	$3,117,075
Average Shares Outstanding	2,000,000	2,000,000	2,000,000
Net Income/Share	$1.29	$1.42	$1.56
NET INCOME	$2,584,179	$2,832,290	$3,117,075
PLUS Beginning Retained Earnings	911,282	3,150,921	5,638,671
Distribution to Stockholders	(344,540)	(344,540)	(344,540)
Ending Retained Earnings	$3,150,921	$5,638,671	$8,411,206

Sample income statement projections used to derive pro forma earnings.

ANALYZING CAR-E-OKI, INC.

Activity Ratios

	2017	2016
Inventory turnover days = 365/(cost of goods sold/average inventory)	74 days	89 days
Accounts receivable turnover days = 365/ (credit sales/average accounts receivables)	9 days	24 days
Accounts payable turnover days = 365/ (purchases/average accounts payable)	55 days	56 days
Cost of goods sold	$654,325	$543,604
Average inventory (average of last year and this year)	$132,078	$133,031
Credit sales (assume 50% of total sales)	$1,085,726	$837,728
Average accounts receivables (average of last year and this year)	$25,892	$54,607
Purchases (cost of goods sold + change in inventory)	$644,825	$551,199
Average accounts payables (average of last year and this year)	$97,071	$85,006

Overall, the activity ratios of CEO reveal that the company is showing slight improvement in its ability to turn inventory, with dramatic improvement in its ability to collect receivables. These improvements, combined with a stable turnover of payables, are helping the company achieve the highest levels of activity efficiency.

Liquidity Ratios

	2017	2016
Current ratio = current assets/current liabilities	4.82	2.63
Quick ratio = (cash + marketable securities + accounts receivable)/current liabilities	4.03	1.71
Cash ratio = (cash + marketable securities)/ current liabilities	3.87	1.64

The company continues to show improving liquidity ratios and is well above the industry averages. The cash ratio alone reveals sufficient cash reserves to cover any near-term liabilities.

Long-Term Debt and Solvency Ratios

	2017	2016
Debt-to-capital ratio = total debt/(total debt + total equity)	13%	23%
Debt-to-equity = total debt/total equity	15%	30%
Times interest earned = EBIT/interest	96.15	96.61

Additional Information:

	2017	2016
Total debt (lines of credit + short- and long-term debt)	$140,194	$111,976
Total equity (shareholders' equity)	$922,282	$368,143

The company shows declining debt levels and a strong ability to service what little debt exists. We believe, however, that the company should consider issuing more debt to bring it in line with industry standards. Proceeds from a debt issuance could be used for expansion efforts as well as share buybacks.

Profit Ratios

	2017	2016
Gross margin = gross profit/sales	69.9%	67.6%
Operating margin = operating income/sales	65.8%	61.6%
Profit margin = net income/sales	41.4%	38.9%

The company continues to show steadily improving profit margins that are among the highest in the industry. Concerns over new entrants have raised speculation that strong gross margins will not continue indefinitely. The company has issued statements regarding this but has promised to initiate any required operating expense reductions to keep operating margins strong.

Return Analysis

	2017	2016
Return on assets = net income/total assets	75%	109%
Return on total capital = net income/(total debt + total equity)	85%	136%
Return on equity = net income/total equity	97%	177%

Additional Information:

Total debt (lines of credit + short- and long-term debt)	$922,282	$368,143
Total equity (shareholders' equity)	$140,194	$111,976

Returns on assets, capital, and book equity are strong although declining gradually. Although the company appears healthy overall, this underperformance raises questions about the company's sustainable growth prospects.

Market Analysis

	2017	2016
Price-to-earnings ratio = stock price/earnings per share	44	30
Earnings yield = earnings per share/stock price per share	2%	3%
Dividend yield = dividends per share/stock price per share	0.86%	1.86%
Dividend payout ratio = dividends per share/earnings per share	38%	57%
Price-to-book ratio = stock price/book price	43	54

Additional Information:

Stock price (price per share at year end)	$20.00	$10.00
Earnings per share	$ 0.45	$ 0.33
Dividend per share (dividend/shares outstanding)	0.17	0.19
Book price (shareholders' equity/shares outstanding)	$ 0.46	$ 0.18

CEO has seen a near doubling of its stock price each year for the past four years. However, double-digit increases in earnings reflect the fact that growth is consistently priced into the stock, yet the company has been slow to achieve fair value. Nonetheless,

T. Soprano Associates (Note: Not Intended for IRS Use)

tertainment Division Revenues	$ 70,000
nstruction Revenues	$100,000
orts Revenues	$ 80,000
reased Accounts Receivable	$ 70,000
reased Merchandise Inventory	$ 20,000
preciation	$ 20,000
reased Accounts Payable	$ 40,000
Liquor Suppliers	$ 4,000
Cement Suppliers	$ 2,000
reased Salaries Payable	$120,000
st of Goods Sold	$ 40,000
aries	$ 8,000
erest	$ 22,000
her expenses	NA
es	$250,000
quisition of Buildings and Equipment	$ 16,000
idends Paid	$100,000
ceeds from Long-Term Debt Issued	
Loans from Friends"	?
Net Change in Cash for Year	$160,000
h, January 1	?
h, December 31	

we believe that this will be the year for CEO and are reiterating our recommendation of STRONG BUY and holding our year-end price target of $31 a share. With new products and new markets on the horizon, it won't be long before the Car-E-Oki machine is as common as the seat belt in most cars, and this does not include the potential for other vehicles. Combine this with a strong balance sheet, solid cash flows, and increasing profits, and we have a formula for success.

APPENDIX B

Sample Problems

FINANCIAL STATEMENTS P[...]

This problem set is an effective way to capture[...]
between the balance sheet, income statemen[...]
statement. First, construct an income statemer[...]
income. This will form the starting point for th[...]
ment, which takes into account the changes in [...]

Problem: Help your client with his finances[...]
following into an income statement and cas[...]
Make sure to include:

- Sales
- Expenses
- Cash Flow from Operations
- Cash Flow from Investing
- Cash Flow from Financing
- Net Change in Cash

FINANCIAL STATEMENTS SOLUTION

T. Soprano Associates
(*Note*: Not Intended for IRS Use)

Income Statement

Sales		
	Entertainment Division	$ 70,000
	Construction	$ 100,000
	Sports	$ 80,000
	Total Sales	$ 250,000
Less Expenses		
	Cost of Goods Sold	$ 120,000
	Salaries	$ 40,000
	Depreciation	$ 20,000
	Interest	$ 8,000
	Other Expenses	$ 22,000
	Total Costs and Expenses	$ 210,000
Net Income		$ 40,000

Cash Flow Statement

Operations		
Net Income		$ 40,000
Additions		
	Depreciation	$ 20,000
	Increased Accounts Payable	
	Liquor Suppliers	$ 40,000
	Cement Suppliers	$ 4,000
	Increased Salaries Payable	$ 2,000
Subtractions		
	Increased Accounts Receivable	$ (70,000)
	Increased Merchandise Inventory	$ (20,000)
Cash Flow from Operations		$ 16,000
Investing		
	Acquisition of Buildings and Equipment	$(250,000)
Financing		
	Dividends Paid	$ (16,000)
	Proceeds from Long-Term Debt Issued "Loans from Friends"	$ 100,000
Cash Flow from Financing		$ 84,000
Net Change in Cash for Year		$(150,000)
Cash, January 1	$ 160,000	
Cash, December 31	$ 10,000	

VALUATION PROBLEM

Compare valuation numbers based on the discounted cash flow method and comparable multiple method. This is standard practice in most M&A transactions.

Part A

AB Pharmaceuticals has invented a new drug to eliminate those unsightly wrinkles that form around the elbow with age. The new drug, Elbowtox, is expected to revolutionize the market for elbow rejuvenation products. Its rival company, Pharmacia ZY, has launched a hostile bid for AB and asked that you construct a discounted cash flow analysis to help evaluate this acquisition. The cash flows created as a result of this transaction are detailed in the following table:

	Year 1	Year 2	Year 3	Year 4	Year 5
Incremental cash flows	$500,000	$800,000	$1,100,000	$1,300,000	$1,500,000
Discount rate (r)	10%				

Note: Year 5 and beyond cash flows remain flat.

a. What is the value of the gain from this merger? _____

b. If the acquisition price is $5 million,
   what is the NPV? _____

Part B

Looking at the acquisition on a comparable basis, what would be a fair price for AB?

	Share Price	Earnings/Share	P/E
ZY	24	$2.00	12
CD	36	$1.00	36
EF	66	$3.00	22
GH	30	$1.50	20
Industry average			22.5
AB	?	$2.00	

a. The share price for AB should be: _____

b. With 100,000 shares outstanding, a fair price
   would be: _____

VALUATION SOLUTION

Part A

	Year 1	Year 2	Year 3	Year 4	Year 5
Incremental cash flows	$500,000	$800,000	$1,100,000	$1,300,000	$1,500,000
PV	$454,545	$661,157	$826,446	$887,917	$931,382
Discount rate (r)	10%				
Terminal value year 5	$15,000,000				
Terminal value today	$9,313,820				

Note: Year 5 and beyond cash flows remain flat.

a. What is the value of the gain from this merger? <u>$13,075,268</u>

b. If the acquisition price is $5 million,
   what is the NPV? <u>$8,075,268</u>

Part B

	Share Price	Earnings/Share	P/E
ZY	24	$2.00	12
CD	36	$1.00	36
EF	66	$3.00	22
GH	30	$1.50	20
Industry average			22.5
AB	?	$2.00	

a. The share price for AB should be: <u>$45.00</u>

b. With 100,000 shares outstanding, a fair price
   would be: <u>$4,500,000</u>

APPENDIX C
Summary Formulas

Here is a handy guide to the main formulas found in the book.

ACTIVITY ANALYSIS

Use the following formulas to evaluate revenues and output generated by a firm's assets:

Inventory turnover days = 365/(cost of goods sold/ average inventory)

Accounts receivable turnover days = 365/(credit sales/ average accounts receivables)

Accounts payable turnover days = 365/(purchases/ average accounts payable)

LIQUIDITY ANALYSIS

Use the following formulas to measure the adequacy of the firm's cash resources to meet its near-term cash obligations:

Current ratio = current assets/current liabilities

Quick ratio = (cash + marketable securities + accounts receivable)/current liabilities

Cash ratio = (cash + marketable securities)/current liabilities

LONG-TERM DEBT AND SOLVENCY

The following formulas are used to examine the firm's capital structure, including the mix of its financing sources and the ability of the firm to satisfy its longer-term debt and investment obligations:

Debt-to-capital ratio = total debt/
(total debt + total equity)

Debt to equity = total debt/total equity

Times interest earned = earnings before
interest and taxes/interest

PROFITABILITY ANALYSIS

Use the following formulas when you want to measure the relationship between a firm's costs and its sales:

Gross margin = gross profit/sales

Operating margin = operating income/sales

Profit margin = net income/sales

RETURN ANALYSIS

The following formulas measure the relationship between profits and the investment required to generate them:

Return on assets = net income/total assets

Return on total capital = net income/
(total debt + total equity)

Return on equity = net income/total equity

MARKET ANALYSIS

Here are formulas you can use to measure value, income, and dividends relative to one another:

Price-to-earnings ratio = stock price/earnings per share

Earnings yield = earnings per share/
market price per share

Dividend yield = dividends per share/
market price per share

Dividend payout ratio = dividends
per share/earnings per share

Price-to-book ratio = market price/book price

TIME VALUE OF MONEY

This formula allows you to calculate present value for a single amount. The formula is for present value (PV) of a lump sum (FVn) given at the end of n period at an interest rate of r percent, discounted once per period:

$$PV = FV_n/(1 + r)^n$$

VALUATION

Valuation of an Asset

For this formula, we assume the value of an asset with expected cash flows CF$_t$ at times $t = 1, 2, \ldots, n$, with required rate of return r:

$$\text{Value of asset} = \sum_{t=1}^{n} \text{cash} = \frac{CF_1}{(1+r)} + \frac{CF_2}{(1+r)^2} + \cdots + \frac{CF_n}{(1+r)^n}$$

Cost of Capital

Dividend Growth Model

$$r_E = (D_1/P_0) + g$$

where

$D_1 = D_0 \times (1 + g)$
D_0 = most recent dividend payment
P_0 = current stock price
g = estimated dividend growth (use historical rates or analysts' forecasts)

Cost of Equity (r_E)

Using the capital asset pricing model (CAPM):

$$r_E = r_f + \beta (r_m - r_f)$$

where

β = beta coefficient of the stock
r_f = risk-free rate
r_m = expected rate on the market portfolio

Weighted-Average Cost of Capital (WACC)

$$r_{WACC} = (1 - T)r_D D/V + r_E E/V$$

where

T = tax rate
r_D = rate of return on debt
D = total debt outstanding in dollars
E = market value of equity in dollars
V = total value of company = $D + E$
r_E = rate of return on equity*

*Can be derived using either the dividend growth model or CAPM.

GLOSSARY

10-K   A financial statement covering a company's annual performance that is filed with the Securities and Exchange Commission.

10-Q   An unaudited statement of a company's quarterly performance that includes reports similar to those found in a 10-K.

accounts payable   The amounts owed by a company to vendors and suppliers.

accounts receivable   Payments owed to a company by customers.

accrual accounting   The recording of transactions as they occur rather than when the cash actually changes hands.

activity-based costing   Managerial accounting method that assigns costs to a task or product based on resource allocation.

alpha   An investment's return in excess of the overall market return.

amortization   The dispersion of expenses or payment for an obligation over an extended period.

annual report   A condensed version of the 10-K, with more emphasis placed on marketing a company to investors through colorful charts and pictures.

arbitrage   The simultaneous purchase and sale of an asset or security to capitalize on price differentials between different marketplaces or exchanges.

assets   The resources of a company that are expected to yield some future benefit.

auditor's report   A report issued by an independent accounting firm hired to determine that a company's financial reports are in conformity with GAAP standards. Auditors are required to disclose any red flags in their reports.

backwardation   A situation in which the futures price for a commodity trades below its expected spot price.

beta   Measurement of an asset's volatility relative to the overall market.

book accounting   A system of financial reporting designed to comply with GAAP standards but not necessarily with IRS rules and regulations.

call option   A contract that allows the holder to purchase a security at a fixed price within a specified period.

cash   The most liquid of all assets.

cash accounting   The recording of transactions when cash changes hands.

cash ratio   The ratio of cash and marketable securities to current liabilities; the current ratio with the exclusion of inventory and accounts receivable.

CDO (collateralized debt obligation)   A security backed by payments on debt instruments such as mortgages.

CDS (credit default swap)   A credit derivative in which payments are made periodically to a seller who makes a lump-sum payment when another party defaults on its debt. Like other derivatives, it can be used as a form of insurance or can be traded for speculative purposes.

conglomerate merger   A merger that occurs between two companies in unrelated industries.

contango   A situation in which the futures price for a commodity trades above its expected spot price.

contribution margin   Calculated by subtracting cost of goods sold and other variable unit costs from unit sales.

cost   What is paid to produce or acquire goods and services.

covariance   Measures the extent to which asset prices move in tandem.

cross exchange rate   The exchange rate between two currencies, neither of which is the official currency of the country where the rates are given.

current assets   Liquid assets, those that can be most readily converted to cash, consumed, or sold (usually within one year).

current debt   Any type of short-term bond or note issued by a company.

current liabilities   Forms of short-term obligations, including lines of credit outstanding, accounts payable, current debt, and current portion of long-term debt.

current portion of long-term debt   The amount due in the present year on long-term issued debt.

current ratio   The most common measure of a company's liquidity, the ratio of current assets to current liabilities.

debt-to-capital ratio   The most common form of long-term debt and solvency analysis. The proportion of total debt relative to total debt and equity.

debt-to-equity ratio   The ratio of total debt to total equity.

depreciation   The loss of value of a fixed asset over its expected life.

derivative   A security based on the movement of another underlying security or index.

direct owners' equity   The funds invested directly into the company by its shareholders; usually listed as *paid-in capital*.

dividend   A periodic payment made to shareholders in a company.

dividend payout ratio   The ratio of dividend per share to earnings per share.

dividend yield   The ratio of dividend per share to market price per share.

double entry accounting   An accounting system in which every transaction occurring on one side of a financial statement has one or more accompanying transactions occurring elsewhere in the financial statements.

earnings release   A condensed form of a company's income statement that highlights the company's performance on the basis of profits.

earnings yield   The ratio of earnings per share to market price per share of a company.

EBIT   Earnings before interest and taxes.

EBITDA   Earnings before interest, taxes, depreciation, and amortization.

EBT   Earnings before taxes.

economic value added (EVA)   A performance measure of a company that deducts the cost of capital from tax-adjusted operating profit.

expenses   What is paid to run a company on a day-to-day basis.

FASB (Financial Accounting Standards Board)   The overseeing body in charge of establishing and improving financial accounting and reporting standards.

FIFO   The first-in, first-out method of accounting for inventory in which the first good produced or purchased is the first one sold.

Fixed exchange rate system   A currency exchange rate system in which the exchange rate between the local currency and a foreign currency is static or moves within a tight range.

Floating exchange rate system   A currency exchange rate system in which the exchange rate between the local currency and a foreign currency is determined by market forces.

flow time   Total amount of time that unit spends in a particular business process.

Form 144   A registration form that discloses when insiders buy or sell stock.

Form 8-K   A form due to the SEC after any material event (any major change in ownership, capital structure, or auditor).

forward   A contractual obligation to transfer an asset at a specific price on a specific date.

future   A contract to buy or sell an underlying asset on a particular date; generally traded on an exchange.

GAAP (generally accepted accounting principles)   The overall principles used in financial reporting.

goodwill   The difference between the price paid for an asset and its fair market value.

gross margin   The ratio of gross profit to sales.

horizontal merger   A merger that occurs between two companies in the same industry.

IASB (International Accounting Standards Board)   A privately funded organization that created and revises IFRS (International Financial Reporting Standards).

IFRS   (International Financial Reporting Standards)   A system of accounting used in many countries around the world. The standards are issued and revised by the IASB (International Accounting Standards Board).

indirect owners' equity   Equity built up through the generation of income. Also known as *retained earnings.*

interest   A payment made to finance debt.

inventory   Goods that a company has produced or purchased but has yet to sell.

leveraged buyout (LBO)   An acquisition that is financed through a large amount of debt.

liabilities   Obligations due in the future based on activities from the past; what the company owes.

LIFO   The last-in, first-out method of accounting for inventory in which the last good produced or purchased is the first one sold.

line of credit   The amount a company has drawn from any credit facilities; similar to credit cards in personal finance.

locational arbitrage   An arbitrage opportunity created by discrepancies in currency exchange rates between two banks. Buying the currency at one bank and selling it to the other creates a riskless profit.

management's discussion and analysis (MD&A)   A strategic overview of a company's performance during the prior year, including expected changes for the coming year. Found at the beginning of most annual reports and 10-Ks for publicly traded companies.

management's report   A supplement to the MD&A that details the responsibilities of the individual managers in preparing the financial reports.

marketable securities   Short-term investments listed under current assets on the balance sheet.

mark-to-market accounting   Occurs when certain financial statement line items are listed at their fair market value.

money laundering   The practice of taking money from illegal sources and passing it through a business to make the money appear legitimate.

net income   A company's profit; the residual amount when all expenses and costs are subtracted from revenues.

net present value (NPV)   The present value of future returns minus the initial investment.

noncurrent assets   Assets that cannot be liquidated within the course of one year.

noncurrent liabilities   Any long-term debt that comes due after the course of one year.

OPEC (Organization of Petroleum Exporting Countries)   Consortium of countries whose representatives meet to determine the supply of oil produced by the member countries.

operating income   Revenue minus expenses involved in the day-to-day operations of a business.

operating margin   The ratio of operating income to sales.

option   A contract that gives the owner the right to buy or sell something at a specified price within a specified period.

owners' equity   The book value of a company; the difference between its assets and liabilities. Also known as *shareholders' equity.*

prepaid expense   An expenditure for a good or service paid in advance of its due date; listed on the balance sheet and reduced as payments come due.

price-to-book ratio   The ratio of market price per share to book price per share.

price-to-earnings ratio   The ratio of stock price to earnings per share.

pro forma financials   Any type of adjusted financial statements.

profit margin   The ratio of net income to sales.

property, plant, and equipment (PP&E)   See *tangible fixed assets*.

proxy statement   A financial report, offered at a company's annual meeting, detailing management compensation, management stock options, related-party transactions, and auditor changes.

put option   A contract that gives the holder the right to sell a security at a fixed price.

quick ratio   The current ratio with inventory excluded from current assets.

REIT (real estate investment trust)   An actively managed investment real estate vehicle in which the tax liability is passed on to the shareholders, who pay taxes on their distributions.

retained earnings   See *indirect owners' equity*.

return on assets   The ratio of net income to total assets.

return on equity   The ratio of net income to total equity.

return on total capital   The ratio of net income to the sum of total debt and equity.

revenue   Payments received in exchange for goods or services.

Securities and Exchange Commission (SEC)   The independent regulatory agency of the US government in charge of regulating all publicly traded companies.

selling, general, and administrative (SG&A)   The day-to-day operating expenses of a company as listed on the income statement.

shareholders' equity   See *owners' equity.*

standard deviation   The square root of variance; often used to measure risk.

swap   A type of derivative in which two parties enter into an agreement to exchange their streams of cash flows.

tangible fixed assets   Noncurrent assets, including all property, real estate, and equipment. Also known as *property, plant, and equipment (PP&E).*

tax accounting   A system of financial reporting designed to ensure that income and deductions reported on tax returns are in compliance with IRS rules and regulations.

throughput   Number of production units flowing through a business over a given period of time.

times interest earned ratio   The ratio of EBIT to interest.

transfer pricing   Price at which one company division sells goods and services to another division.

triangular arbitrage   An arbitrage opportunity created by converting one currency into a second, the second currency into a third, and the third back to the first. In this process, a riskless profit is earned as a result of pricing discrepancies.

variance   Measures the extent to which data points deviate from the mean.

vertical merger   A merger that occurs between two companies involved in different stages of production within an industry.

volatility index   Index reflecting expected volatility in the stock market.

warrant   A volatile option with a longer duration than a standard option that usually originates as part of a new bond issue.

RECOMMENDED READINGS

Borghese, Robert J., and Paul Borghese, *M&A from Planning to Integration: Executing Acquisitions and Increasing Shareholder Value*, McGraw-Hill, New York, 2002.

Brealey, Richard, Stewart Myers, and Franklin Allen, *Principles of Corporate Finance*, 12th ed., McGraw-Hill, New York, 2016.

Koller, Tim, Marc Goedhart, and David Wessels, *Valuation: Measuring and Managing the Value of Companies*, 6th ed., Wiley, Hoboken, NJ, 2015.

Malkiel, Burton, *A Random Walk Down Wall Street: The Time-Tested Strategy for Successful Investing*, W. W. Norton & Co., New York, 2016.

Ramesh, Ram, *Financial Analyst's Indispensable Pocket Guide*, McGraw-Hill, New York, 2001.

Rickertsen, Rick, *Buyout: The Insider's Guide to Buying Your Own Company*, AMACOM, New York, 2001.

Schilit, Howard, and Jeremy Perler, *Financial Shenanigans*, 4th ed., McGraw-Hill, New York, 2018.

INDEX

INDEX

Return:
    expected, 238
    internal rate of, 147–148
Return analysis, 88, 97, 284
Return on assets, 97, 284, 293
Return on equity, 97, 284, 293
Return on investment (ROI), 97
Return on total capital, 97, 284,
    293
Returns on real estate, 218–219
Revenue:
    defined, 293
    on income statement, 37, 38,
        42–45
    increases with M&A, 185
    manipulation of, 71–72
Reverse repurchase agreements,
    176
Rigas, John, 15–16
Risk and beta, 121–124
Risk-free rate, 120–121
Risk management, 245–246
RJR Nabisco, 196
ROI (return on investment), 97,
    218–219
Roosevelt, Theodore, 182
Round-tripping, 7

Sales:
    on income statement, 38
    as investment banking, 249–250
    net, 37
Sales and trading groups, 249–250
Sales comparison valuation, 215
Sales projections, pro forma
    financials, 78–81
Sales shifting, businesses and
    operating subsidiaries, 69, 71
Sales skimming, 69
SEC (See Securities and Exchange
    Commission)
Secured debts, 152
Securities:
    convertible, 151
    debt, 150
    marketable, 19, 292
    mortgage-backed, 221

Securities and Exchange
    Commission (SEC), 9–10, 13–14,
    42–43, 76, 293
Segment information, and fraud
    detection, 75
Sell side of finance, 247–252
    commercial banking, 248
    investment banking, 249–251
    retail brokerage, 249–251
SG&A (selling, general, and
    administrative), 38–39, 293
Shareholders' (owners') equity,
    24–25, 292
Shifting sales and expenses, 69, 71
Short selling, 159–161
Smart beta, 246
Speculation, currency, 204–205,
    208
SPEs (special-purpose entities),
    31–33, 71
Spot market, commodities, 228
Staff Accounting Bulletin 101 (SAB
    101), 42–43
Standard deviation, 239–242, 294
Statement No. 95,FASB, 62
Stock options, fraud detection, 75
Stocks, 157–161
    defined, 150–151
    discounted cash flows, 157–158
    dividend valuation, 158–159
    equity advantages, 150–151
    short selling, 159–161
    valuation, 158–159
Structured notes, 176
Supermajority provisions, 189
Supplementary information,
    financial statements, 15–16
Supply and demand, exchange
    rates, 201–202
Surplus funds utilization, M&A,
    184–185
Swaps, 172–173, 294

Tangible fixed assets, 20, 294
Tax accounting, 11–12, 294
Tax benefits of M&A, 186
Taxes on income statement, 39

305

ABOUT THE AUTHOR

Reuben Advani founded, built, and sold a financial training company. In addition, Mr. Advani launched a popular series of MBA-style seminars that are offered at corporations and law firms in the United States and Europe. Mr. Advani began his career with Morgan Stanley & Co., Inc., the Wall Street bank, where he worked in the firm's corporate finance division. In that capacity, he performed detailed valuation analysis on acquisition targets for Fortune 500 companies and oversaw the coordination of several debt and equity issuances. Mr. Advani's next position was with Sony Corporation of America, where he was active in the development of Sony's online initiatives. Mr. Advani has provided consulting services to companies throughout the United States and Latin America and has held interim positions with several of them, including CFO and COO. He is a frequent speaker on topics ranging from corporate valuation to financial reporting.

Mr. Advani holds a BA from Yale University, earned an MBA from the Wharton School, and is a university lecturer.

Follow Mr. Advani on Twitter @reubenadvani.